DIVING TO ADVENTURE

This time Joerg followed the regiment of jack fish to the bottom

DIVING TO ADVENTURE

Harpoon and Camera
under the Sea

By

HANS HASS

Translated from the German by
BARROWS MUSSEY

With over 60 Illustrations

JARROLDS *Publishers* (LONDON) LTD
FOUNDED IN 1770
London   New York   Toronto   Melbourne   Sydney   Cape Town

Originally published in Switzerland under
the title, *Drei Jäger auf dem Meeresgrund*

First published August 1952
Reprinted   -   October 1952
Reprinted   - February 1953
Reprinted   -   March 1953

Printed in Great Britain
by The Anchor Press, Ltd.,
Tiptree, Essex

ACKNOWLEDGMENT

The extracts from *Battling With Sea Monsters*,
by F. A. Mitchell Hedges, are reproduced by
permission of Gerald Duckworth & Co., Ltd.

LIST OF ILLUSTRATIONS

7

8

9

"The boy must learn to swim," said Uncle Fritz when I was four, "and I'll see to it that he does!"

Mother was willing. And unsuspecting. After all, she couldn't have known that Uncle Fritz—normally a most amiable soul—was at the moment occupying himself with problems of educational psychology. "Human beings can swim naturally," he defended his theory afterwards, "only you have to get the child into the water before he quite realizes what's going on, and you should do it without much fuss. Then the natural instinct will come out, and the child will swim without needing a lot of tedious instruction."

Uncle Fritz took me by the hand, and we trudged across a meadow to the swimming pool. Mother was busy for the moment, because Aunt Marta was telling her how much she had to reduce under the arm. Stitches, she meant, in knitting a sweater. But then her eyes widened . . .

Uncle Fritz and I stood by the diving board, where of course the water is deepest, he said something to me, and I jumped. And while I was obviously drowning, he kept his eyes on his watch!

How the experiment would have turned out remains uncertain, because it was never finished. A young sports instructress —the same who subsequently dealt Uncle Fritz such a dreadful box on the ear—fished me out. She said I had been a good six feet under.

That was the greatest depth I achieved at that age.

Uncle Fritz had no scientific satisfactions from me. I threw up at least a pint of water, and thenceforward hated it like poison. Not until four years later did Mother succeed by guile in winning me back to the watery element and thus to my later work.

We spent the summer at Valbandon, near Pola. Mother was knitting again, this time a pair of bathing trunks, and I raced around on the beach. With Indo, my silent love—silent because the child with her black curls understood not a word of German. But otherwise we understood each other splendidly. Nobody ever built finer castles of withered agaves than we.

For her sake I even went into the water, though only where it was shallow. I hunted shells and coloured stones for her, and once a crab bit me in the process. Or it may have been a shrimp, or perhaps only imagination, but it was something, anyway. And in Indo's eyes I was a great hero. She nursed the wound in our agave castle. But I never did really conquer her heart until I could swim, and this I owe to Mother. She went into the water with me, and we played "floating man". She said that I was to lie down on my back in the water and she would keep her hand under the back of my neck, so that I couldn't go under. It worked first-rate. I shut my eyes and really lay at ease upon the waves, rocking to and fro as if I were in a hammock. When I opened my eyes again, Mother was long since on the beach. She had quietly withdrawn her hand, and I was floating all by myself!

That was how I learned to swim, though only on my back. Not until later did I pluck up courage to turn over on my side, and finally on my stomach. By then, unfortunately, Indo was gone.

2

One especially fine day we went by boat from Valbandon to the island of Brioni. Mother got seasick, so they put her down in a *chaise longue*, at the hotel. Everybody was interested in her, nobody in me, and before long I vanished.

I stalked—I was an Indian at the time—through the old, run-down deer park, and wound up by a little bay fairly remote among the cliffs. There, on a jutting crag, sat a fat man in a white hat, fishing.

He spoke German, and put me to work finding snails for him. Then he would crush them, fetch out the creatures, and impale them on his hook. The fish relished the bait, and the old man made a good haul. From time to time he would drink from a small bottle.

Suddenly he got up.

"Now we need a few more that have got to be caught differently," he said, grinning. He took off his shoes, pulled a fork from his pocket, and, thus equipped, waddled into the shallow water of the cove. There he bent down, reached cautiously for a stone with his left hand, snatched it away in a flash, and at the same time stabbed with the fork. Naturally there was nothing on the fork, and I rocked with laughter.

But at the third attempt a fish was flapping on the fork after all, and a shrimp, and then some more fish followed. When the old man had enough, he waddled ashore with his prey, put on his shoes, and crawled into the bushes, whence he produced a pot and a bag of tomatoes and all sorts of green vegetables. Then he built a stove out of stones, and while he had me fetching and piling wood he boiled a marvellous soup, which we drank straight from the pot. We ate the fish in our hands. Then the old fellow stretched out his legs, belched audibly, and reached for his pipe.

"The sea," he growled, "is more to me than the most beautiful woman that ever was!"

"Yes," said I, stretching out my legs also, "I can well understand that."

The old man roared with laughter. "You little squirt! What do you know about women and the sea? They're both so deep and dark . . ."

He rolled up his jacket and elaborately pillowed his head on it. "I knew a diver once who forgot what the very sound of laughter was like. But I don't know why it was—because of something that happened to him down below, or because of his wife. On the bottom, he said, there were flowers, even lovelier than the evening sun, and shining with colours such as no one up here has ever seen. If you touched them, they scorched your hand as if you had put it into burning sulphur.

"I knew perfectly well that his wife was deceiving him, but he never found out about it from me." The old man sucked at his pipe, and shut his eyes blissfully.

"On the bottom of the sea there are creatures that no man has ever seen. Only the drowned people down there know those creatures—but none of them has ever told the tale. There are monsters bigger than a hundred elephants, with shining eyes and so many arms that you couldn't count them all in one day. Down around Cape Horn we once met a big sailing ship moving all by herself. We yelled and waved, but not a soul was to be seen on board. The men thought it was a ghost ship. There was a storm in the east, but I rowed across to have a look for myself. Never a soul anywhere! Dinner was on the table and half eaten—even an egg that the top had just been sliced off of. The men's things were still lying around in their quarters, and the fire was still warm in the galley stove. The writing in the logbook broke off in the middle of a sentence. But nowhere did I see a sign of fright or confusion. The sailors had simply vanished. How and where? God only knows. And if He doesn't happen to know, the devil must.

"And that same year my friend the diver was lost on the bottom. But I still insist it was better so."

The old man stretched, yawned, and turned over on his side; and each time he snored, a shrill whistle followed. Meanwhile, I sat motionless, pondering. About the sea and about women. . . .

When I got back to the hotel late in the afternoon there was great excitement. They had been hunting for me everywhere. Only Mother had remained calm, for she had a philosophy of her own in such matters. "Everything happens the way it's going to happen," she said. "If the boy is destined to have an accident, nobody can prevent it. Otherwise, his guardian angel will look after him all right. And it'll do him good to be a little independent."

14

To me, however, "If you run off again without asking, you get whacked—do you hear?"

"You know, Mother," I replied, "I'm never going to marry. But I'd like to be a diver!"

3

At that time—I was nine by then—another problem also came up. "So far as smoking goes," Mother said to me one day, "I'm not going to make rules. I'm going to start giving you pocket money, and if you feel like it you can spend the money on cigarettes. Of course smoking isn't healthy—you know that anyway—and anyone who wants to be a real athlete won't even start. Some boys think it's particularly smart and manly to smoke, but since practically everyone does, obviously it's much smarter if a person is the only one who doesn't. But you can think that all over for yourself. After all, you're grown up now."

Naturally I didn't smoke.

But otherwise I did mischief enough. Once a friend turned up with the wonderful news that you could explode bottles. You put unslaked lime in a beer bottle, poured in water, stoppered the bottle, and ran away. But nothing happened. We waited; then my friend said perhaps you had to shake the bottle. So I went and shook it. And this had the desired result. I was just in the midst of shaking when the bottle burst with a dreadful bang. Broken glass flew in my face, and the boiling lime splashed in my eyes. When I looked around, I was suddenly in a thick fog. I could just barely see a few yards; everything beyond was dim. I raced into the house, and my friend shouted after me to hold my eyes under the tap. Who gave him this idea I do not know—probably my guardian angel. I put my eyes under the running water immediately, and so saved my eyesight. When the doctor made his examination, he found that some of the lime particles had already eaten their way deep into the cornea. He fetched them out individually one by one.

For two weeks I lay with wet cotton wool over my eyes —the longest fortnight of my life. Privately I vowed to myself that if I should be cured I would not live so thoughtlessly as before. I would thank God for everything every day. Just so long as I could see again!

My eyes recovered, and the vow was soon forgotten. I sank back into the carefree life of boyhood, which knows only the moment and cares for nothing else. Nevertheless one trace remained. Somewhere in my subconscious I cherished the knowledge that seeing is not to be taken for granted, but is a most wonderful gift which one can never appreciate too much.

The years flitted past with school, sports, and pranks. Our cook said a wasp was stinging my tail. I'm afraid it still is.

Things were always specially lively on the Old Danube, a branch of the real Danube on the outskirts of Vienna. My parents had a week-end house and a raft from which we used to go swimming. The moment the weather got warm I could invite all my friends, and we would gambol about in the water until we were blue with cold. Here I made the discovery that the raft had a secret; you could dive under, and at one particular point you could breathe unseen below the planks.

One Sunday, when a lot of people were along the bank, we were playing in the water with a big wooden ring. We held it upright, then pushed it under with united strength, and let it shoot up in the air. Each time it would slap back on the water with a terrific bang. Before long a sufficient crowd of spectators had gathered on the bank, and suddenly they saw an alarming sight: the ring flew up in the air and landed right on my head! Nobody noticed I had ducked under water the instant before. The ring went on floating, I had vanished, and my friends took no notice.

16

1. A strange brown creature moving soundlessly among the rocks

2. The octopus I took there had tentacles with an eleven-foot span

3. These gold-striped fish have just one aim in life : to eat until they burst

4. The mullet seemed transformed : the god of love had bewitched them

Promptly the first shouts came from shore. When my friends did not react, a fat little man with a bright face broke out of the crowd and came running down to the float, brandishing his umbrella. From my hideout I could also see that he wore red garters.

"Hey!" he roared across the water. "Didn't you see?"

What was the matter? came the reply. Would he please get off the float? This was private. The hotel float was farther down . . .

The man above me danced with excitement. "Why, didn't you notice," he roared, "that the ring fell on your friend's head?"

"On whose?" came the long-drawn reply. "Oh, his! That never does him any harm at all!" Boisterous laughter followed.

The dance over my head was suddenly frozen into immobility. The man was gasping for breath from sheer indignation. Footsteps rang out, and people came rushing down to the float. Some with, some without garters. I heard shouts of "Ambulance!" and "Police!" which indicated to me that the high point of the fun was already past. So I dived as noiselessly as possible, and swam back under water as fast as I could to my friends. Half a minute later I suddenly reappeared quite abruptly inside the ring, and we went on playing as if nothing had happened.

People shook their heads in astonishment and gradually scattered. Only the man with the red face stayed on the raft. He was perfectly quiet now and poked thoughtfully between the planks with his umbrella. Then he sat down, put the umbrella ready to hand across his knees, and showed no signs whatever of going away.

That day we stayed in the water an awfully long time.

4

Once, on my way to an appointment with one of the girls of my heart, I ran into my schoolmate Janossy. As usual he had shiny horn-rimmed spectacles on his nose. It was his birthday, on which occasion he had been given a microscope that he wanted to show me. Since I was early anyway, and he lived near by, I dropped in at his place.

The microscope was really something. We studied the insides of a drop of water, and discovered the most incredible creatures in it. Some were propelled by countless tiny oars and looked like galleys; others recalled a dragon with a crocodile's head; others, again, resembled Canterbury bells, were transparent, and had a mobile stem and glimmering bristles around the calyx. Suddenly we came across a little creature that was lying perfectly quiet, dividing itself down the middle. Right before our eyes it split into two equally large parts, both of which then swam off. One individual had become two.

How did this happen? What became of the original ego of the creature? Did it die? And if it died, where was the corpse?

I arrived at my cinema date fifteen minutes late, but just in time to see the girl walking inside—with Klinkhoff, my hated rival! I went back to Janossy's.

5

My mother was a beautiful and charming woman. Since Father was usually detained in Vienna by business, the two of us generally went on our summer vacation by ourselves. We might have been taken for brother and sister, because she looked very young, and we got along together extraordinarily well.

When I was fourteen, we went to Royan, at the mouth of the Gironde, and, finding it too cold there, the next two summers we went to Juan-les-Pins on the French Riviera. Mother sent me at the age of seventeen to southern England as an exchange student, and at the age of eighteen to Paris alone. She was of the opinion that it now was time for me to sow my wild oats, and I was fully resolved to comply with the maternal wish.

I stayed three weeks in Paris, made acquaintance with the International Exposition and a few other things, and then I had had enough. The only thing I had not enough of was money—it had shrunk alarmingly. So, with manly resolve, I left Paris, and went to Hosségor, a bathing resort near Biarritz, which friends had particularly recommended. When I arrived it was pouring buckets, and wretchedly cold. Besides, the hotels were scandalously expensive. Walking dismally through spruce woods in the rain, I figured and figured, and finally, totting up, decided to move on. Once again half across France, to the familiar and always sunny Juan-les-Pins.

After this decision I felt much better. I ate lunch in a small restaurant, and then went down to the sea. The rain had stopped meanwhile, but the wind rose to storm force. Jumbled tatters of clouds raced across the sky, and white pennants whipped over the sea. The surf was six feet high, pounding the beach with giant fists. But far out, where scattered sunbeams painted the ocean arsenic green, dolphins were playing and making sport of the storm.

I could not help thinking of the old man of Brioni and his tale of the monsters in the deep. And I thought of a fish, too, that my uncle, Professor Erich Zugmayer, the explorer, had shown me, which he had fished up himself from ten thousand feet down, and which now bore his name. It had looked like a severed head, with a tiny tail grown on in the rear. And there were even far more fantastic creatures in the

19

icy depths, Uncle Erich had said; the deep sea was the last stronghold on earth of untouched nature. Surely it must be glorious to roam there like Jules Verne's Captain Nemo, penetrating a completely unknown world where each step would lead to new adventures.

A black flag on top of the weather station forbade swimming. But far and wide not a soul was to be seen. I undressed and raced with loud yells into the surf. The waves took care of the rest.

The very first breaker landed on me full force, and spun me so fast that only the feel of the stones told me which was up and which was down. When the whirling finally slackened, and I was about to gasp for air again, the next wave broke upon me, and I found myself inhaling salt water. Coughing, spitting, and raw from head to foot, I finally ended in deeper water. Here the sport was really worth while. It was glorious to dive through the tall, racing walls of waves; some of them towered seven or eight feet high.

Things were less pleasing when I had had enough and wanted to get ashore again. No matter where I set foot, the water streaming back snatched the sand from under me, and I kept falling again and again. The one chance of reaching shore was in surrendering myself passively to the force of the breakers. And so I did finally get to dry land again; but now I know why the stones on that coast are so round. . . .

6

When six fish are so close together that only a little oil can squeeze between them, they are usually in a sardine tin. If a few hundred people are lying so close together that not even a toe dancer can pass among them, they are undoubtedly on the beach of Juan-les-Pins. You never know whether it's a waiter from Toulouse, an American film director, an English lord, or an international pimp.

The slim figure playing ball with a well-known English jazz band leader yonder behind the red parasol was a princess. The onlookers were two American girls, a Swedish lawyer, my friend Jacques, a Parisian *comme il faut*, Locatelli, the Italian ex-world champion welterweight. The yells that kept coming from the sea originated with the water polo team, which was training there; the somewhat shriller yells from the other side were from the throats of the fifty "children" of Professor Thirreay, who was giving modern gymnastic lessons around a huge rubber ball. The three portly ladies, gleaming with fat, who were roasting beside me in the sun, were Russian *émigrés* who had opened a restaurant "A 12 Francs" near the Palais Wilson, and the weeping girl with bangs was the ordinarily so cheerful soubrette from a local bar. I asked whether anything had happened to one of her fiancés, but nothing had. She had merely come from a session of having her eyebrows plucked for twenty minutes. At the Caraval Café up above people were dancing the rumba in bathing suits. The little thing with the red hair who was dancing with two full cocktail glasses in her hands had staged two suicide attempts that week.

An elegant lady passed by. She was almost without make-up, her expression was chilly, and she wore a high-buttoned dress. An unusual sight in these surroundings. Where *had* I seen her?

Of course—at the Casino! It was Joan Warner, the strip teaser.

For a month I romped with this menagerie, and thought it exciting and splendid. Then I succumbed to an unhappy love—you can find even that at Juan-les-Pins—and started taking walks in solitude.

That was how I got to the remote Cap d'Antibes, near which is Eden Rock, one of the most luxurious hotels in Europe. It was a marvellous day. Not a breath was stirring, the air quivered over the hot cliffs, the sea was tired and gentle. Every now and then a wave would grumble, having gone astray in a cave under the bank and angrily sought its way back.

I undressed mournfully and was getting ready to bathe when I noticed a human body among the rocks. It floated motionless on the surface, the head hanging under water; at first I thought the man was dead. But then the head rose; the swimmer took breath. He wore rubber goggles over his eyes, and in his right hand he had a long stick.

I now watched the man disappearing from time to time beneath the waves. He did not dive as one usually does, but sank away absolutely without a sound, so that no waves betrayed where he had vanished. Each time it would be astonishingly long before he reappeared, somewhere, at quite another spot, as noiselessly and unexpectedly as he had gone. And never a sign of being out of breath!

Inquisitively I climbed out on a jutting crag. What was the man doing?

He had dived again now, and was swimming past me about ten feet under, a big brown creature below the waves. The water was so calm and clear that I could follow his movements perfectly. He swam remarkably carefully and cautiously, and pointed his stick at a coloured bunch of seaweed. I looked closer—there was a fish! And at the same moment his stick flashed forward. A brief gleam in the water, then the man came to the surface. On his spear gleamed a fish, pierced through the middle!

The man finally came ashore, and I made his acquaintance. He was an American by the name of Guy Gilpatric, and, I discovered later, a well-known writer and correspondent for the *Saturday Evening Post*. He told me he had been pursuing his under-water hunting for some years; ordinarily he hunted with two friends from a small yacht. The man must have been at least in the forties, but seemed considerably younger. His skin was tanned by water and sun, his hair like a bundle of straw.

"A harpoon?" was his ready answer to my question. "The best man to make you one is Martin the mechanic at Antibes. He wants three hundred francs. But don't go swimming alone in deep water, because sharks sometimes come over to the cape here. And watch out for octopuses too!"

Then he thrust the knife with which he had killed the fish back into its sheath, pulled his goggles over his eyes, and vanished again in the sea. A strange brown creature, moving soundlessly among the rocks. (Illus. 1.)

7

The first time anyone looks under water through watertight goggles he is amazed. Whereas with the naked eye you see everything under water so blurred that you cannot even decipher the headline of a newspaper, with goggles you can see just as plainly as in the air. The reason is that the light is refracted differently under water from what it is in the air, and our eyes are not adapted to the change. In order to see clearly, you have to put an air space between eye and water, such as watertight goggles provide. An important point is that the glasses of the goggles must be exactly parallel, otherwise you get a double image.

The eyes of fish are adapted to the refraction of water by having, not lentil-shaped lenses like ours, but spherical ones, with the corresponding disadvantage that a fish's eye—photographically speaking—has only a very small depth of focus. It must be focused fairly accurately for any given distance, and objects at other distances are blurred. A further peculiarity of the fish's eye is that in repose it is focused close up. Whereas we stare idly into the distance, a fish in off moments looks into the foreground. In addition, its eyes are not parallel, but look to the sides, which gives a wider field of vision, but also destroys the capacity to see things spatially. For these reasons a skilful and careful swimmer can creep up on a fish unobserved. Even if the fish's eye is upon him, that is no sign the creature will necessarily see him.

Monsieur Martin welcomed me cordially, proclaiming his fondness for Vienna. He regretted that he could not deliver the harpoon before next week, and even then only at four hundred francs. I sighed, and gave the order anyway. I was luckier at the optician's in Cannes, where one pair of water-tight goggles was still in stock. They were not cheap, either, but the man vowed that they were the best kind, the same as the pearl divers in the South Seas use. I tried them on, and they fitted as if made to measure, so I scraped up the money, and set off forthwith.

Fifteen minutes by motor launch will take you from Cannes to the Isle Sainte-Marguerite, the far-famed "Pearl of the Mediterranean". In reality its little sister, Saint-Honorat, hiding modestly behind it, is the true pearl. This island is almost completely uninhabited. Only in the centre, where the spruce forest is thickest and the bramble hedges are highest, an old monastery hides, and on the south coast a great, lonely tower rises up, a ruin from the time of Louis the Fat. Anyone who likes solitude and can get accustomed to the incessant chirp of cicadas will find Saint-Honorat a paradise. I had been there often before with Mother, and we had discovered an ideal picnic ground. It was here I wanted to try out my goggles.

The first attempt was a failure. I saw nothing at all. The goggles steamed over on the inside. Luckily I remembered that just before Guy Gilpatric went back into the water he had spat copiously into his goggles. I spat into mine, and that did the trick.

The water was crystal clear, and now I could see into a strange and oddly glimmering world. The reflected sunlight on the waves danced over the jagged rocks below me, across chasms, and through gaudy seaweed shrubbery, constantly changing colour. There were fish here, too, some even fairly big. But when I happened to glance at my hands, I realized that the fish could not be so very big after all, because my hands likewise looked much bigger than they actually were. Like a wrestler's paws, in fact. The refraction of the light in the air space within the goggles makes everything seem a third bigger, just as your finger looks bigger if you stick it in a glass of water.

When I dived, the fish didn't seem particularly timid. I even got so close to one with big pop eyes that I tried to grab him. But again refraction fooled me. Through the goggles everything looked not only a third bigger, but correspondingly closer; my reach always fell short. I started practising on quieter targets, diving for shells and red starfish that contrasted gaily with the green-covered rock, and I chanced on a big sea snail that weighed nearly five pounds.

Peering about and diving ever deeper, I worked my way along the coast. The world above water and my unhappy love were forgotten; a new world and a happier love had come to me. So I was all the more surprised when I popped up in a little cove and saw three young women sunning themselves here in the solitude, as unclad as Eve in Paradise. When the three discovered me, they sprang up and tried in confusion to cover themselves with something. But their clothes were far away and stones would not serve the purpose. The three sprang boldly into the water beside me. To escape my eye. . . .

8

In China there are all kinds of strange things. For instance, cormorants, which catch one fish after another from dawn to dark, and are always hungry. These poor creatures are on a string, with a ring around their necks so small that they cannot swallow any of the fish they catch. The owner of the birds, meanwhile, sits at ease in the boat, smoking his pipe, and not troubling to do anything but pull in one cormorant after another, examine its gullet, and praise this one and scold that one. In the evening the ring is taken off, and each cormorant gets its reward: a fish.

The South Sea Islanders catch turtles in much the same way. They attach a remora to a long line, and then let it swim at large. The creature can think of nothing better than to hunt out the nearest turtle, and fasten its sucker so tightly to the armour that the Islander can drag the turtle into the boat. While the remora is being sent out on a renewed search, the poor turtle has an unenviable fate awaiting it. In the shade of a South Sea hut it gets a piece of ground for a bed and a stone for a pillow, and has time to reflect on the well-known kindness of man to animals. Since turtles have great vitality, they stay alive in this position for weeks. They may pant every ten minutes, though certainly not from indignation, but merely to take another breath, which is rather hard for them lying on their backs. When an unexpected guest turns up, the South Sea woman need not worry: she always has fresh meat ready to hand.

The poor turtle! my esteemed reader will think, but in a fish market has he ever thought, the poor fish? They lie out on a plank side by side or one on top of another ("All fresh and still alive!"), panting desperately for water, while their gills slowly dry up. This suffering is the fault of the good Lord, because He gave fish no voice. If they could howl or simply squeak or miaow, like dogs and cats, they would certainly not be tormented so. But as for creatures that do not make a sound, who feels sorry for them? Anything that doesn't yell certainly can't feel pain.

Almost all fishing is cruel and a dirty trick. The creatures are jammed together quite ruthlessly in the nets, and put into casks alive by thousands. That is to say, occasionally one still has some life left. It may be impaled on a hook, and allowed to swim around in the sea again. The more lively it is, the better the fisherman is pleased. Then at last a predatory fish comes past, thinks, How delightful! makes a mouthful, and the next moment is yanked upward by the invisible line. It, too, is a victim of base treachery. But the fish have no complaint: of recent years fishermen have been firing a compressed-air cartridge into whales, so that they cannot sound and float like live balloons on the water.

26

In comparison with these methods, goggle-fishing is most assuredly fair. You confront the fish in its own element, where almost every advantage is on its side. It can swim faster, stay under water indefinitely, never suffers earache, and needs no nose clip. The goggle-fisher's harpoon and his intellect are his only strong points, but even then not always, because neither avails him against the teeth of a shark. In battle with the great predatory fish of the sea the goggle-fisher has no advantage at all. Surely this is the height of fairness.

Probably the first goggle-fishers were the natives of the South Seas: old sources tell how naked divers of Penrhyn Island caught great turtles. On Nauru the natives dived and took sea eels and morays with a noose. Under-water fishermen were observed on Mbangu. It is asserted that the Hawaiians used to go after sharks with a knife, but once when I was in Hawaii and inquired, people hotly rejected any such suggestion. Guy Gilpatric told me he had learned his art from an American naval officer. I presume that he in turn had gained his skill in the South Seas.

Spear-fishing has rapidly grown popular as a sport; within ten years after Gilpatric's earliest publications it had disciples all over the world. California has a spear-fishing club with an entrance examination and a constitution. In Florida there are under-water archery contests. Along the shores of the Mediterranean you can buy specially built catapults, which render under-water fishing considerably easier. In Italy I met a spear-fisher who could neither dive nor swim, and yet took fish with her catapult even so. She would lie on an inflated rubber mattress, hang her goggled curly head into the water, and from this position shoot comfortably into the depths. I suggested that she make her work even easier—use cormorants!

9

At last the great moment came—Monsieur Martin handed me the finished harpoon. It consisted of three parts screwed together and was nine feet long. At the top, on a short iron shaft, gleamed the artfully forged head. In the fish's body it would instantly come free of the shaft, leaving the fish on a shot line that was in turn fastened to the pole of the harpoon. In that way I could pull my prey to the surface.

I hastily pressed the money into Monsieur Martin's hand, and was off like the wind. It was very hot, and the road was dusty, but still I ran as if the devil were after me. Today was a special occasion. Never had the sky been so blue and the oleanders so red, and never had pretty girls interested me so little.

A few friends, past whom I rushed with shouldered harpoon, shouted after me. But I had no time. I was long since gone from Juan-les-Pins, somewhere in remote, unknown seas, where monsters lived, "bigger than a hundred elephants". Ah, how indescribably vast was my new hunting ground! How immeasurably extensive the shores of the sea! Reefs everywhere, everywhere islands and coral banks, everywhere new landscapes and new creatures! How was I ever to see even a fraction of it? I quickened my pace yet more.

Finally I got to the cap, and here everything went like lightning. I hid my clothes under a rock and belted the dagger in its sheath around me. Harpoon in hand, I clambered down across the rocks. Then I spat into my goggles, and off I went.

It was the same place where I had watched the American a week before; today the fish should meet a new adversary! Cautiously I glided into the water, peering around, anxiously avoiding any splash. Fish have a delicate sense for vibrations in the water; that much I had noticed the previous days, when I was simply diving with goggles. Any splashing, any quick motion in the water frightens them. I must grope forward with slow, harmonious swimming motions. Silent as a snake. . . .

Down yonder was a fish!

I clenched my teeth. Calm, calm above all; I dived, or rather tried to dive, because with the long pole it was far from simple. The moment when I turned my body downwards my feet splashed the surface. The fish was off.

I had first to practise the art of noiseless diving with the harpoon. Standing erect, with the harpoon pointing diagonally downwards, I had to sink as deep as possible, then pull myself farther by the shaft, then turn downwards and take several strokes with my free left hand in order to get deep enough to stretch my legs without breaking the surface of the water. This was no easy matter, particularly because you have to breathe in deeply before diving, which makes you very buoyant. I tried it several times, until I could do it successfully.

Nevertheless I could not get any of the fish. Heaven knew why it was: the same species of fish which, on previous days, I had come so close to that I thought I could touch them with my hand were now so timid that I could not get within fifteen feet of them. The creatures squinted up at me with nervous anxiety, and often fled even before I dived. Was it the harpoon? Did they guess my evil intentions?

Once I got fairly close to three fish that were pushing their plump bodies sluggishly among the seaweed. This time I crept up so slowly that in ten seconds I scarcely advanced thirty feet and the blood was pounding in my temples for want of air. Nevertheless I could not approach even them. They fled, and I thrust after them with the harpoon, at least getting the satisfaction of seeing them scatter like scared chickens. I noticed that one of the creatures had a diagonal scratch across its back. Of course. Gilpatric had been fishing here! Probably that was why the fish were so shy.

That would be it. I decided to swim across a cove to the next headland; perhaps it would be better there. It was a fairly long and tedious swim, which took me past the bathing beach of the Eden Rock Hotel. Everything here was very grand: little terraces with beach chairs and coloured umbrellas, tarpaulins, rafts, a fresh-water pool, and even a little bar at the top. Among them a few abandoned rubber animals, inflated

29

to bursting in the midday sun. Probably the guests were eating now. On a raft out front I saw two feminine figures.

Damn! Now I had actually gone and harpooned myself! In the act of swimming I drove the harpoon into my left palm, and fairly hard at that. The wound bled freely, and, much worse, I was so startled I dropped the harpoon. I dived right after it, as fast and as deep as I could, but in vain; I could not overtake it; it sailed downwards faster and faster. Now I was back on the surface, gasping for air, and staring once more into the depths. Neither harpoon nor bottom was to be seen. This was the end of my hunting!

But I would not give in. I swam to and fro, dived as deep as I could, and shaded my eyes, accustoming them to the twilight of the depths. Gradually I could make out that an endless meadow of seaweed spread below me. It was perfectly flat and montonous, with nowhere a harpoon to be seen. Just a tiny stick at one spot, that was all. Could that be the harpoon? Only now did I realize how deep it was. Of course that was the harpoon, standing erect because the heavy head dragged the front end down! There it stood, tiny as a matchstick. The bottom was at least eighty feet down.

I studied the spot carefully, surveyed it by landmarks, and then swam to shore. A beach attendant had turned up, and I asked him politely for court plaster and a long rope, but evidently nobody except guests of the Eden Rock Hotel existed for the fellow. Not until the two feminine creatures came to my assistance—American girls interested in my bleeding hand—did his manner change. Then he hurried off, bringing back iodine and a plaster and also the desired rope.

While the ladies were using the iodine in generous doses, I explained my mishap to them. I was awfully sorry, I added: ordinarily I always had a few fish with me; but if in spite of my wound I should manage to catch something, I would make bold to send my booty to the ladies.

Then I swam back to the scene of the accident, tied a big running noose in one end of the rope, and lowered it, wide open. I repeated this twice, five times, ten times, twenty times, and more, thus gaining the opportunity for exhaustive study of the contrariness of a hemp rope and the various local currents. The loop never stayed a loop for more than thirty feet; then it would twist and tangle, and, at fifty feet, would be caught by a side current, wound into a snarl, and driven sixty feet away. It was the same thing every time. Not once did the loop go down decently to the bottom. I was blue by now, trembling all over, but it was no use, I had to have the harpoon back. Four hundred francs meant thirty lunches; I couldn't afford to lose them.

Meanwhile the bathing beach had come to life again. Several times friendly swimmers visited me and inquired what I was doing. But I could only growl. I was completely frozen stiff. Even breathing came hard to me. With mechanical regularity I kept throwing out my noose. An hour passed, two hours passed.

Finally the two American girls came out in a boat, bringing me a thick sandwich to restore my strength. And it worked. At the next attempt the loop actually settled around the harpoon! With trembling hands I pulled it up and waved it in farewell across the waves.

I had now only one desire in life: to get back and out into the sun. I panted like a rusty old motor-boat straight across the bay. As I got to the craggy shore of the headland, I noticed a big fish, resting motionless beside a bunch of seaweed. This bunch of seaweed struck me as oddly familiar. I located myself by shore points: it was actually the same place! Here Gilpatric had taken his fish, here, by that very same bunch of seaweed! That was a good omen, if anything ever was!

With my last strength and last warmth I dived and stalked the fish. My movements were infinitely slow, and before my mind's eye I could see myself already in the dining-room of the Eden Rock Hotel, the beautifully cooked fish before me and the two American girls opposite. But the fish was still alive. It nibbled at the seaweed, never dreaming what disaster awaited it. I tensed my body with the utmost concentration, and then, just as the fish looked up, I thrust home, thrust with all my strength—into the rocks!

The fish moved slightly to one side, and swam off without haste. But there was really no need for him to hurry now. The spearhead, my precious, expensive spearhead, was broken.

31

If you paddle around barefoot in the Orinoco you find yourself suddenly falling over, paralysed. The natives will say regretfully, "arimna," meaning by this a snakelike creature whose mysterious powers have caused more than one scientist to rack his brains. In the whole animal kingdom there is only one other creature, a fish, equipped with a disastrous power like the arimna's. As chance would have it, this very one was the first fish I ever harpooned.

I was not hunting alone now. I had chanced to meet in Juan-les-Pins my old friend Burli Marischka, who promptly joined me, likewise acquired watertight goggles, and was no less enthusiastic than I. Our first stalking hunt together took us to the reefs at the east tip of Saint-Honorat, which were alive with fish. Suddenly Burli pointed downwards. Just below us, on the edge of a seaweed meadow, rested a strange creature, flat and round like a potato pancake, with a dainty little tail. I dived at once, and it was anything but a heroic achievement. The fish did not stir. I simply nailed it to the sand.

"What kind of wretched brute is that?" cried Burli when I came up again. But when he touched the "wretched brute", he cried out in fright.

It was a torpedo, which gave off an electric shock when you touched it. The body of this fish contains an organ that generates and stores electricity. How this living battery functions is something the savants have not quite decided even yet, the more so because the creature can discharge it absolutely at will. The torpedo paralyses and kills small fish in this way; arimna, the South American electric eel, can paralyse a horse with one jolt.

5. Cheerly, I, Heinz, Egon, Haemmerle, and Guido aboard
the *Sokol* before our first expedition

6. "Catch fish
by hand? Why
any child in
Austria can do
that!"

7. In the clear waters of Uljan we snapped everything there was to be snapped, viz. ourselves in the diving helmet . . .

8. . . . the unappetizing sea cucumbers

Down at the beach a gramophone was playing "La Paloma". Beside it sat the old Turk, obviously drunk again. His gaudy caftan hung open in front; he had taken off his red fez; the rugs he peddled along the beach all day lay beside him on the sand. He was watching some fishermen poke around with long switches in the knee-deep water. When we sat down beside him, he began to cry, and confessed that he was not really a Turk at all. He said he was born in Naples, and had been a fisherman there.

"Just like those fellows out there," he wailed, "that's how I used to go fishing with a switch. With beautiful red-and-white tassels on it. Because red and white are the octopus's favourite colours. If you come near his hole with the tassels, he grabs at them, and hangs himself up on the hook—ho ho! And what eating—tee hee!"

He wept, and re-wound his gramophone.

"But I've caught bigger ones, too," he went on, "with a mirror. You have to let down just in front of the octopus's hole. Then the monster sees himself, thinks there's another octopus, and grabs the mirror to fight it. And hangs himself up on the hook—ho ho! And what eating—tee hee!"

We let the old fellow gabble on. He told about Turkey, which he had never seen, about octopuses, about Naples, and also happened to mention a wreck that he said was on the sea floor not far from Cannes.

The next day we went to the place. It was called Château de la Galère; the ship was some thirty-five feet down, with the tip of one mast still rising above water.

As a boy I had read a story about a diver on a wreck, and had cherished romantic ideas on the subject ever since. The present reality, however, was rather prosaic. Nevertheless we found it most exciting. We dived down to the old captain's bridge, commanded now solely by jellyfish and starfish; to the smokestack, which lay like a battered plug hat; and to the forecastle, which had collapsed into a heap of rusty iron. The hull was split into several parts, bedecked with bearded seaweed. Fish both large and small swam everywhere among the twisted iron sheets.

I dived to an open door, and was peering into the darkness of the compartment when I noticed to one side of me a massive body creeping shapeless and slimy from a crevice and gliding like slow ooze across the deck.

I saw by the tentacles that I was dealing with a big octopus. Its slit eyes glared at me, cold and evil. Guy Gilpatric had warned me never to harpoon an octopus, because sometimes the impaled beast would climb up the shaft.

I swam to the surface, and looked around. Burli was far off. Aboard the wreck below the octopus was already moving back towards a crevice. If I meant to do anything, I must be quick about it.

I hesitated no longer, but plunged, and drove the harpoon square into the slimy body. With the same movement I snatched it back so that the head would come off the shaft, and the octopus could not climb up the harpoon. This yanked the beast off the deck. It immediately squirted an inky fluid into the water, and shot jerkily hither and thither like a smoke rocket.

I sped upward, dragging the creature behind me, and had barely managed to reach the surface when I felt a slimy arm clutching my legs. In an instant the octopus had fixed all eight tentacles upon me, and I could not shake it off. Though I had a knife, I could scarcely go jabbing around my legs in the turbid water. Besides, I needed both arms to stay on the surface. The octopus hung to me like a leaden weight.

I yelled for help, and luckily Burli was soon at hand. He and another man who rushed to my assistance from shore pulled me in. Once ashore we tore the tentacles off my legs; each of the many suckers left a red circle on my skin. The octopus was eleven and a half feet across, and we had to stab its slimy head innumerable times before it was dead. (Illus. 2.)

"Stabbed it in the head?" cried the horrified Turk when we showed him our prey that evening. "You mustn't ever kill

34

an octopus with a knife—that only destroys his body but not his evil spirit!"

He explained that you must reach into the monster's pouch-shaped body and turn it inside out like a glove. Only then would the creature really be dead, body and spirit. Having made good our omission, he took a club and began pounding the now doubly dead brute. Very few people knew, he leered, that octopus meat was just as good eating as lobster. Tinned lobster was almost half octopus—he knew, because he had worked for one of the canning companies himself.

After counting out ninety-nine blows, he dropped bits of the creature into boiling water. The skin turned red and pulled off; the white meat was delicate and really tasted delicious. We ate it with mayonnaise until we were sick to our stomachs, playing "La Paloma" the while.

12

When you are swimming around in the depths of the sea, you never know what will happen the next moment. It's just the same when you are courting a girl.

Two weeks after my melancholy expedition of Cap d'Antibes it turned out that my unhappy love was not unhappy at all; she even followed me into the solitude, and waited on the cliffs while I fished. Only now I had nothing but fish in my head. By day I saw fish in the sea, at night I fished in my dreams, and meanwhile I compared the two.

So my love remained unhappy.

Twenty-five feet away from me swims a silvery fish with an arched, high back and a pointed little mouth. He swims somewhat comfortably, yet briskly, from seaweed to seaweed, from cliff to cliff, nibbling at a rock here, taking an interest in a small crab there, then swims on a bit, encountering a colleague who apparently has something to tell him, and finally, quite elaborately, picks out a spot for a rest between two rocks. I know the fish: it's a sea bream. I dive quickly, because a cleft is the easiest place to outwit the bream, but before I get down there the restless spirit has already left his hiding place. So I shall have to try another way. I swim slowly and very carefully behind him, and before long he grows irresolute. He knows something is going on behind him, but does not know what it is, and would like to. Shall I make a run for it, he seems to be wondering, or mightn't I better look first to be sure it's necessary? He keeps squinting back at me first from the left and then from the right side. Although desperately short of breath, I keep up my pursuit, and finally the bream's curiosity grows to the point where he can no longer control it. He turns, places himself crosswise, and squints back. And at that moment I thrust!

Swimming on, I reach a spot overgrown with sea kale, where a school of fat gold-striped salpa are grazing. They look as if they must burst at any moment. (Illus. 3.) The entire meaning of their life seems to be gluttony. They are always eating—morning, noon, and evening, possibly even at night. Mostly you see just their tails, because their heads are burrowing in the lush green. Nevertheless it is almost impossible to get near them unnoticed. One of the creatures always discovers the danger in time, the warning flap of a fin shrills through the water, and the next moment they are all in flight. One conspicuous point is that in a moment of danger the school immediately assembles; individuals that have strayed while grazing race blindly after the rest. I hope to make use of this observation now. I wait until a fair-sized fish has separated from the others while gormandizing, and then I dive perpendicularly to the bottom some distance from him. Creeping like an Indian just above the floor, I succeed in getting between the single creature and its school unnoticed. As soon as I am sure of myself, I make a motion, and then watch sharply. The school flees, and my expectation is justified: the single fish comes rushing straight at me, obviously with nothing in his head except to get back to the school by the shortest route. Not until he is right upon me does he swing about—and at that moment I thrust!

With the gold-striped salpa in my game net I swim on, and then I notice a grey shadow beneath the waves. My friend branzino, a dashing, predatory fish, is a regular daredevil. He comes straight at me, glaring defiantly like a German university student trying to pick a duel. At first I never knew the etiquette of the situation, because I couldn't spear him from in front. I have since learned a good dodge. I wait until the branzino is as close as possible to the tip of my harpoon, and then startle him with a short, harmless jab. He dodges like a flash, and whisks a few yards away. Then he immediately collects himself, and—obviously to take the ignominy out of his flight—comes back with a graceful sweep. Impudence! you can see his eyes flashing. With quivering fins he fixes his gaze on the harpoon head. And when nothing more happens he turns haughtily to one side, slowly, the more fully to express his superiority. And at that moment I thrust!

Fish are not nearly so dull and tiresome as most people think. On the contrary, their natures are as varied and colourful as their shapes. Many of them have pronounced traits of character that positively challenge comparison with human beings. Almost each species has particular habits, and is distinguished from others by its own character, intelligence, and temperament. In many species these peculiarities are so pronounced that you can recognize the fish just as well by their behaviour as by their bodily characteristics.

But since these differences are apparent only in nature,

not in an aquarium and oceanographers have seldom had the chance to observe on the spot, psychological characteristics have scarcely been used in classification. Here the under-water huntsman has a chance to do valuable scientific work. He is in constant intimate contact with the creatures; his every movement produces certain movements on the part of the fish in reaction. From hunting them he gets to know them so well that he can often tell beforehand what they will be doing the next moment.

It is very interesting, too, that wounded fish of different species behave differently. Some try for a crack in the rocks regardless, others always stay on the surface, others, again, always flee towards the deep sea. If you injure a fish in the gills, it swims to the surface bleeding profusely, and often seeks out shallow water. Since the fish's gills are its lungs, it suffers from want of breath, and floats helplessly at the top.

In the first week of my hunting with Burli we once fished near the little village of Theoule, where at a certain distance from shore the flat, stony beach plunges off to a great depth. On this threshold I took several fish in rapid succession, among them a five-pound mullet that I hit right in the gill. The creature flapped violently, yanked itself off the spearhead, and fled, bleeding, towards shallow water. I followed as fast as I could, but a fishing boat got in my way, and I lost sight of the creature. Meanwhile Burli, along shore, was hunting shells and crabs, while a few fisherfolk and bathers sitting on the beach watched him.

Suddenly they saw an odd spectacle. Burli stopped, looked fixedly ahead, then took a few steps and flung himself headlong into the water. There was a huge splash, and when he stood up he pulled a big, flapping fish out of the water with his bare hands.

The mullet gasped for air, and the people gasped even more. This was a complete novelty indeed!

Only Burli lost none of his aplomb. "Catch fish by hand?" I heard him say. "Why, at home in Austria any child can do that!" (Illus. 6.)

14

The episode that gave "Death Bay" its name began with an idyll. We had made ourselves comfortable in a sheltered spot among the cliffs. Burli was lying on his stomach, groaning from time to time, while I sat astride his back, poking around in his heel with a needle. The poor fellow had stepped on a good dozen sea-urchin spines, all of which were deep under the skin. The spots were edged with blue, and there was a certain fascination in performing the operation neatly. You first carefully raise the upper layer of skin, and then, with the needle point, start wiggling the end of the broken spine to and fro. If you do this skilfully, it slowly comes out. But usually the patient rears up at the crucial moment, and the spine breaks off, so that you have to penetrate with the needle into far deeper regions.

After the sixth spine Burli vigorously shook me off. We ate a sandwich, and watched some mullet that were lying almost motionless on the surface.

By nature, mullet are equable souls. Usually you find them swimming in small groups along the rocks, where they burrow in the moss with their fleshy lips. If you startle them, they spit out their titbits and flee for ten feet, after which they forget their fright. The previous week this familiar behaviour had suddenly changed. They seemed to be transformed. They danced about one another, shot to and fro, and it was quite impossible to bag one. Sometimes they would float in twos, snuggling close together with vibrating fins, then suddenly they would be off like arrows. That love was rearing its head here was obvious. The madness lasted for a week, then all was over. The creatures hung tired and worn near the surface, and we could have harpooned them by the dozen. But a person has some sentiment, after all. (Illus. 4.)

We lay down, and I fell asleep. On this occasion I had my first meeting with two mermaids. They swam through an avenue of red coral, making a charming sight. Particularly the smaller, with fins like veils, and bangs. However, as I approached, a shark suddenly appeared. The mermaids began to cry and clutched me so tight that I could scarcely stir. Luckily an iceberg floated between us and the shark. I woke up, feeling cold. The sun had gone, leaving me in the shadow.

Where could Burli be? The harpoon was gone, so he must be fishing; it was to be hoped that he would bring it back with the head still whole. I shifted over into the sun again, and tried to go on with my dream, but instead of veil-like fins and bangs I saw my professor of Latin, which was a most inferior substitute. While he was giving me an examination, as thorough as it was disastrous, on the *Odes* of Horace, I woke up again, and discovered that Burli had not yet returned. Judging by the height of the sun, at least an hour had passed.

I clambered up on a high rock, but Burli was nowhere to be seen. So I swam to the next bay. He was not there, either. It was fairly dark under water by now; I began to feel quite uneasy. In spite of myself I peered into every cave in the bank. Could he have dived in somewhere and run into an octopus? Hadn't the comic Turk told us that big octopuses made a habit of crouching among the shore rocks, clutching the passing swimmer with suddenly out-thrust tentacles? Could he have met a shark? Since the British naval flotilla had cast anchor here in the gulf, sharks had been sighted twice.

The wind freshened considerably; clouds moved across the sun, which was already sinking towards the mountain-tops; under water, it was already completely ghostly. I swam on and on along the shore. My anxiety turned more and more to fright.

Then the blood froze in my veins: close beside me I felt a motion! I whirled, but in the dim light could see nothing. I felt plainly that a big creature was close to me. Instinctively I drew in my arms and legs, peered in every direction, and held my breath longer and longer so as not to interrupt my underwater survey. Finally I could hold it no longer, and gasped for air. And just at that moment it happened.

I can still remember that I was looking towards shore, that the cliffs were already deep in shadow, that the caves in the bank reminded me of the ugly gaps in a row of teeth, and that the water between me and the shore looked black and uncanny. Then I felt the same motion again, heard a hissing, and not fifty feet from me a giant body shot up out of the water. It rose straight skyward, hung for an instant in the air, glittering and gleaming in the light of the setting sun, then turned and plunged like a radiant projectile into the dark flood. Its stream-line shape was so perfect that it split the sea almost without a splash.

It was a dolphin, a creature more than seven feet long. I saw it for one moment more under water, then it vanished in the depths, like a vision dissolving into nothingness.

With quaking knees I reached shore, and now discovered Burli, who was standing high up on the cliffs, brandishing the harpoon. His long absence was also explained. He had pursued a big fish until he was too cold to go on, and coming back by land he had got lost climbing among the rocks. The wind had blown his shouts away.

We baptized the bay that I had searched so anxiously for him "Death Bay", and agreed thenceforth not to go fishing alone.

15

"I can't sell the fish to you," I said to a woman who stopped me along the way. "But I'll be glad to give you one."

I gave her the biggest one I had taken, and strolled on, feeling very pleased with myself. A few hundred yards farther I was already beginning to be annoyed—I might just as well have sold her the fish. After all, I had expenses, too, and my finances were far from robust. Not at all a bad idea, in fact! Why shouldn't I sell the fish?

At the next restaurant I passed I still had too many inhibi-tions, but at the second one I drove myself to the attempt. I was quite bashful about it, but the proprietor made no fuss at all, offered me a decent price, and I was rid of the fish. As it turned out, good fish was very much in demand here. The professional fishermen, who knew perfectly well that the restaurants were dependent on their supplies, caught correspondingly little, and charged correspondingly high prices. Besides, the very fish that were easiest to harpoon—branzinos, dorados, mullet, and sea bream—are the most popular food fish, but are seldom taken with net or hook and line.

Whistling a merry tune, I jingled in my pocket the first money I had ever earned myself. What should I do with it? Go to one of the local bars that evening? Or have a really grand feed at the Casino for once? I wavered for a while, then came to a serious and noble resolve. Now and for all time I would never use the income from my under-water fishing for anything except more fishing. In this way each enterprise would finance the one to follow. I was so serious about my decision that I went straight to a stationer's, bought an account book, and started keeping strict accounts. On the left, under debit, I wrote down my expenses so far; on the right, under credit, my first profit.

That was the eighteenth of August, 1937, and the debit was the larger by four hundred and seventy-six francs.

16

The sale of fish conspicuously improved my financial situation. I was soon able to rent a bicycle, and came to know the whole coast as far as Saint-Raphael. I fished off Cap Miramar, off the rocks near Trayas, along Cap Roux, near the little island of Anthéor, and finally even near the romantic cliffs of Drammont. And I soon acquired a good eye for fishing grounds.

There is a science, called ecology, that deals with the relationship between the peculiarities of a region and the

42

animals and plants that occur there. In those days I knew as much about this as a pig about flying; but even so I made a good many ecological observations.

I encountered very few fish on sandy bottom or seaweed meadows obviously because there is not enough food there. Things were better in coves, among seaweed, sand, and boulders, and along much-split rocky shores, where caves and clefts offered refuge to the innumerable tiny beings. Here all the fish abounded that were after worms, molluscs, crabs, and other small fry. Where they stayed, the predatory fish were not far behind. The most interesting fishing was along rock capes with outlying reefs and along cliffs that plunged off abruptly to a great depth. Here the denizens of the coast encountered those of the deep sea. The currents drove great quantities of tiny organisms past, which were devoured by swarms of small fish; these in turn were consumed by bigger fish, which hid in the surf caves; and sometimes huge deep-sea visitors arrived, in whose stomachs the chain came to an end.

I kept striving to dive deeper and deeper, but at forty feet the pressure in my ears grew so heavy that I could not go any farther. At first my nose complained also, but it soon became resigned to its fate. If I dived deep, water would get into my sinuses, but it did not hurt, and as soon as I reached shore again it would run out of its own accord.

So far as the length of time I could stay under goes, I don't believe I ever lasted more than one and a half or at most two minutes that summer. Burli, however, thinks otherwise. It happened this way:

In "Death Bay" we were exploring some surf caves, and happened on a cavern below the water level, which seemed to lead fairly far into the bank. While Burli waited outside, I dived with the spear and pushed my way inside. As soon as my eyes were used to the darkness I saw that the cavern widened towards the back. A few smaller side caves also branched off, from which colder water poured in. Not seeing any fish I was about to turn back, when I noticed a dull gleam of light, which came from inside one of the rear side caverns. I followed the light, swam around a corner, and now saw that

43

the cavern had a second exit here. To get there, you had to pass a fairly narrow spot. As there was a good-sized fish beyond, silhouetted against the bright circle of the opening, I hesitated no longer, but forced my way through the bottleneck. The fish did not see me coming from the darkness, so I had an easy time harpooning him. Pretty well out of breath, I surfaced in a tiny pool some distance within the shore line. I killed the fish, took a rest, and then went back as I had come.

Burli was beside himself. I had been under water at least five minutes, he declared. And he must have known.

17

Once when we were hunting along Cap Miramar people told us that a French naval officer named Le Prieur had been there fishing the day before with a diving outfit and an underwater gun. As far as we could discover, he loaded the gun with a powder cartridge, and so fired off little harpoons, which were attached by a line to a piece of cork. After the shot these would float to the surface. When Le Prieur had had enough fishing, he would come to the surface and collect the corks along with the fish attached to them.

The traces of his activity were plain enough: not a fish anywhere! The few there were, were so nervous and timid that you could not do a thing with them. Feeling fairly put out, we swam to a reef some hundreds of yards from shore, and then I heard a gurgling cry behind me. Burli was waving his arms in the air and pointing frantically downward.

"Tunas! Tunas!" he yelled, quite beside himself.

The water below us, yawningly empty but a moment before, now flashed with thirty gigantic fish. They had plump, silvery-gleaming bodies and swam around in a circle like mad. And there were more and more of them.

44

I took a breath, but swallowed the wrong way in my excitement, and had to surface again in order to spit out the water and get a better breath. Then I hurried down as fast as I could go to the gleaming, silvery merry-go-round. The creatures paid me no attention at all, but simply swam round and round in circles. I clutched the harpoon, and set after the first one I met. The fact that the creature was at least as big as I was did not occur to me in my huntsman's fever. I thrust, but missed. Then, controlling my excitement, I replaced the head on the harpoon shaft, whence it had fallen off, and took aim at another fish. This time I was calm and careful, and drove the harpoon into his body with all my might. As I did so I could feel how hard and compact the flesh was, and for a moment I was reminded of canned tuna. Then the giant saw to it that I should think of live tuna. He tugged at the cord like a mad thing. I clutched the harpoon handle, managed to catch a quick breath of air on the surface, and then the creature dragged me pitilessly into the depths. I fought back, trying to brake his pull by swimming, but the tuna was considerably stronger than I. He gave me no time to think, but kept on dragging me downwards, while I yanked desperately at the shaft. Suddenly the pull stopped. An ounce of tuna meat clung to my harpoon; the rest of the creature made off at high speed.

Another day we were back hunting along the reefs on the eastern tip of Saint-Honorat, at the same place where we had taken the torpedo. I first harpooned a few mullet and sea bream, and a dorado, whose gills turned a golden red in death; then thirty feet down, off the outermost reef, where the bottom sinks away almost perpendicularly, we spied a big fish with a green-and-brown pattern. He hung quietly before the entrance to a cave in the rock and goggled rather stupidly. While so doing, he fanned his tattered pectoral fins with dignity.

Him we had to have!

So as not to frighten the creature, we swam back cautiously to the crag and held a council of war. The creature was so big that we could not possibly overpower it with the short line. We needed a long rope. Then we would fasten one end to the harpoon head and the other to Burli. He would sit on the

45

crag and hold the fish fast; then, together, we would pull
it up.

We swam back to the island, where he found a fisherman
who had a ninety-foot rope. At first he did not want to lend it,
but when we described our purpose and the size of the fish, and
offered him our clothes as security, he agreed. By way of payment we were to give him the head of the fish; he wanted to
make a soup of it.

Meanwhile the sky had clouded over, and a thunderstorm
was coming up from the east. The sea was stained greyish-blue
and the first squalls were already whistling over the waves.
We leaped into the water with our rope, and found the sea
astonishingly warm. When we came to the crags, the surf was
already so high that a mountainous wave would sometimes
carry us up as high as the rock. Seconds later we would be twice
as deep below.

Burli now tried to climb up the outermost rock, but the
waves kept washing him down again. He went head over heels,
and was rolled across the jagged rock covered with sea urchins.
When I tried to help, the rope caught in the rocks, and as Burli
was on one end and I with the harpoon on the other, everything got hopelessly tangled up, and we were fairly at the mercy
of the waves. One lifted us up and plumped us down in the
middle of the rocks, then the next wave came, broke over us,
and tumbled us back across jagged stones and sea urchins.

When we finally got loose, we were flayed alive. We un-
tangled the rope, and arrived pretty well exhausted at the spot
where we had seen the fish. Visibility under water was now
very much worse on account of the heavy surf. At each breaker
clouds of spray went downward like air fountains. We had to
dive a dozen feet or more to see clearly at all. But luckily the
fish was still there. He was still in the same place, still fanning
his pectoral fins with dignity.

While Burli stayed behind close by, near the rocks, I swam
a little farther out into deep water, where I could dive better.
It was a queer situation: we were not seventy feet apart and
yet saw each other only occasionally. When one of us was high
up on a wave, the other would be at the bottom of a deep

trough. Only when we were raised simultaneously by neighbouring wave mountains did we see each other.

On a signal from Burli that he was ready, I dived and swam downward among the clouds of spray. Countless small fish were hanging close to the cliff here, probably because the surf killed a great many small creatures that drifted down the rocks to the bottom.

I cast a last glance backward: the rope, attached to my harpoon head, led upward in a sweeping curve and vanished in the clouds of foam that hid Burli from my sight. He had fastened the end to his belt. The moment the fish was on, we had agreed, he was somehow to clutch the rocks. Then I would come to his assistance as fast as possible.

The monster fish goggled dully at me. As I got closer, he withdrew, swimming slowly backwards, into the entrance of his cave. At that moment a current came to my aid, carrying me within thrusting distance of the creature. I took careful aim, the fish turned slowly, and I thrust. That is, I was about to thrust, for at the very moment when I was shooting my arm forward, the harpoon was yanked backwards out of my hand. The fish gave me one last, surprised glance and vanished into his cave.

I swam back up, determined to throttle Burli. But he was innocent. A high wave had grabbed him and swept him away, and with him the rope and my harpoon.

After these two failures I finally discovered the ideal solution. I tied the harpoon head once more to a long rope, but this time did it up in coils, which I fastened to my belt with an ingenious knot. The moment there was a pull at the rope, the knot would untie itself and the coils would fall free. I could then swim up to the surface, quickly climb the rocky shore, and from there I could tire out and land the fish.

This knot, an invention of my own, came within an ace of costing me my life.

The summer was over, and we went fishing one last time along the romantic cliffs of Drammont. That day I had already taken a capital branzino by the new method, and then I met two big groupers, perhaps the most beautiful creature of the

Mediterranean. Among all the fish I know, not one makes such a majestic impression. The creatures are big, sometimes up to forty pounds, nobly shaped, dark blue, conspicuously shy, and usually they sweep past in twos or threes at unattainable depths. I had often tried to take one of these splendid creatures but had never succeeded. This time chance came to my assistance. I encountered the two fish in a narrow channel between two reefs, which they were trying to pass through in one direction, I in the other. Exactly in the middle we met. Since big fish generally dislike to go out of their way, and groupers scorn all undignified haste anyway, the two of them swung around fairly leisurely, which was fatal to the leading fish. Or rather, it was really fatal to me. I hit the creature with a good thrust, but my patent knot would not let go. The fish whizzed off, straight downward, towing me ten feet after him. I tried everything I could think of to make the knot see reason, but rope, belt, and bathing trunks fused into one entity.

I have not always told the upshot of this adventure quite truthfully. The real course of events seemed to me too ignominious. I usually asserted that I had drawn my knife and cut the rope, but in reality I had forgotten and left the knife ashore. The fish kept pulling me ever downwards, and no matter how I tugged at the line, this time the head sat fast. I lost my nerve, beat about me, got water under my goggles, coughed, swallowed, and did not realize until the last moment what a serious fix I was in. There was nothing for it but to bend frantically backward and force my way out of the bathing trunks, which were drawn very tight. But while they, along with rope and patent knot, were left at the disposal of the grouper, I got back to the upper world, and Burli gaped mightily when he saw me coming ashore.

48

9. Hunting with the camera was no less exciting than with the spear

10. The surface is the sky of the underwater world, the waves its clouds

The evening before I went home there was a great celebration at Juan-les-Pins, which I happened to blunder into.
A side street served as a dance floor, tables and chairs were
borrowed from a restaurant, an accordionist and a gramophone
provided the music, there was all the wine you wanted, and
everybody who passed by was invited—in a word, it was the
birthday party of an American.

A young man came up to me and bowed. The young man
wanted to dance with me. I told him I would rather make use
of a lady for that purpose, whereupon he expressed his regret.

Everything was in complete confusion. Some young lads
were dancing with elderly matrons, some elderly gentlemen
with very young and very dubious ladies. A black-haired
woman was revolving, closely entwined with a platinum blonde.
Next to them whirled three figures, one of whom perched on
the other two, and a drunken Hungarian, who was dancing
alone, but did not know it, for he kept whispering "Natasha!"
whereas his Natasha had in fact long since vanished down the
side street with somebody else. Some chorus girls were dancing
in complete costume, just as they had come from the Casino,
a man was dancing in a tail coat, another without shoes, an
Italian girl as greasy as she was bewitching in coloured ker-
chiefs, a Spaniard stripped to the waist. And in the midst of all
was the generous fat American with an upturned champagne
bucket on his head and a little fox terrier, which had been fed
on champagne, and which kept turning in circles. . . .

Suddenly the music stopped, and everyone was on the move.
Why and how, nobody knew, but everyone ran down to the
beach. In the lead was the accordionist with the chorus girls,
the man with the gramophone bringing up the rear. The fact
that nobody had a bathing suit with them didn't matter; soon
there were screeches and splashing everywhere in the dark.
Everyone swam out to the diving tower.

I stayed behind and let the waves carry me. The cries in the distance died away, soon all was quite still, and only the little ripples lisped around me. The night was dark, the water warm and soft, my heart pounded.

"I love you," I whispered into the ear of the ocean. "Ever since I've known you I've loved you. I must see all your marvels, know all your beauty. . . ."

And the ocean listened, and snuggled still closer to me.

19

Back in Vienna, life resumed its accustomed course. I matriculated at the university and entered for a law course, because I was to take over my father's office later. I had really meant to study zoology, but Father said zoology was all well and good if you had money enough to spend; if not, however, you could easily starve at it. With great luck I might be a museum curator or a university professor, both jobs equally ill paid, and I might be an old man before the government would treat me to an expedition. As a lawyer, on the other hand, I could easily make money enough to afford such extravagances on the side.

And so I stuck to the law.

I crammed Roman law for two terms, and it was no waste of my time. If I soon forgot the difference between a tort and a writ, I did learn once and for all the clear, logical thinking that is fundamental for any scientific work. And the more clearly and logically I thought, the clearer it became that I should not spend the rest of my life among writs and summonses.

So I didn't stick to the law after all.

On the way home from Juan-les-Pins I gave my imagination free play about the furore I would create with my experiences. Particularly among the girls. Actually it turned out differently. The fact that I could harpoon fish under water was something that some people believed and others did not, but mostly they simply were not interested. I swallowed the bitter pill that it is easier to start something new and special than to convince the rest of the world that it really is something new and special.

Uncle Erich, who made me tell him my experiences in detail, consoled me. A person could cross the Himalayas, he said, and his acquaintances would simply remark, "Why, how interesting!" and then turn right back to their bridge. Or football. Though of course if there was an article about it in a weekly magazine, that was different. Then you were a hero at one blow. And in that case it wouldn't matter much what you had done, if anything; you merely had to appear in the weekly magazines.

All right, then, a weekly magazine! I wrote a glowing account and sent it to the three big papers. At the same time I subscribed to the following numbers, which, however, turned out to be a waste of capital. I did not even get the manuscripts back. Only when, on another attempt, I enclosed the return postage did they inform me with regret that the subject was too remote, and I had really better try a fishing paper. As a matter of fact the article did appear in an anglers' journal. Nobody I know of ever read it.

At least I got a fee of two hundred marks, though, with which I bought a camera. Then I had a mechanic build me a watertight case, because I was determined to bring back under-water photographs from my next trip as evidence of what I had done. I also tinkered away at new harpoon heads, and got a pair of swimming fins from France, where they had just been introduced at the World's Fair. These fins, patented by a Monsieur Corlieu, were as yet quite unknown in Vienna. I demonstrated them at a swimming pool, beating one of the best Austrian swimmers by two good lengths with their help, and instantly my fins were the talk of the town. Now, all of a sudden, people also believed my stories about the octopus and the tuna, and my first lecture at the Academic Sport Club was a success. No less than eight of my athletic friends wanted to go with me on my next trip. The girls, however, admired me as the inventor of the fins. I hope Monsieur Corlieu will forgive it.

21

The story of how Old Wabble escaped scalping at the very last moment is fairly well known. After pursuing him through impassable mountains for several days, the Sioux surrounded him on the south bank of Lake Shenandoah. When the trapper saw that escape was impossible he uttered a fearful curse, set spurs to his horse, and bounded through the reeds into the lake. The Indians shot at him from every direction, and Old Wabble almost instantly fell off his horse. With wild cries of triumph the redskins rushed to the spot, but found only the injured horse and Old Wabble's broad-brimmed hat which was floating on the bloody water. The chief had the lake probed with poles for a long distance around, but the corpse was nowhere to be found. This threw him into such a rage that he scalped Old Wabble's horse. The night was devoted to an orgy, and next morning the redskins departed. Shortly thereafter Old Wabble reappeared. He had hidden under water between two rocks, and breathed through a hollow reed that he had poked to the surface.

This was the system I wanted to use in the future for fishing. I proposed to dive with a rubber tube in my mouth, floating the upper end on a cork above water.

Unluckily there was one catch to it. Old Wabble must have stayed quite close to the surface, because even at three feet below the surface the water pressure on one's chest is so heavy that a person cannot suck down air for any length of time. A Viennese professor even figured out that an experiment of this sort was bound to end fatally at six feet down. As it would be an unusually quick and simple death, the method was suggested for purposes of execution. So my project of diving by Old Wabble's plan came to nothing.

I now studied the subject more carefully, and learned that a person can breathe at any considerable depth under water only if the air he breathes is under the same pressure as his body. This is the principle on which the diving helmet used by the American explorer William Beebe and by his countryman and colleague Longley works. The helmet is open at the bottom; that is to say, in principle it is a small diving bell put over the head; the air is supplied through a tube by a hand pump. Beebe's accounts excited me so much that I had a similar helmet built. We tried it out that spring in the Old Danube.

Neither my parents nor those of my newly acquired hunting companions were particularly delighted with these diving attempts. But we did not let that stop us. I was the first off the raft down to the bottom, about twenty feet below, and everything went beautifully. Of course the water was very muddy, and the air that was pumped down to me smelled like old rubber tubing—and far too little of it came, so that I kept tugging imperiously at the tube—but otherwise I thought it glorious. For the first time I could move under water without any difficulty in breathing!

It was not long before tugs at the tube came from above. My friends wanted to dive too. I clambered up and gave them expert instructions. If the pressure in their ears got too strong, they were to swallow. If this was not enough, they were to press their noses against the glass to shut off both nostrils, and then blow hard. This second rule I had discovered in a diving text book, and we concluded that the author must have had a most unusual nose.

One after another of us went below, and each tried to outdo

53

his predecessors. The first man went in for long-distance running, so that the tube kept travelling back and forth from one raft to the other; the second tried broad jumping, and achieved thirteen feet, so he said; the third went in for high jumping, and suddenly appeared, swimming, on the surface. All three wound up with wicked headaches. In order to reassure the various sets of attending parents, we also practised throwing off the helmet in case of danger, which we did without difficulty. In fact we even managed to do the reverse: we would swim down to the bottom, put on the helmet our predecessor had left there, and stay below.

That afternoon I wanted to undertake a crossing of the Old Danube, and my friends immediately took charge of the technical organization. They appointed the float of the Café Lesgoschek as the starting point of the expedition, because conditions on the bottom were alleged to be particularly favourable—actually because some pretty girls were sitting on the float. These last were ruthlessly crowded back into one corner of the float. Then tube, pump, and helmet were produced and gravely tested by each man in turn, a boat was prepared in which the pumping crew were to accompany me, distress signals were arranged, photographs taken, and when enough spectators had finally gathered I was permitted to take to the water.

Conditions on the bottom at this spot were very far from favourable. The bottom was covered with tiny shells so sharp that you cut yourself on the slightest contact. This was the first thing I did. My cut finger smarted, and I discovered, to my regret, that I could not even put it in my mouth. Through the window in my helmet I mournfully watched the blood leaving my finger in a smokelike streamer, but I decided not to turn back on that account.

So I started off, and the first thing I encountered was a pike that looked like a painted stick. He dodged to one side, and then hung motionless again. I regretted very much not having a harpoon with me. Next I came to a thick, tangled forest of water weeds, in which I forthwith got lost. I suddenly had no idea what direction I was moving in. Everywhere the same soft bottom and the same snarl of weeds. Furthermore, my stamping raised the mud, so that I could see hardly six feet. The boat, which was really supposed to guide me, had vanished from my sight at the very start, and the direction of the tube offered no guidance, because it was much too long, and curled in every direction. I ransacked my entire store of knowledge, gained from William Beebe's books; but how you were to find your way under water once you had gone astray was something I had never read about. "If a wild sea tosses you on razor-sharp coral needles . . ." flashed through my head. "When walking under water at night with strong phosphorescence . . ." None of this suited my case. All I could do was to take off from the bottom now and then, swim up with all my might, peer briefly above water—in each case I was received with thunderous shouts of applause—and, in sinking back, take care that I did not revolve. In this fashion I went slowly forward. It was a painful journey.

Hours later—hours, I thought!—when I finally reached the far bank, nothing in the world mattered to me. I saw neither the many boats nor the people, nor did I hear the triumphal yells of my friends. There was room for only one thing in my head—headache!

22

The room in which I was pacing to and fro like a caged tiger was twenty-three feet long and ten feet wide. It was a long, narrow tube; at one end was a window, desk, and book-shelves, at the other end a door, chest, and bed. In the middle stood a big armchair, a round table, and a radio. The room, my cage, was on the fourth floor of an old Viennese house, and thus easily four hundred miles from the Dalmatian coast.

What did I think I was doing?

I wanted to conduct ten of my friends to Dalmatia that summer, five the first month, five others the second. I wanted to teach this throng how to hunt under water, I wanted to dive and take photographs, I wanted to have a lot of experiences and organize everything efficiently—and that was by no means a simple matter.

In the first place, we needed a vessel. For this purpose I had already conducted an extensive correspondence with a Mr. Zenic in Zara, who was an old friend of my father's. He had found a cutter that would probably serve our purpose. It was named *Sokol*, a twenty-six-footer, had a small auxiliary motor, and cost two hundred dinars a day, plus, according to local laws, a native captain. Mr. Zenic suggested a man by the name of Belic, who would go only if he could also have a sailor aboard. For this post Captain Belic proposed a man by the name of Kovacic, and this man luckily made no further requirements. Of course both had to be paid and fed extra. And there was no tender.

Second, the ship's outfit. After all, what were we six passengers to sleep on? If on straw ticks, they could be bought here and filled down there; if in hammocks, then we would have to make sure there was room below decks to swing them; if on pneumatic mattresses, a rubber-patching kit must not be forgotten.

We would also need an oil or carbide lamp; torches with enough batteries, a first-aid kit, hand tools, pots and pans for cooking, and a container for drinking water if there was none already on board.

Victualling would be a special problem. Of course we could live mostly on the fish we took, but what else would we need? And who was to cook? Yes, who indeed was to cook? But somehow it would be managed.

Third, the hunting outfit. Harpoons and helmet were all ready. I was getting a more powerful air pump next week, but a non-return valve still had to be installed. I already had a hundred feet of garden hose—the only question was whether it would stand the outside pressure. The new brass harpoon heads were beautifully shaped, but the points were too soft.

56

Would it be possible to screw on interchangeable steel points? For the big harpoon I had ordered five hundred yards of real Hardy line, from England, and Uncle Erich was giving me an old fishing reel. Belic sent word we were to bring along fish-hooks, too, but of course that was preposterous. Fishhooks! I would show Mr. Belic how to catch fish! For the fins and goggles I had to make a second foreign-exchange application so that the people in Paris could get their money at long last. It was each man for himself in the matter of bathing caps, ear plugs, and nose clips.

The under-water camera was still not watertight. And the view finder had to be altered to lie flat, or it would break off at the first opportunity. The spare glasses were ordered. I would get the photographic material on the last day, so that it should be fresh. I still needed all the junk to develop with. Must we take along distilled water? Glass marbles were necessary to keep the jars of developer full. The bottle had to be brown, with a ground-glass stopper. I put the films in a watertight rubber bag with some chemical that absorbed the moisture.

Also, we need spare harpoon shafts, spare wire, rope, and swivel hooks, a sewing kit—would there be a soldering outfit on board?—clips for the nose, stainless knives, and suitable sheaths. Finally, portable packing cases—or should we move the things in trunks, after all? And anyway, how were we to get the whole thing over the frontier? The customs! Yes, the customs! Something more would have to be done about that, but it would go through somehow or other!

Fourth, paperwork. I groaned, and paced faster and faster. If only all this nonsense were already behind me! If at least I knew who was coming with us! Heinz, Guido, and Cheerly were certain, Alfred had declined, and then I had six other names, and three more as substitutes. But there was some difficulty with each one. One couldn't give any definite word yet, another had no money, the third was sick, and the fourth didn't want to come if the fifth did. They all needed exit permits, tickets, foreign exchange, and visas, and to cap it all, the regulations had all changed. The travel agency had no instructions whatever about a good deal of it. Most of the boys

57

were subject to military service, too. Egon was a Croatian, and entirely different rules applied to him. He was coming by motor-cycle with Hinze, while the rest of us went by train to Split and thence by boat. On 8 July we were all to meet at Biograd na Moru: the *Sokol*, the two Croatians, me, and the two on the motor-cycle. Would it ever work?

I kept pacing my cage. The sun was shining outside, my friends were playing tennis at the Academic Sport Club. Mother said it was insane to make life so hard for myself. But actually she understood me. Life was a cage: twenty-three feet long and ten feet wide. If you didn't like your cage, you'd simply have to use your head a bit.

And somehow it all did go through.

23

Anyone who takes the trouble to notice will find that the sun is not always the same size. Sometimes it creeps through the clouds like a mere dwarf, and then, again, it swells as if to burst with power. One explanation may be that the earth moves farther away from the sun in summer; another that the peculiarity of the landscape where you see the sun makes it look bigger or smaller. But these explanations alone are not enough. For myself, anyway, I have seen big and little suns at every season and often in the same spot, depending on how happy I was.

The evening in Split, when I saw the sun again, it was unusually large. Red-hot and heavy, it hung like a tropical fruit in the sky, and the gay little clouds around were like a wreath of flowers twined about the fruit.

"It's out of the question for us to go to bed tonight!" trumpeted Cheerly. "Why, I saw a girl on the plaza that . . ."

Guido patted me gaily on the back. "Surely you don't believe we came to Dalmatia just for the fish sticking!"

As there was time enough before the steamer left, we put our things on board and then hurried down to the plaza. Cheerly, who was tall as a bean pole and will some day look like Don Quixote, had turned himself into a very seductive character by means of a silk muffler, and Guido outdid him with chamois shoes. Both of them insisted on beginning by wetting down the "welfare of the expedition", and since we were so particularly concerned with this toast, and the wine was good, we made a thorough job of it. Then we plunged into the colourful turmoil along the Corso. We did not find Cheerly's girl, but we saw a lot of others instead whose eyes were so black and whose lips were so red that I became thoroughly uneasy about the "welfare of the expedition".

There was no holding Cheerly; he accosted every girl he liked the looks of. As he spoke German and the girls nothing but Serbian, it was not easy to reach an understanding. But he cleared that hurdle at a bound. What he lacked in language he made good by pantomime that would have done honour to a deaf-mute. Before long he vanished, accompanied, behind a dark archway, and when Guido and I went back aboard late that night there was not a sign of him anywhere.

As the night was so particularly lovely, we sat out on deck. It was marvellously calm round about, and I felt marvellously calm inside. All the rush and worries of the last few months had fallen from me; the die was cast, and now matters would take their own course. There was nothing more I could do about it. But at any rate the hardest part of the enterprise was behind me. Henceforth each one of my companions would be doing his own share for the success of the voyage. Since they had come along, it was in their own interest.

"I'd like to build myself a house around here," said Guido abruptly, filling his pipe. "High up above the sea, with a lot of climbing flowers running wild over it, and with blossoming agaves over the rocks. And a nice car and a motor-boat—it wouldn't be a bad life at all!"

Guido puffed at his pipe, and asked me what was my real object in the trip. Was this under-water hunting just a sport and fun for me, or did I look for something more from it?

59

I did not know what to say. I had not even asked myself so plainly as that.

"Well, yes," I said, "as a matter of fact I do look for quite a good deal . . ."

Guido seemed to be interested in nothing but his pipe.

I talked on. I said I must manage this summer to take some good under-water photographs. I could publish them, and maybe give lectures as well. In that way I should make money, and then in the next holidays I could go on a bit farther, possibly to the tropics, perhaps to the Red Sea, or Ceylon, or to the South Seas. That was where things would properly start: hunting really big fish, battles with sharks, coral reefs—and take films of it all! In this way a person could surely earn enough to finance a really big expedition, with a ship of his own, with better equipment and scientific aims. Undoubtedly there would be a chance for wholly new investigations, which you might be able to put to scientific use.

So I raved on.

The smoke from Guido's pipe rose perpendicularly, straight to the sky, which was sprinkled with countless stars. The sea was like a dark disc. In the distance the moon was just rising, silvery gleaming and gigantic. It was even bigger than the sun.

24

Next morning I slept late. When I woke up, we were just putting into Sibenik. I was about to get up, when I remembered that this was the first day when I had nothing at all to do, that things were taking their own course now. So I burrowed deeper than ever under the blankets.

It was nearly eleven when I finally deigned to come on deck. Biograd na Moru was already in sight. The sky was slightly overcast, and gusts of wind lashed across the sea. Over the white-capped waves gulls sailed ahead of the ship. Cheerly was the first whose eagle eye spied Heinz, Egon, and Hinze on the mole. They wore white shorts, and brandished harpoons in welcome. Next to them stood another waving man—obviously Mr. Zenic, my father's friend.

The meeting on shore was tempestuous. Hinze and Haemmerle told of their experiences with the motor-cycle; Cheerly told of his experiences with the girls. I thanked Mr. Zenic for his exertions, and then Egon took me to one side. He indicated a small cutter with an awning at the far end of the harbour: that was our *Sokol*. (Illus. 5.) She was not exactly big, and as for how we were all to find room aboard—— But somehow we should manage. Captain Belic and Kovacic were both very nice. Egon had already bought some provisions.

"Do you know, Egon," I said hesitatingly, "is there any possibility that you'd take on the worry about our daily bill of fare? It's a thankless job, I know, but seeing you're the only one that can speak the language . . ."

Egon was willing. He also subsequently managed the joint treasury and kept our accounts. In contrast with the others, he did not regard the trip simply as a jolly holiday that had to be made as amusing as possible. He was always concerned for the success of the enterprise, and shared with me every one of the many worries that came up in the course of the voyage.

"Cooken gut eat for you!" was Captain Belic's welcome aboard to us. He was obviously nearing sixty, had sunken cheeks, and looked as if his professional activity would soon come to an end. Kovacic, on the other hand, was young and muscular, a cheerful, high-spirited fellow. He served us the "good eat", a mutton dish that Cheerly and I ate with relish. Guido poked at it rather dubiously, Hinze remarked gleefully that he would have to get used to a lot worse things than that. How right he would prove to be he probably did not dream.

The weather was not exactly inviting, but still I could not resist temptation. I put on my bathing trunks, took goggles and harpoon, and slid into the water amid the boisterous shouts of my friends. As I swam along the mole, they accompanied me above, "to pick up the supper".

61

The water was muddy, and the few fish I saw were shy. Besides, the expectant onlookers upset me. As I swam along I had certain misgivings. Was the hard part of the enterprise really behind me? Would the ship and the many hands really make light work? And was the region suited for under-water hunting? Suppose it should turn out there were not any good fishing grounds around here at all?

I reassured myself. After all, I had spent time enough over maps. The islands of Uljan and Incoronata, with their many outlying reefs and islets, were bound to be a veritable Eldorado for under-water fishing. There was no possibility of mistake.

Finally I harpooned a very small fish, the smallest I have ever speared. I aimed at a big one that dodged, and it was unfortunate for him that the small one was behind. The hole I drilled in him with the harpoon was almost bigger than the whole fish. I took a glance upwards at the mole, where my expectant friends were standing, then furtively pulled the tiny fish off the harpoon and put it out of the way. I had to be thinking about my prestige now.

At three in the afternoon we took leave of Mr. Zenic and set our course for Preko, a place on the island of Uljan. Our two Dalmatians were not pleased; they had wanted to stay the night at Biograd. "Strong wind coming!" they had maintained. But we were not to be taken in. Egon had observed good old Kovacic in the port with a dark-haired señorita. We knew where that "strong wind" was blowing from.

After three hours' sail we reached Preko, a tiny remote fishing hamlet, such as there are plenty of in Dalmatia. Nets were hung up to dry outside a few dozen white houses, some gaily coloured fishing barks rocked along shore, and children tumbled about in between, picking their noses.

Leaving our ship in the little harbour, we started out on a thoughtful evening stroll along the shore.

Our talk no longer consisted exclusively of jokes. An expedition spirit began to make itself felt. We talked about the voyages of Alexander von Humboldt, and then the problem of free will was discussed. A prickly plant was studied, and an insect sitting by the wayside was imprisoned in a matchbox.

Each of us regarded himself as a savant exploring strange countries. I was delighted with this serious, constructive mood, little knowing that it would never once recur during the entire trip.

When we came back from our stroll, it turned out that Preko was by no means prepared for tourist trade. We had started with a hearty appetite, which promptly turned into full-scale ravenousness as we found ourselves obliged to go tramping back and forth among the three *gostionas* in the village. Nowhere could anything edible be found. The lofty atmosphere vanished, and a mood of irritation spread abroad. The words "faulty organization" were not actually uttered, but I could feel quite plainly that I, as "leader of the expedition", was being held responsible for the inhospitable attitude of the taverns. So matters were not going to take their course!

Luckily Egon and Kovacic finally succeeded in talking one of the publicans into making us a big dish of spaghetti and tomatoes. The price the man demanded for it was scandalous; we charged it to "once bit, twice shy", and consoled ourselves with the reflection that starting tomorrow we would be eating the fish we caught. The general temper improved again. Over steaming noodles and red wine we drank to Alexander von Humboldt.

But the evening was not over yet. The hardest problem still lay ahead of us. When we got back on board it was deep, dark night, and each man started hunting in the dark little cabin for his property, for pyjamas, blankets, and rubber mattresses, and the more we hunted, the worse grew the confusion. It also turned out that there was not room enough for us all to sleep below. In the bow Captain Belic and Kovacic lay wrapped in blankets; the space aft of the mast, reserved for us, was too small for six men and the accompanying bags. As this was a matter of principle for the whole length of the trip, nobody cared to give in. Finally Egon and I sacrificed ourselves. We bedded down on deck. During the first few nights it was fairly cold, but later, when it warmed up, the others envied us our airy berths.

In the cabin, however, everything was still far from quiet.

Guido was determined to brush his teeth, and could not find his toothbrush. Cheerly burrowed everywhere in search of his revolver.

"What does he want with the damn-fool shooting iron now?" came an irritated growl. But Cheerly was not to be put off. He said he knew exactly what he was doing, and we would all be grateful to him yet. Finally he tripped over a leg, fell full length upon the others, and a battle royal began. Yells and laughter were mingled, and the ship rocked as if tossed by a storm. The details of what was happening we could only guess at on deck, but the fact that something was going on you could see clear to the village.

This touchy situation was smoothed over quite unexpectedly. Egon, who seemed to be paying no attention at all to the others, had perched himself in the bow, and started playing his harmonica—softly, not at all insistently, and within a few minutes all was still again on board.

Nothing keeps a mob of people together better than a common task, a common adventure. After a stirring indoctrination address I set out next morning with my pupils in pursuit of fish. With our long spears we offered a warlike spectacle, and were instantly the sensation of the place. Even the children stopped picking their noses for a moment.

"So catch nix—panula good," rasped Captain Belic, brandishing a hook he had just attached to a piece of lead. We looked scornfully at his hook, and laughed at him. We knew better.

At the proposed scene of the crime, a rocky headland jutting far out into the sea, I gave a brief object lesson in how to put on the goggles and how to dive noiselessly, and then led my pupils in slipping into the briny.

What I saw there I shall never forget. I was quite aware that on the ocean floor you must always be prepared for every possible or impossible surprise, and the sight of a red-checkered hammerhead shark would therefore not have caused me to turn a hair—but what I saw here on the coast of Uljan made me turn a hair all the same.

The islands, outliers of the Zara region, were pure chalk—

11. Joerg with a twelve-pound perch

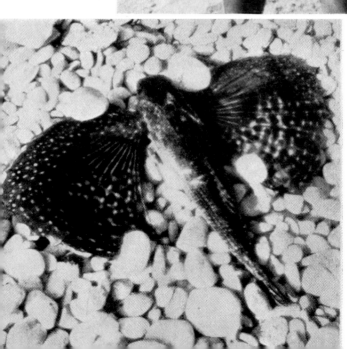

12. Cheerly's fish, a flying gurnard, "with wings and four legs"

13. The marbled sea bream suddenly straightened up and
began chewing meditatively

14. The wrasse, sometimes—and not without reason—called the lip fish

15. I deck myself in borrowed plumes: the shark Joerg harpooned

16. Diagonally below us was a most peculiar reddish forest, its trees completely rigid

17. Colourful and glimmering like sunlight is the life among the coral limbs

bare, rounded ridges with scarcely anything growing on them. And under water it looks exactly as it does above water: white rock, here and there a stunted tuft of seaweed, nothing more. The ocean floor is practically bare. Small wonder that plant-eating fish are lacking also. And of course where they are not the predatory fish will not go.

So far as I could see—and in the extraordinarily clear water I could see nearly a hundred and fifty feet—there was not so much as a fin of a fish anywhere. By way of poor con-solation, hundreds, nay thousands of unappetizing black sausages lay around on the bottom: sea cucumbers. As far as my eye would reach—sea cucumbers! (Illus. 8.)

"This seems to be the outlet of a very high-powered latrine!" came Hinze's voice behind me, followed by roars of laughter.

What more can I say? After my crew had let off their huntsman's ardour on the innocent sea cucumbers, and I had swum a few coves farther in my desperation, we gave up and went back on board. At the same moment our two Dalmatians came home, having been out fishing in deep water with a hook and line. And they ate fish for dinner.

"Panula good," Captain Belic smirked.

25

Just a word more on the subject of sea cucumbers.

These extremely ugly, though in tropical waters most colourful, sausage-shaped creatures, which the Chinese palate finds savoury, are relatives of the sea urchins and starfish, and very peculiar characters indeed. They lie motionless on the bottom, not looking in the least like animals, with neither head, eyes, nor any limbs at all, but simply an opening in the front that is surrounded by tentacles, and another behind, which may, however, offer some surprises, because it is by no means confined to the purpose characteristic of rear openings. If you take a sea cucumber out of the water a powerful stream of water immediately squirts out of this opening. It comes from the creature's water lungs, which also discharge through the end of the intestines. If the sea cucumber feels itself in greater danger, it ejects a whole network of sticky threads through the opening. If this is still not enough, all the internal arrangements follow, bowel included—which, however, by no means signifies the death of the creature, because these innards can be very quickly renewed. Sometimes sea cucumbers go so far in their exasperation that they part themselves across the middle. Then a new rear grows on to the front end, and a new front end on to the old rear, and one animal has become two—all from exasperation.

But to get back to the rear opening, whose surprises are not yet exhausted. Still other things may happen. A small crab will be crawling on his way by night and encounter a sea cucumber. Safety first, he thinks, and goes not to the front, where the tentacles are, but past the aforementioned hole in the rear. And here his fate overtakes him. A toothy maw suddenly appears in the opening, and two wicked eyes sparkle at him. "And science maintains that sea cucumbers have no eyes!" breathes the crab. And, so saying, breathes his last.

The explanation? A wormlike fish, fierasfer by name, hides out in the sea cucumber's water lungs. He feels quite at home there, swims in and out at pleasure, lies in wait by night at the entrance to see whether small creatures will come past. Sometimes several fierasfers will live in the same sea cucumber, and there is quite a brisk traffic through the rear opening. But this fish does not live only in the body of sea cucumbers; it also inhabits the interior of shellfish, where it sometimes suffers a kingly fate. If it goes astray between the flesh and the shell of the oyster, it is mummified in calcium and coated with mother-of-pearl. With fierasfer and man alike, or its equivalent, then, you find one living merrily in the rear end of a sea cucumber, another mouldering in his costly splendour.

66

26

We sailed from one island to another, and they were all
barren and dismal alike. Nowhere were there fish, except at
unattainable depths. There were not even villages on the
islands. Aside from the remnants of a smoked ham that Egon
had managed to find in Preko, a few crusts of hard bread, and
oil to fry non-existent fish, we soon had nothing left to eat. The
temper on board deteriorated accordingly. To penetrate into
hospitable regions as an explorer was no doubt fine, my companions felt, but wandering around in the holidays among
godforsaken islands where there were no fish or anything else,
let alone girls, was not at all to their liking.

"And yet I'm convinced," said Guido, expressing the
general feeling, "that Split is just swarming with fish." And
everyone agreed most enthusiastically.

So what could I do but give in?

We shouldn't have gone to Split again. Or at least we
shouldn't have gone along the Corso again. Heaven knows
why, but we didn't see a single pretty girl. Of course they were
still wearing red-and-white flowers in their hair, and the
flowers were still beautiful and sweet-smelling. But aside from
that . . .

"Guido," I said, "can we possibly have drunk as much as
all that?"

Nevertheless each of us found something in Split to reward him. Cheerly still liked the girls as much as ever. Guido
became a steady patron of the best restaurant. Heinz and
Hinze, who were the proud possessors of a Baedeker, followed
the trail of antiquities laid by Diocletian—and wound up at
the swimming pool with two girls from Prague. The two of us,
Egon and I, crept ashore as inconspicuously as possible. Because
we were still going hunting under water.

I was not very happy those days. True, there really were
considerably more fish in the region around Split, but this did

me little good. While Egon was pursuing them to his heart's content with his harpoon, I hunted them—with the camera. Considering my future plans, good photographs were more important than captured fish. So I swallowed my annoyance, and snapped my scaly friends from in front, behind, and both sides.

But within a few days I began to enjoy the new form of hunting. Fundamentally it was no less exciting, and as a matter of fact a successful photograph was an even better trophy than a dead fish. Furthermore, this photographic hunting was decidedly harder than harpooning. I had to creep up still closer, that is to say still more skilfully, and at the same time keep an eye on background and lighting, so that the fish would come out well in the picture. Also, I usually had to stay a good deal longer under water. And in addition I needed both hands to work the camera, so that I had to dive wholly with my legs. The fins were a big help. I could not move them too fast, however, or the fish would flee, obviously thinking some big predatory enemy was on its way.

We had made our first test shots at Uljan. We had gone walking on the bottom there in the diving helmet, and had snapped, with various lens apertures, what there was to snap, namely, ourselves and the sea cucumbers. (Illus. 7 and 8.) We had got the film developed by a photographer in Split, a very keen businessman, as it turned out. When we picked up the film, we found several enlargements of our pictures in his window. And, less agreeable, some weeks later I saw splendid reproductions in a Yugoslav illustrated paper. The name of the under-water photographer was there too—a Croatian name.

These test shots had shown us how to figure our exposures at various depths. Since the watertight case of my under-water camera allowed me to work only the shutter release, not the aperture, shutter speed, or range, I had to make up my mind on shore what depth and particularly what range I wanted to take pictures at. In order to estimate distances under water correctly, I carried a rule with me at first. We discovered that not only did everything under water appear closer and larger to our eyes, but that the camera was subject to the same illusion. If, for instance, I wanted to photograph a fish thirteen feet away, I had to focus not for thirteen, but for ten feet. In case you think this is not complicated enough, let me tell you that the proportion is not constant, but varies with the temperature and the salt content of the water.

This fixed-focus photography was a severe handicap. If I had set my focus for fifteen feet in order to catch Egon hunting, I could be dead sure that the most beautiful fish would go dancing around eight feet in front of my lens. If, on the other hand, I focused for close-ups of fish, it was equally certain that Egon would spear something before my eyes—though this, as a matter of fact, did not yet happen often. So I had to let a good many fine chances for photographs pass by, including one that I still regret to this day.

Egon, the hero of this story, took a poke at every fish he saw, and, being still a beginner, he usually missed. Often the scales would fly, and I not infrequently encountered fish bearing unmistakable marks of his activity. Once I was there when he approached a fat, extremely blasé salpa. He hit it, but low down, so that the harpoon tore out. The result was that the salpa had a large hole in its belly, and it stopped fairly well at a loss among the rocks. Egon raced to the surface to get air; obviously the fish needed only the *coup de grâce*. I was waiting below to see the final combat when I noticed that a long, thin end of intestine was curling out of the aforementioned hole in the salpa's belly. And like a flash—heaven knows from where— a perch appeared, swam eagerly to the scrap of intestine, and began calmly nibbling at it. The salpa was beside itself. It rolled its eyes backwards and forwards, turned indignantly, and swam on a few yards. Meanwhile Egon was back, but the little perch was quicker. Quite ignoring Egon and his harpoon, it was nibbling at the intestine again. The salpa dashed on farther, with Egon and the little perch after it. Twice more Egon tried to thrust, but each time the perch was ahead of him. Finally the salpa made off, and Egon jabbed savagely at the little perch—which, however, was as hopeless as trying to swat a fly with a club.

27

Even under water the photographer is subject to the weather, only the under-water weather depends on different circumstances. If the wind is blowing offshore towards the sea, it drives the dirt downwards, and the water clears. If it blows towards shore, the swell whirls up sand and dirt, and there is fog under water.

The surface of the water is the sky of the under-water world, the waves are its clouds. Sometimes they are dainty, woolly lamb clouds, moving evenly across the under-water sky; again they will gather, wild, heavy, oppressive. With a swell going, an under-water storm rages through the seaweed forests, and the fish flutter about like frightened birds. But when it is calm and the surface spreads like a monstrous mirror, there arches over the depths a silver dome more boundless and mysterious than anything we know above water. (Illus. 10.)

In the rain, I found the under-water sky dappled with countless tiny dancing points. I surfaced, and felt the wet drops on my body. So I dived again—to keep dry.

28

Egon, who was amazingly familiar with the history of his native country, was determined to show me how you could trace, by the buildings of Split, the countless changes of ownership in the city's turbulent history, but I stood him off firmly. It was really far too lovely a day. The bluff at the east end of the city gleamed reddish-yellow and bluish, and a sea of yellow blossoms surged below the old cemetery wall. From that old cemetery at the foot of Monte Marian you get a magnificent view. We stood in the shade of melancholy stone pines, cypresses, and ailanthuses, among iron crosses covered with elaborate curlicues and tombstones amid a flood of white oleander, and looked down upon the broad circle of the deep blue sea at our feet, upon the gleaming white decorations of the city, and the abrupt mountains in the distance. Egon had been quite right to talk me into this stroll. The last storm had stirred up the sea so much that there was no chance of underwater hunting, so we climbed Monte Marian together.

We kept going higher among vineyards; unfortunately the grapes were not yet ripe. Then we clambered up the steep slope to the former dwellings of the mountain monks, who had carved their cells, several storeys deep, in the perpendicular cliffs. Nobody troubled their solitude up here, and yet the world lay open to their eyes. Yonder, apparently within arm's reach, lay the sweet island of Bua, beyond it honeyed Solta, once called Olintha, and Brač, which legend called the home of Emperor Constantine's mother. The weather was so brilliantly clear that we could see all the way to Hvar and Vis, and in the far west to Trogir, the two-thousand-year-old city of the Venetians.

Slowly the sun sank down upon the horizon. The ringing of bells came up to us from far below. We were sitting on a stone parapet, eating oranges, and Egon announced that he wanted to accompany me on future expeditions as well. I had found a comrade, then, and we contrived plans for the following summer. But Egon was not there to see that summer. . . .

29

One of my least pleasant memories is connected with our departure from Split. We had decided to shift our operations to the seaside resort of Makarska, and were going to leave harbour at nine in the morning; then it turned out that our anchor was fouled in the bottom. In spite of all our exertions there was no hoisting it. Captain Belic groaned and wailed and told us in detail how many lovely round dinars a new anchor would cost and how many bottles of beer you could buy for the price.

"You good dive," he tried to encourage us; "you anchor up bringen und wir alle drink beer!"

Anyone who knows the harbour of Split will realize that this beer interested us but little. Countless fishing cutters and freighters are moored side by side, and all the garbage from these ships, of course, goes overboard. In addition, the sewers of the city empty into the harbour. The water is black, quite black and heavy, and a million different things float on the surface.

Since we did not want to put off our departure, I suggested that we draw lots. The others were willing, and naturally I drew the short straw. I must say that I put on the diving helmet with very mixed feelings. Hinze asked me derisively whether he shouldn't put an open bottle of eau-de-Cologne at the intake valve of the pump. Recommending my soul to God, I lowered myself bravely away. I can still remember the many onlookers staring across at me from the mole; I saw them for a moment more through my window, and then I was through with seeing. I had been prepared for a good deal, but the reality exceeded my worst expectations. Even three feet below the surface all was perfectly black around me, so black that I could not see my hand at arm's length. When I reached bottom, I sank up to my knees in a soft, warm morass. If I had not known what my legs were sunk in, the situation might have reminded me of a pleasant mud bath, but the smell that came up to me permitted of no illusions. Painfully wading, I groped my way along our anchor hawser, and discovered that it had become fouled with another, bigger anchor. I tried to lift it, but only sank in the deeper myself. The anchor did not stir, so I clambered up on it, jumping and rocking, and thus contrived to turn it a little. Our hawser was free!

Heaving a sigh of relief—so far as it was possible in that

72

atmosphere—I groped farther, and fell into a deep, soft hole, in which I sank up to the hips. A stupefying stench filled the helmet. What I wouldn't have given for Hinze's eau-de-Cologne!

Somehow I managed to get out of this pestilential pit, too, and, with a splitting headache, attained our anchor. How I cursed it when I found it had fouled itself with another anchor again! I very nearly gave up. Then I gritted my teeth, clambered up on it as well, began hopping and rocking again, and finally this obstacle also gave way. By the time I had brought the sixty-five-pound anchor to the surface I was completely exhausted.

Cursing profusely, I was just in the act of scraping the thick crust of oil from my skin with a knife when a man came running along the mole. His anchor was fouled, too, he shouted, and how about another try? Perhaps for some beer?

30

When William Beebe descended in a diving helmet to the bottom of the sea for the first time—on 9 April, 1925, at Darwin Bay in the Galapagos Islands—he picked out a convenient boulder, sat down on it, shut his eyes, and said to himself: "I am not at home, not in any city, or among any people. I am far out in the Pacific Ocean on a desert island, sitting on the bottom of the sea. I am deep under water, at a spot where no human being has ever been before. This is one of the most important moments of my entire life. Thousands of people would give a great deal, would make great sacrifices, to have the same experience for only five minutes."

When I dived from the headland close to Makarska, I also sat down on a boulder, shut my eyes, and imagined myself looking back upon this experience as something in the past.

What would I most like to take a closer look at in that case? What action would I repeat if I could turn time and space backwards?

This was a good prescription. When I opened my eyes, I was really much more aware of the strangeness of my surroundings. True, no blenny shaped like a spotted prize bull appeared before me, as it had to William Beebe, but anyway I did notice a sea anemone that struck me as more admirable than any I had seen before. I took the time to examine it more closely. Was it a flower or an animal? I hauled out all my academic knowledge, but there was very little to haul out. Here was a being grown fast like a plant, with a long tube for a stalk. At the upper end was a delicately feathered flower, brightly coloured in concentric circles. When I approached it with my finger, this flower vanished like a flash in the tubular stalk. Later I learned that they are really the tentacles and gills of a worm, whose sensitivity is owing to the fact that it has tiny, dotlike eyes on the gills. An animal, in other words, that can see with its gills.

Farther down the slope I spied a three-foot brown sponge in the shape of a gigantic funnel. With an unusual feeling of security I hurried down the slope. In the diving helmet I barely weighed seven pounds; I could stand on any tiny jut of rock without fear; there was no danger of slipping and falling. If I encountered an obstacle, I had only to push off from the bottom and float in slow motion across gorges and crags, to land gently on the far side.

I picked the sponge, which was fairly rotten, and then down the slope I saw a bigger one still. Without stopping to think, I hurried on down. But as I stooped for it I felt a tug at the hose. The upper world was calling! What was above I had quite forgotten. I looked behind me, and only now did I realize how deep I had dived. The hose went straight and stiffly upwards, vanishing somewhere in the silvery heights. From down here I could not even see the boat any more! I shivered. The water was very cold down here. This, too, I noticed only now.

Before I set about climbing again I stepped out on a pro-

74

jecting crag. Below me the wall fell away almost perpendicularly—a bottomless, strangely tempting abyss. "Where a lunar light revealed waving sea whips and circling fish", William Beebe wrote after standing by a similar abyss on the sea floor of Haiti. Now I could sympathize with the yearning he had felt at the spectacle of the boundless deep. What mysterious creatures might be living yonder in the infinite spaces of ocean? How might those landscapes look? His yearning had since found fulfilment. He had been the first human being to look into that other world, through the window of a steel globe, and watch the denizens of the deep sea as they came up, luminous, from the dark, only to flee again into the murk of their unknown sphere.

With the big sponge funnel and an old grave cross that I found by the way on my road back, I clambered up the steep slope again. "A lunar light revealed waving sea whips and circling fish", kept sounding again and again in my ear.

31

Makarska reminds me of a little city in Switzerland. It lies at the foot of the tremendous, plunging cliffs of the Biokovo Mountains, on the shore of a blue lake, surrounded by green forests. Actually the apparent lake is an almost enclosed bay of the sea, a splendid natural harbour. Even the Phoenicians are supposed to have come here to fetch the snails from Dalmatia for their purple dye.

Each of us was satisfied with Makarska, because each found what he wanted. The fact that Egon and I were the only ones who still wanted fish I need scarcely mention. Mostly we never saw the others except at meals or in the evening on the Corso, and I was glad to let things run as they would. Egon, meanwhile, had developed into a skilful under-water hunter, so that a keen rivalry developed between us. During this time our ship was demoted to a hotel, the captain to a cook, and everybody was satisfied.

I met a lot of old friends in Makarska. In the turbid water of the bay mullet burrowed among the seaweed; near a slaughterhouse big branzinos wandered about. By swimming out of the bay we reached a steep rock cliff, where monstrous shoals of fish sometimes produced a strange gleam in the water. Below, in the caves of the cliff, hung great groupers, and still farther down majestic bream swept past. A flatter rocky coast beyond this was simply teeming with salpas, smaller bream, and dorados, and a little farther on, off a sandy beach, there were rays.

Mingled with these old friends there were new ones. Along the cliff we saw dark green fish with beautifully shaped fins and large, expressive eyes; the fish were always to be found in small groups near a cave. If we approached, the fish retired smoothly and without any sign of fear into their hiding place; they were almost always alone; apparently they wanted to avoid all contact with other beings. Their motions were gentle and harmonious, and even when they ate they were not avid, but simply casually, dreamily brushed the moss with their lips. The German name for these creatures is "Shadow Fish", which, for once, suits them. We harpooned very few of them; we liked their calm, aristocratic bearing.

There was a second fish, until then strange to us, that we met by the sandy beach of Makarska. We would see peculiar clouds of sand rising from the bottom, and soon recognized that it was caused by comparatively small, cross-striped fish burrowing with their extensible snouts in the sand. It was amusing to watch one of the creatures. It would bore into the sand with great vigour, dig around for a while, then suddenly straighten up, chew reflectively, and finally spit out with some force anything it did not relish. This process was repeated with great regularity, and it was a relatively simple matter to outwit the creatures. We would wait until the sand clouds rose up, when we could swim down fast and without precaution. On the bottom we would keep watch until the creatures stopped

76

burrowing and the sand cloud drifted away, then we could harpoon the fish. (Illus. 13.)

Once I injured one of these marbled bream—the fish's scientific name—that had just eaten its meal of sand in the company of another. It fled towards the beach, and I noticed that its companion stayed by its side. To test this unusual behaviour, I stabbed at the faithful friend as well. And in fact he remained faithful! I could not manage to part the two creatures. Sticking close together, they hurried into the shallow water, and swam around among the legs of some bathers, where I could hardly do much about them.

32

When the first month of our hunting was approaching its end, I had the disheartening news from Vienna that with the exception of Joerg Boehler everyone who had been expected for the second month was unable to come, including Burli, who was sick in bed, and wrote me a heartrending letter.

At first I was crushed, then I realized that there was a silver lining. As a matter of fact the ship and all the members of the party had really been more of a burden than a help. I decided to give up the ship and go by steamer to Dubrovnik along with Cheerly, who wanted to accompany me farther, and thence on to Lopud, an island near Dubrovnik, which had been recommended to me as abounding in fish. I made the necessary arrangements, and wrote to Joerg that we would await him at Lopud.

The two Dalmatians were very much distressed at this turn of events, but by means of appropriate quantities of beer I succeeded in reconciling them to their fate. When we parted with the ship, it was a great weight off my mind. Henceforth I would not need to worry about seven different people, seven different stomachs, and seven different opinions. And, my particular delight, I no longer had anything to do with port authorities. Red tape is unlovely stuff at best, and in Dalmatia it is tied into a million knots. Every time you put out with the ship, you need the approval of the port authority, and almost invariably the official concerned is having his *siesta*. Haste in those parts is a red rag. What's the hurry? everyone asks; tomorrow is another day. There is an Arab joke which could just as well be a Dalmatian one: in Libya a camel takes a fortnight to get from one town to another. The new bus does the trip in one day. The camel driver asked the bus driver, "Tell me, what do you do with the other thirteen days?"

33

Of all the fish I know, none has exasperated me more or become a better friend of mine than the grouper, a rugged, ungainly character, thick-skulled as a country bumpkin, always waiting suspiciously outside his cave. There appear to be groupers everywhere. I met them on the Riviera and in Dalmatia, later in the West Indies, the Pacific, and the Aegean, and everywhere they behaved the same.

They always sat fat and clumsy near a cave or some sort of hiding place, they always goggled up at me with round eyes, always waved their pectoral fins with dignity. Since groupers are unusually sensitive to vibrations in the water, I very seldom succeeded in approaching them unnoticed. If I stalked closer, they would goggle mistrustfully at me, and then withdraw, swimming slowly backwards, into the entrance of their caves. If I came yet closer, they suddenly whirled around and vanished in the hole, where, however, they would immediately spin round again. The next moment I could see their inquisitive eyes gleaming out of the shadow in the hole. There they obviously felt safe, and it was now possible to approach them within thrusting distance. I learned that in harpooning it was best to aim between the eyes because at the moment of the thrust the fish turns, and you thus hit him a good blow behind the gill. The next moment is the crucial one. If you do not succeed in yanking the grouper out of his cave immediately, fish and harpoon head are almost invariably lost. It is worth remarking that harpooned groupers all over the world behave exactly alike. They flee as fast and as far as they can into their caves, where they jam themselves tight with out-thrust fins and inflated gills between the rocks. They seem to freeze in this position, and do what you like they will not stir.

During the first two days in Lopud I harpooned five groupers, and lost seven of my expensive harpoon heads in the process. Each time the creatures wedged themselves in so skilfully that I could not manage to pull them from their retreats. I tried everything. I tugged at the line until it broke, forced my own way into the crack, harassed the creatures with harpoon and knife, and even drove two more harpoon heads into one grouper. It was no use; they stayed put.

The third day I swore I would never pay attention to another grouper. And exactly at that moment I saw a particularly big one. He hung lazy and at ease in a rock channel. The nearest cave was at least sixty feet away. I wavered. Then I decided to risk one last head—the eighth. I crept nearer, and landed a good thrust. And that was the end of my initiative. The fish whirled off with incredible fierceness, dragging me after him like a motor-boat. By the time I had recovered from my surprise I was at the entrance of his cave, holding the very outer end of the harpoon shaft, while the rest, along with the ten-foot harpoon cord, had vanished in the dark of the hole. Served me right! But I swore a great oath that I would not lose that eighth head, after all. I would sooner blow up fish and cave together with dynamite!

Hurrying to the surface, I fetched a rope we had deposited on the cliff. I gave one end to Cheerly, who was to sit on the rock above; the other I tied to the harpoon line, so that the fish could no longer get away. The rocky cleft into which he had fled went down twenty-five feet between a cape and an out-lying reef, and was so narrow that I could force my way in only about six or seven feet. By a feeble gleam of light that fell from above into the cleft I could see the grouper. He lay jammed between two rocks at a narrow spot far in the back, not stirring. Even when I tugged at the line, he remained motionless. I now tried, with frequent interruptions for air, to chase the creature out with the harpoon shaft. If I forced myself far into the cleft—which was not easy, because the waves kept scraping me up and down on the rough rock—I could just barely reach the grouper with the end of the shaft. I tried kind-ness first. I tickled his tail, and tapped him on the nose; but this did not have at all the desired effect. Instead of leaving his retreat the grouper swam a little farther into a quite remote part of the cave, where he jammed himself in, and stayed once and for all. I could still see him plainly, but now the harpoon shaft was too short to reach him. I dived several times, and finally found a somewhat deeper spot, where I could force my way a little farther into the cleft. Here, of course, a sharp point of rock bored directly into my spine. But, on the other hand, I could reach the grouper again. I was now determined to go the limit. Quite coolly and objectively I brought the pointed end of the harpoon shaft up to the wounded creature, and bored it several times into the hard, muscular body. At the first jab the grouper gave a sort of jerk, then remained motionless. Obviously he was dead. But that did very little good. The spearhead was still in his body, and his body was still wedged between the rocks as firmly as if the creature were part of the stone. I dived again and again, each time getting the sharp rock against my spine, but all my efforts were in vain. The fish and the spearhead stayed where they were.

Meanwhile the sun had passed the zenith and was slowly but surely descending upon the mountains. By four in the afternoon I was so exhausted that with the best will in the world I could do no more. I was already bleeding from many raw spots. Since Cheerly, too, refused to sit any longer on the rocks, we tied the rope to a jutting crag, and I renewed my vow that this eighth head should not be lost in spite of all.

80

18.   A creature that looked like a toy fish made of
coloured cardboard

19. When the file fish is asleep has dark diagonal stripes

20. When agitated, he loses them and changes colour

21. In an equable mood he looks like this

22. When the hedgehog fish finds himself in danger, he pumps himself up

23. He stared out of the coral hide-away with big, anxious eyes

24. This ray was even bigger, even darker, even fiercer

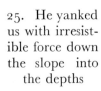

25. He yanked us with irresistible force down the slope into the depths

The next morning I came back with renewed strength and a huge, long trident. By this time a high surf was running. The line had worn through and was floating in the waves. I dived, but it was not easy to find the right entrance to the cleft through the clouds of foam raised by the surf. For just a moment the wildly bubbling foam gave me a clear view, and I saw that the body of the fish was no longer in the same spot. It now lay in the darkest corner of the cave. I next strove to introduce the more than ten-foot trident into the cleft, and it was just about the hardest job I have ever undertaken. Clouds of foam obscured the view; the water kept rising ten feet and falling back; the breakers snatched the long pole out of my hand again and again. It was a good two hours before I finally had the trident in the proper position. And now I discovered that it was just a little too short! I could indeed barely reach the fish and even push him aside a little, but no matter how I dislocated my arm, no matter how deep I bored the rock point into my spine, I could not penetrate the body of the fish.

With grim fury I once more renewed my vow, and walked back to the village, where, however, no longer trident was to be found. Finally I scared up a carpenter who cut me a sixteen-foot pole, upon which we mounted the fork. With this murderous weapon we went back to the scene of the crime. Meanwhile, however, the surf had grown so strong that a further attempt seemed hopeless. The following day, too, was stormy. Only on the morning after that did the decisive battle occur.

I crept expectantly into the familiar cleft, and sure enough, the body of the fish still lay in the same spot. It was probably not edible by now, but surely spectacular enough for photographic purposes. With Cheerly's help I guided the monster fork into the proper position, and then, slowly and with relish, drove the five points into the solid body. It was a moment of glorious triumph. Only now, as I drew the fish towards me, did I see how big he was. He really did not look decayed at all. The skin was vivid green, with brownish spots, the staring eyes still looked positively alive. I reached for him. And then my heart stood still! There was no doubt about it, the fish corpse began to flap again! The creature hit about savagely, yanked himself off the points, and vanished with perfectly normal, confident motions into the depths. . . .

From all I know of groupers, this character was undoubtedly in good health again within a few weeks, and unless I am much mistaken he has long since gone back to crouching outside his old cave, obstinate and thick-headed, sedately waving his pectoral fins—and with my eighth harpoon head in his belly.

34

As there were plenty of other fish besides groupers along the coast at Lopud, we almost always came home with an ample catch. Cheerly, who had not yet succeeded in harpooning a fish himself, always offered to carry the fish on the way home, an honour I gladly accorded him. Our entry into the village was always a sensation. People came and felt the fish, and Cheerly happily gave information about everything. We also began to sell the fish here in the tried and tested way, but in so doing we roused the envy of the native fishermen, which soon had unpleasant results.

One morning there came a summons to the police-station. There we were informed that according to information received we had been poisoning fish under water, that this was strictly forbidden, and that we were to desist at once or else leave Lopud. I asked how they pictured this crime—did they suppose that we put the poison into the fishes' mouths under water? But the clerk refused to get involved in any argument. According to section so-and-so fishing with poison was prohibited, and we were to cease and desist or leave Lopud.

We strove to explain the basis of our work to the man, but he would not believe that you could get close to fish by diving.

82

I proposed that he should come with us; I would lend him goggles, and he could swim with us and see for himself how the thing went. This came to nothing because the man did not know how to swim. Finally, most fortunately, the mayor of the place (who was also the proprietor of the biggest hotel) volunteered to make this inspection in person.

The show started at noon. Cheerly had seen to it that half Lopud was present; a throng was massed along the shore. Well aware of the significance of the moment, I most formally adjusted the goggles to the eyes of the somewhat portly mayor. Then I went into the water, and he followed with the dignity of an ambassador. But the moment he had had his first glance under water he squeaked with pleasure and was as enthusiastic as everyone is who looks at the sea through goggles for the first time. I showed him some fish, showed him how to dive with fins and spear, and had the feeling that he was already wholly on our side.

Now, however, a fish had to be harpooned, and that was far from simple. No less than three police boats were beside us —probably to prevent me from poisoning the mayor under water. Besides, my companion puffed like a walrus while swimming, and I was naturally excited. I kept missing my aim. Nevertheless the mayor was delighted even at these attempts, and when I finally did succeed in bagging a fish as point of honour, I was the hero of the day. I was now taken in the police boat from one "particularly good fishing spot" to another, and each one of the policemen who was able to swim determined to have his chance at a look through the goggles. When I came home hours later, chattering with cold, I had become a local celebrity, and had learned how wearying that is.

"Everything's all right with the police," said the mayor when I called on him at his hotel that evening. "You can fish all you like. One thing, though—you mustn't sell the fish."

35

Whenever anyone asks me whether you don't have to be a champion swimmer to harpoon fish under water, I tell the story of Joerg.

From the very start he pointed out that he was a non-swimmer. He said he could keep his head above water, and that was all. He was fond of sailing, though. And since, as a medical student, he might be of some help aboard, he thought perhaps we would have some use for him. I took his name down as a substitute member for the second month, and, as I have already said, he was the only one who came.

Joerg had spoken the absolute truth: a swimmer you could not call him. Nevertheless he harpooned several fish on his first attempt and very shortly became the best under-water hunter I know.

Our first day's hunting began with Joerg jabbing the harpoon into his foot as he was about to enter the water. It was not a deep cut, but happened to hit a vein, and blood spurted as though from a broken garden hose. We took this as a good omen. After all, on my first expedition I had not harpooned myself for half an hour.

As soon as the flow of blood had been stanched somewhat we went into the water, and I witnessed a most impressive performance, Joerg, who was making his first attempt with fins, scrabbled around in circles a few times like an unfledged bird, then started moving his fins, and suddenly buzzed off. He seemed to have found limbs that he had lacked before. He swam straight down into the depths.

We roamed along the coast, and I introduced Joerg to the various species of fish. I explained to him how you had to dive and creep up without a sound. I was just about to demonstrate when he dived noiselessly himself, stalked forward, and shortly afterwards came to the surface with a neatly harpooned fish. So I kept my wisdom to myself, and took pains to catch something of my own; but when I finally had a fish, Joerg was already brandishing his third above water.

Of course there was luck to it, and some setbacks followed. But within less than a week he had learned practically all the dodges. And from that date forward there was no unanimity in fish circles as to which of us it was better not to meet.

Cheerly, too, went hunting successfully under water—for sand mussels. As the name indicates, the mussels have their lower ends stuck in the sand. They are red, grow up to more than three feet long, and since they rise perpendicularly from the bottom, looking down from the surface you can see only the dark cleft of their slightly open shells, so that it is not easy to recognize them from above. Cheerly had heard somewhere that you occasionally find pearls in these mussels, and so he began looting the ocean bottom. Instead of pearls, however, he found in almost every fair-sized mussel nothing but a couple of small domestic crabs. Believing them to be young lobsters, he imprisoned them all in a pickle jar, to take them to Vienna alive and feed and raise them there.

Joerg and I were loafing around in the sand when Cheerly came out of the water very much excited, insisting he had seen a fish with four legs and blue-spotted wings. He said the creature flew around in the water with the wings, walked on the sand with the two hind legs, and used the front two like hands to eat with.

I smiled. Joerg did not even smile, but Cheerly stuck to his story. The creature would surely still be there, and we should come along and see for ourselves. Sighing, we followed him into the water.

This time Cheerly had not exaggerated: we saw the creature with our own eyes, and it was exactly as he had described it. The fish was about eight inches long, with a broad armoured head and a compact, plumpish body; it had big, round, butterfly-like wings on each side, and on its breast it had two pairs of pointed vestigial fins, with which it actually ran around on the sand as it would have with legs, using the front pair to hunt for food. It was a flying gurnard, one of the most remarkable and also most savoury of Mediterranean fish. (Illus. 12.)

85

When approached, the creature sailed through the water like a great exotic butterfly. We followed, and after a while it made a landing on the sand, where it rested quietly. Joerg murmured something about honour where honour is due, and handed Cheerly his harpoon. It was accepted with great excitement, and Cheerly launched the harpoon with great force —and missed. That is, he did not quite miss, but grazed the creature's head, which caused it to swoon and lie motionless on the sand. Beside himself with excitement, and puffing loudly, Cheerly appeared on the surface, took a breath, and raced downwards. Here he pierced the sand with two more extremely powerful thrusts, and then came to the surface again. As the fish was still in a swoon, its chances were poor in spite of all. At last Cheerly recovered his composure. He dived for the third time, now with a desperately resolute face, put the harpoon point directly on the creature's armoured neck, clutched the harpoon shaft with arms and legs, and then made a jerking motion downwards. This sporting manœuvre was successful. The creature, pierced through, unfolded its beautiful wings for the last time. Cheerly rejoiced: he had his first fish!

Unfortunately it was also his last. The day afterwards a letter came, summoning him back to Vienna at once. The last time we saw him he was standing high up at the rail of the steamer, brandishing his harpoon over his head in farewell. He kept shouting loudly, "Hallo, boys!" which made it obvious that an English girl whom he had for some time been anxious to meet was also leaving on board the vessel.

36

The ocean lies quiet, only clucking with tiny wavelets against the rocks. Over it arches the glimmering, endless expanse of summer sky. High, high up above hang two lonely, woolly-lamb clouds, the last ones that the sun has not yet devoured. Schools of fleeting anchovies whisk across the surface of the ocean, and sometimes a faint breeze drifts past, scented with blossoming twigs afar.

Joerg is all ready, and is just sharpening his harpoon head with a file; I make haste to get into the water ahead of him. Ever since Joerg and I have been hunting together we have noticed that the one who gets into the water first invariably harpoons the first fish. This time I am the one, and our superstition is promptly confirmed. I have scarcely gone under when I see two big branzinos roaming shadowlike through the reefs, and very shortly the bigger one is flapping on my line. I brandish him triumphantly above the water. Joerg grins and hurries after me. I look downwards again, and see the head of an impressive grouper, peering out briefly between two rocks. Quickly I get the harpoon ready again, and before the grouper can count three I have harpooned him and yanked him out of his cave. When I kill him, he spits out three gull bones.

"Hoy, hoy! One to one!" comes a shout across the waves. Joerg, too, is now brandishing a fish above water. He has harpooned a dorado.

"No—five to one!" I yell back, lifting up the grouper as best I can; it must weigh at least sixteen or seventeen pounds.

An hour later I come ashore again and lay out the fish I have taken in a neat row, according to size, in the shadow of a cliff. While I am waiting, I see that Joerg is still diving at the same spot. After a while he shouts to me to come over if I can. He says he has a fish that is tangled under a rock—the stupid brute.

So I go back into the water, swim over, and am determined to get the fish loose at the first attempt come what may. But it is a fairly hopeless task. Joerg has been using a heavy hundred-and-fifty-foot fishing-line, which is now completely snarled under a big boulder. And the fish is in such an awkward place that I cannot reach him with my hands. Nevertheless I do everything to get him loose, stay under water much longer than usual—and my patience is rewarded. Just as I am about to give up, the fish comes out of his hiding place of his own

87

accord, voluntarily, so to speak—or perhaps just to annoy Joerg. I grab him, and shoot upwards as fast as I can, because I am really at the end of my powers so far as air is concerned. Then suddenly, ten feet below the surface, a sharp jerk at my leg stops me, and I feel a burning pain around my ankle. Turning in alarm, I see that my leg has caught in a noose. I am tied to the line whose lower end is still snarled under the rocks below!

In my first excitement I tug at my leg, but my knife—the sheath is empty! I've gone and left the knife on shore again.

With grim determination I grit my teeth, conquering the agonizing want of air. That I cannot free the line from the rock below is obvious. There is nothing for it but to untie the knot. But it is drawn tight and hard as a rock now, whereas my nails are completely softened by soaking in the water! I work like a madman, trying again and again. Tears come to my eyes, a dull pain descends upon my head, my chest rises and falls frantically—surely this can't be the end! All because of that stupid noose.

With unflagging patience I try again and again. And slowly, very slowly, the noose finally loosens. Then I get hold of a loop, pull at it, something lets go—and I am free! With my last ounce of strength I manage to reach the surface. . . .

When I recover somewhat, I see that Joerg is very pale. He, too, had had no knife with him, and so all he could do was to sit by and watch. If he had not kept calm, I should probably not be alive now, for together we should never have undone the knot.

37

"Do you expect the fish to eat that?" one of the townsfolk said, eyeing our harpoon head. Another thought that it must be a blinker.

We were now in Cavtat, not far from the Boka Katorska.

Our last few days at Lopud had been very successful. Too successful, in fact! Our fish peddling had flourished in secret. We had even worked to order—branzino? Groupers? Or would you rather have dorado this evening, sir?

At night we would sit in the hotel and eat the best table-d'hôte. Without a fish course, naturally. There was no satisfaction among the native fishermen over our flourishing trade, and this it was that led to our somewhat abrupt departure. The mayor came to us, all excited, wringing his hands, and informed us that a deputation of fishermen had just been to see him. We must leave at once; he could not answer for our safety any longer.

As we had fished the Lopud region fairly bare anyway, we were not broken-hearted at going. We went to Dubrovnik, where we fished off the Lapad Peninsula, and where, most fortunately, even better prices obtained. But we were not destined to stay long. Within three days we heard privately that a charge had already been laid against us; this time, by way of variety, we were supposed to be fishing with dynamite. Wanting nothing more to do with the authorities after our previous experiences, we took leave of our own accord, without further encouragement.

We thought we had finally landed in Cavtat, but here, too, public opinion was already turning against us. True, nobody could prove that we were selling the fish this time (we traded them to our host for rooms and meals), but we were boycotted just the same. No fisherman would rent his boat to us any more —except for the eldest of all, who rowed as slowly as a gondolier on a moonlight party.

We had him row us out several times to a little island, and the last of these expeditions had an unexpected upshot. Overnight the water had turned so cold that under-water hunting was not to be thought of. But we did not discover this until the old man had deposited us on the island. So we had to wait until five in the afternoon, when he would come for us. We sat around in disgust, freezing, and when the sky clouded over we froze even worse.

Now it happened that in addition to ourselves there was a loving couple on the island, whom at first we kept away from in order not to intrude. But when, about noon, a savoury aroma of pork and beans drifted towards us, we abandoned our reserve, crossed over, and—happy people usually being generous as well—we made up a foursome to eat the beans. They were truly unique, not alone in their exquisite flavour, but also in their consequences to me. I hasten to add that I am referring to an involuntary bath, which the generous donor imposed on me. As the meal was drawing to a close, the girl, hitherto so charming, had the loathsome idea that we ought to catch a fish for her. To my objection that complying with this desire involved a polar expedition, she murmured in reply that some people were grateful and some were ungrateful. So there was nothing for it but to draw lots—and naturally I got the short straw again. So, with rage in my heart, I descended into the liquid refrigerator and brought back two wrasse, sometimes very rightly called lip fish. (Illus. 14.) But it was a long time before I could eat pork and beans again.

After that I was not really intending to enter the water again at all. But when we finally got back to Dubrovnik, the sea was suddenly warm again. So we decided to stay one more day, and swam out to the Pettini Reefs, which are situated six hundred and fifty yards off the Lapad Peninsula, rising out of the water like the faulty teeth of a sleeping sea giant. Between the two incisors of these teeth we were to have the last and most exciting adventure of the summer—we met our first shark!

It was not a big shark, not at all as you would imagine one of these man-killers, but still a supple, muscular fellow some five feet long. He swung out through the aforementioned gap in the teeth, and luckily Joerg and I had discussed such an eventuality not once but fifty times. Our parts were so arranged beforehand that not a word was necessary now. Joerg, who had the camera, strapped it tighter, I handed him the harpoon, and he dived to meet the shark, which seemed quite uninterested in what we were doing. Not until the harpoon head penetrated the rearmost opening of the gill close to his heart did his behaviour suddenly change: the shark now raged to and fro. I grabbed for the line, and clutched, because while Joerg was hurrying to the rock with the reel running out, it was my job to check the creature. Luckily the shark did not sound, but stayed close to the surface; I could catch some air, and then pull myself towards him hand over hand. Then I managed to embrace him, and although he snapped and hit about him wildly, I stabbed him in the belly from below several times with my knife. Meanwhile Joerg had reached the rocks and was pulling hard on the line. I helped pull, and took care that the shark should not swim round any projecting rock. He was now bleeding fairly freely, and his strength was visibly ebbing. In triumph we dragged him up over the cliff. (Illus. 15.)

Joerg had the shark's teeth mounted for himself; I fell heir to the dorsal fin and tail. I fell heir also to a rather badly scraped stomach and the adventure itself to which I was yet to be much indebted at home. . . .

38

"Well! So you tangled with a shark, did you?" cried Mr. Witthalm of the Vienna Urania. "Now that's interesting! Well, let's try it in the middle hall; we'll see how many people are interested in your lecture. Of course I can't pay you a guarantee, but you'll have thirty per cent of the proceeds."

Mother was less pleased at the adventure with the shark.

"What will this lead to?" she asked, shaking her head.

"It'll lead to the South Seas!" I cried. "Yes, Mother! To the coral reefs of the South Seas!"

In order to make my lecture as attractive as possible, I arranged a special surprise. When I had finished the first half, and the light was about to go on for the intermission, I announced to the ladies and gentlemen that I had something else unusual to show them. At a sign from me the unusual something came up on the stage. It was Guido in bathing trunks and full battle dress: with fins on his feet, a diving helmet on his head, a harpoon in his hand, and a big dummy fish in a net at his belt.

The success of this lecture could not have been greater. Even in the intermission all kinds of people crowded into the dressing-room, including a particularly excited gentleman who wanted to hand me a hundred schillings on the spot for the next expedition. Inexperienced as I was, I hesitated to accept at once. I courteously asked for his address, and said I would get in touch with him when things had reached that stage. Afterwards my father pointed out to me that this was a mistake. He said you must strike while the iron is hot. So the next day I started an "Exploration" account at the postal savings office, and sent the generous gentleman a money-order form with a cordial letter. Unfortunately the iron was no longer hot. . . .

The lecture was repeated, but Guido declined to act as a "show-window dummy" again. My other companions also showed no interest in this form of celebrity after the resounding laughter that had greeted Guido's appearance, and I had difficulty filling the job, important as it was to my lecture. The matter grew specially acute when I began talking at the suburban adult education centres. In Ottakring I had no choice but to telephone the chairman and ask him to furnish a suitable man, whereupon I was supplied with an usher.

The man had by no means the figure for an under-water fisherman. He was short and rotund, and wore very strong spectacles. Furthermore, when he learned what was in store for him, he bathed and scrubbed thoroughly, so that his skin was as pink as a suckling pig's. This time when I announced a surprise to my audience I was certainly not exaggerating. In order to put on our goggles, the poor man had had to take off his own spectacles, and on top of this he wore the diving helmet, whose window steamed over on the inside. In a word, he could see nothing at all. And then there were also the fins, on which he could walk only most painfully. Groping helplessly forward and sideways, he came upon the stage, a plump, short, pink figure, waddling along on frog feet with a gigantic spear, a diving helmet, and three big celluloid fish at his belt.

People roared with delight. A fat lady in the front row laughed until she cried. But all this only increased the confusion of the under-water huntsman. He turned to seek refuge in flight, but missed his way, and plunged into the auditorium with his lance held before him. He very nearly harpooned the fat lady.

39

And the way things are in life, the merry and the tragic often falling side by side, this is what happened that same day in Kitzbühel.

Egon, arriving by the early morning train, dropped off his things at the hotel, and then went straight to the big ski jump. He was a passionate ski jumper, one of the best of his age group. He quickly mounted the hill back of the jump, and forthwith whizzed down through the air into the valley. Happening to land on a rocky spot with too little snow cover, he fell, and was instantly killed. Nobody was there when he jumped; he was not found until hours afterwards.

That was the first time I had realized the dreadful finality of death—how suddenly it could come and destroy all our hopes and plans. Some chance, some intrinsically quite insignificant trifle, and suddenly all was over. I could see Egon clearly before me as we were discussing our future at the top of Monte Marian, and I remembered the many hours we had spent alone or with Joerg elaborating our plans. Now a rock with too little snow cover had intervened, and all this would never be. I should have to look round for a substitute, and Egon would simply be left behind. I became very conscious of how completely anyone who defies danger in any form is at the mercy of chance.

But ought one really to draw conclusions from this? Should one expose oneself the less to danger and to chance? No. A life spent in constant anxiety over losing it would be no life at all. It would not be worth a single day really lived. We must be thankful to fate for every single moment, but must not turn one step aside from the path we have entered on.

40

There is nothing more wonderful in the world than a plan that completely absorbs you day and night. That was the kind of plan we had. We were going to tropical seas, going to hunt sharks, going to see for ourselves the celebrated beauty of the coral reefs.

If you went up the narrow, winding staircase two storeys from the reading-room of the National Library in Vienna you found yourself in the Geographical Cabinet. Here I had set up my headquarters. Round about me were piled maps and descriptions of all the world's coasts, and as I studied them I was already there in spirit.

The most beautiful coral reefs are in the Red Sea, in the Society Islands, and along the Great Barrier Reef of Australia. Such dainty corals are said to grow along many Japanese shores that not even a Japanese painter would imagine anything more exquisite.

Off Mannar in Ceylon, where the loveliest butterflies and orchids are, the pearl-diving fleet goes out every day to the stormy banks. Gay sails rise above the white foam, bronzed natives dive with stone and basket, dive straight into the spray, for where the surf is strongest, the pearl oyster is most at home.

Nowhere in the world is the ocean bottom so deep as in the Philippine Ditch east of Mindanao. Nowhere do such gigantic seaweed trees grow as in the cold waters around

Patagonia and Tierra del Fuego. Nowhere does the water teem with fish of all kinds as it does along the black lava coast of the Galapagos Islands.

The moon is in its last quarter, the natives sit anxiously in their boats, waiting. Behind them sharp, jagged, volcanic mountains, the symbols and gods of Samoa. Suddenly a shrill cry, and instantly the scene is transformed. Whooping and howling; brown hands dip into the water, scooping up the thick liquid. Yes, it has grown quite thick and viscid, and when someone sticks in a paddle it stands erect! Billions of curling worms fill the sea, thin yellow and brown tubes, full to the bursting point with eggs and seed. When they meet, they burst; eggs and seed unite. Rejoicing, the natives scoop them into baskets and eat them raw by the handful. The palolo is back! Not a moment late! Punctually, as every year in November, when the moon is in the last quarter, it has crept out of the reefs to mate. Yes, the palolo is back. . . .

"You'll have to finish up now," said the attendant, rolling up the maps. "It's seven o'clock; we're closing."

41

A week later the decision was made. I had settled it—we would go to the Red Sea! For that reason I had been sitting two hours in the bathtub, to the great astonishment of our cook, who simply could not imagine what had got into me. But what did our cook know of the Red Sea? How could she know that the salt content of the water there is 4 per cent, or how important it was for me to test the effect of such a solution on my own skin? For safety's sake I had even made a 5 per cent solution, and the temperature was exactly fifty-two degrees. If I shut my eyes, I could imagine myself in the Red Sea already.

There were many points to be considered: in such salty

water, of course, the buoyancy was greater, and consequently the under-water camera had to be made somewhat heavier in order to offset it. Then we had to beware of rust; all iron parts had to be very heavily chromium plated. If we should need any ointment to protect our skins, we must not use oil, or we would be even hotter in this hottest of all seas. Klunzinger, the German doctor who had lived for years in Koseir and studied the reefs, wrote that the heat paralysed all energy. So far we had always been cold; if we spent all day in the water down yonder, surely it wouldn't be too bad. On the other hand, all the poisonous sea creatures were a problem—was the spine of the diadema sea urchin really deadly? It was said to lie hidden in the sand—and the sand, too, was a problem! If the wind was blowing from shore off the desert, undoubtedly the water would be turbid with flying sand; but if it came from the other side the surf would stir up the sand on the bottom, and this would probably be even worse. And then there were various seaweeds, which multiplied sometimes until the Red Sea was really red. So it was important to find out when and where these particular seaweeds occurred, and when and where was least wind. Probably the islands off Massaua would be quite suitable. They were also reported to house the only shark-fishing station in the world where enough sharks were taken to make the business pay. Furthermore, Massaua was Italian, and thus undoubtedly better in view of the political situation than the British Port Sudan. We might go to Koseir, and then we could travel by way of Cairo, up the Nile to Luxor, and from there by camel across the desert.

After two and a half hours' trial I decided that the 5 per cent salt solution had done me no harm. Only my fingers were wrinkled like a washerwoman's. The high temperature of the water was also bearable. I must admit I was fairly exhausted, though. I tottered out of the bathroom, and our cook shook her head. But I reassured her, saying that everything was all right now—fundamentally there was no further obstacle to a voyage to the Red Sea.

96

26 and 27. The shark was so beautiful and so elegant a fellow, and bore so little resemblance to a bloodthirsty man-eater, that my one thought at this moment was how nicely he would photograph. I forgot I hadn't even a knife with me . . .

28. Why did the shark flee from me?

29. If you imagine a midwife's bag with pop eyes, devil's horns, and dainty fins, you have an idea of the appearance of the trunkfish, which frequents the reefs of Curaçao

42

I had no lack of optimism; but neither had I any lack of difficulties in the way of this optimism. The moment was most ill-chosen for our purpose. The annexation of Austria by Germany meant that all important decisions were made in Berlin, not in Vienna. As the political situation was so tense, exit permits were very hard to come by, especially for young people like us who were subject to early draft. And then there were Labour Service, Harvest Help, the difficulties of getting visas, and the still great difficulty of foreign exchange. I am still amazed that our project materialized in spite of it all.

"What agency are you working for?" was the first question every government office asked, and if you could not prove some important interest of state, you had little chance of favourable action. And what government agency would be interested in my plan? For whom could it have the slightest importance? Fish sticking? Photographs on the ocean floor? People looked at me aghast. "No, no, my dear fellow," they would say, "just put that nonsense out of your head. You go to the university like a good lad and then do your military service. Where would we be if all of us wanted to go to the South Seas?"

Besides, nobody thought it possible that you could go swimming around among coral reefs in bathing trunks and fins. Because if it really were possible, people argued, somebody would surely have done it before. Probably we would be eaten by the first shark. I ought to be downright grateful if people did not help me.

What I needed most was references. But where to get any? If Uncle Erich Zugmayer were still alive he could surely have helped, but he was gone; I had not even been able to show him our pictures from the Adriatic. When I thought of him, it suddenly occurred to me that he had once recommended me to a gentleman at the Natural History Museum. Sure enough, I still had the name in my notebook. I set off at once, and I was lucky: Regierungsrat Pietschmann, the director of the Ichthyological Department of the museum, was actually there. I was shown through long corridors, passing between endless shelves with fish in alcohol, and then found myself facing a friendly old gentleman who was ensconced behind huge masses of books and more jars of fish. I introduced myself as the nephew of his late friend, and he listened to my story with interest. He was the first person who did not seem to consider my plan solely a boy's wild idea. He advised me from the experience of his own explorations, and gave me a document with an impressive stamp saying that in the course of a trip to study tropical regions I was to make zoological collections for the Ichthyological Department of the museum, and that all government agencies involved were therefore requested to assist me in every possible way. Then he told me which tropical fish I was particularly to collect, and handed me a book of instructions for collecting. I was to come and get the formalin to preserve the creatures just before we departed.

With this document I now resumed running from pillar to post, and since I met with so much opposition, which forced me to stop and think again and again, my plans gradually took on more tangible shape. Unfortunately I had to give up the Red Sea, because communications were too difficult. On the other hand, I discovered that German ships plied to the West Indies, offering the special advantage that you could pay your passage in marks. The ships went from Hamburg by way of the Azores to Barbados and Trinidad, and thence along the Venezuelan and Colombian coast as far as Panama and Port Limón. I wrote straight to the Barbados, and was told in reply that no entry permits were being issued at present. Trinidad was out of the question because the island lies off the mouth of the Orinoco, whose muddy stream obscures the sea for a long distance around. The local Hamburg-Amerika representatives at La Guaira and Puerto Cabello wrote that the coastal climate was intolerable for Europeans, and living was very expensive. So I hit upon Curaçao, the next place where the ships called, a Dutch island, better known for the liqueur that has not been produced there for a long time than for its outstandingly im-

98

portant oil refineries. My studies in the Geographical Cabinet indicated that Curaçao had coral banks and a healthy climate, and appeared to be suited in every way for our undertaking.

The Dutch consul in Vienna told me that an enterprise such as we planned required a special permit from the Dutch Foreign Ministry. I immediately sent an application, and since I had good connections with the Dutch Government through a relative, I had no doubt that the permit would be forthcoming.

A difficult problem was the foreign-exchange question. I sent off one application after another, and one after another they were returned disallowed. The museum could not help me here either. In my despair I addressed some of the highest official quarters that would admit to having jurisdiction. And yet I was asking for only two hundred dollars, with which I meant to finance the three months' expedition with three members. I figured that we would live in a tent and eat chiefly the fish we caught. But perhaps the very modesty of my request was a mistake. Possibly our enterprise seemed too cheap to be taken seriously. Perhaps they would sooner have given us ten times that amount.

In this predicament chance came to my aid. On the tennis courts I met a Dutch businessman who was attracted by a wild notion like ours. At my suggestion he agreed to transfer eight hundred guilders to Curaçao for us, and in return I undertook to give him a share of the proceeds of the expedition. Of course the agreement also required the approval of the foreign-exchange office.

Along with all this we had to worry about the equipment of the expedition. As I was now studying at the Vienna Technological Academy—my father would still have none of zoology—I had very little free time, and Joerg was the only one who could help me. We paid the bills ourselves, and I was very proud that I could meet my share with money I had earned with lectures, newspaper articles, and my first book. We tried hard to think of everything beforehand, and to improve our hunting outfit in every way. Better harpoons, better fins, an under-water film camera, and a new diving helmetwere built to our designs; the construction of a special under-water camera was entrusted to a photographic firm in Düsseldorf. I ordered the tent outfit with the rubber mattresses and all the kitchen equipment in Vienna; the first-aid kit and the hunting guns were Joerg's department. He also procured a gigantic spring scale, on which to weigh the fish we took. When he unpacked it, he looked most dissatisfied. It would only weigh up to eleven hundred pounds, he said, and we glared most disapprovingly at the thing.

43

One evening Burli came to see me, bringing along a book by Mitchell Hedges, called *Battling with Sea Monsters*, which I drank in like an oracle. Here at last was a man who knew the Caribbean and its inhabitants like the inside of his pocket, who had hunted gigantic fish there for years, sharks weighing more than seventeen hundred pounds, twenty-six-foot swordfish, giant rays, and turtles of absolutely unique size. And he had often looked down from a boat upon the coral landscapes that we now hoped to make our hunting ground. "No painter," I read, "could reproduce the luminosity of the blending colours. There is no expression for the colour, no words to describe it."

I closed my eyes. I should be seeing all this for myself soon! Vienna then would be far, far behind us, somewhere on the other side of the globe, and perhaps I would think back to this moment. I pulled the lamp closer, and read on:

It would take great courage to venture into these unexplored, mysterious depths and penetrate the unknown with its unnamed terrors. . . . There is no jungle in the world that hides such terrors as the deep tropical seas. I have seen tragedies that make the blood run cold. One moment there stood a man in the prime of life—the next, nothing but bloody, frothing water and a weeping wife and fatherless children. I have seen a young man go out to fish with a definite premonition of coming misfortune. He never came back!

I swallowed, and read on.

I have seen something worse yet. Thirty or forty natives were bathing near their little village, among them a father with his grown sons. They were close to the shore, tumbling about in the water. Suddenly one of the sons, sixteen years old, uttered a gurgling scream. His head disappeared under the surface, and the water turned red with blood. The father and an older brother rushed to the spot. At that moment the boy appeared, stretched out his arms, and screamed piercingly. They grabbed his hands, and at the same moment there was a tremendous eddy in the water. A dorsal fin cut the surface, and the great shark flung itself again upon the boy. Frozen with horror, father and son watched the gigantic maw open. They heard the gritting of the jaws as they closed again. They still held the boy's hands, but only his head and shoulders were still there. . . .

I did not sleep very well that night.

44

Three weeks before the ship was to sail I called on my school friend Alfred von Wurzian, and asked him if he wanted to sail for the West Indies in three weeks with me and Joerg. Once he had recovered from his astonishment, he fell upon my neck and accepted. We had known Alfred for years as a trustworthy companion with a great capacity for enthusiasm, whose daredevilry was equally popular in sporting and female circles.

Another side of his character we discovered only in the course of living together. Alfred is one of those enviable people

who find pleasure in being annoyed. It obviously gives him
real satisfaction. As good friends we naturally took care that
he should never be at a loss in this respect, but this was not
enough; he went on hunting for annoyance under water. Later
it became his favourite occupation to lie outside a big coral
bush in whose maze of caverns a fish was hiding. Then we
would see him swimming tirelessly round and round the coral
bush with his harpoon at the ready, lurking now before this
and now before that entrance to the interior. At the same time
the fish would keep swimming tirelessly around inside, always
taking up a position where Alfred's harpoon could not reach
him. Then Alfred would try to fool him. He would scratch
noisily with the harpoon on one side of the coral, and then
hurry around as fast and as inconspicuously as possible to one
of the opposite entrances. Usually the fish saw through this
manœuvre as well, and annoyance and fun would continue.
Afterwards Alfred spent three whole days on one and the same
fish, whose habits he finally knew down to the last detail. In the
evening by the campfire he would tell us with shining eyes what
ruses he had thought out this time, and how the fish had cir-
cumvented even these. Finally, the third evening, Alfred was
quiet, and looked rather downcast.

"Well, did he finally swim away from you?" asked Joerg
sympathetically.

"Oh, quite the contrary," sighed Alfred. "I harpooned him
today."

45

And once again I was racing to and fro like a tiger in a
cage, just as I had done a year before. Tomorrow morning
early the expedition would start. We were to leave by the
eight o'clock train for Hamburg, and go on from there to the

Caribbean, and now came this letter, and ruined everything!

My bad luck had begun two days before, when I broke a bottle riding on my motor-cycle. I had fetched the bottle from the museum; it contained the formalin for preserving the fish. The first fish to be preserved was my new exposure meter, which was unfortunately in my brief case beside the bottle. When the latter broke, the meter drowned in formalin, and breathed out its light-sensitive soul. I rushed to the photographer from whom I had just bought it, and learned that repairs would take two weeks. A new one would cost forty marks. I wept and wailed until the man had pity on my distress. He took the preserved exposure meter to sell on commission, and gave me a new one for the price of the repairs.

Next I headed my motor-cycle for the rubber concern where I was to pick up our new fins, and there I learned that the casting had unfortunately failed. But they would do their best to manufacture at least a few pairs for us by hand, and send them to the ship by air mail, but of course they couldn't promise anything.

Then I went home, where for a change a pleasant surprise was awaiting me. The package from Düsseldorf had arrived, the longed-for package with the new watertight cover for my camera. I heaved a sigh of relief—after all the telephone calls and urgent telegrams! And it really did look glorious. The designers had not exaggerated: it was a masterpiece of technology! It was of cast aluminium, very neat and graceful, and allowed you to make every adjustment of the camera from outside by watertight levers. I showed it to Father, and we put it right into the bathtub, to make it feel at home, so to speak. When I got back half an hour later it turned out that the watertight masterpiece was quite half full of water. Luckily I had taken the camera out of the case beforehand, from some vague mistrust of everything too bright and shiny. Otherwise it, too, would have been full of water.

Since Uncle Paul happened to be there, and he is an engineer, he took the matter in hand at once. It was not hard to ascertain that the water was getting in from the front through the lens window, a plate-glass sheet with eight holes through which ran screws that held the glass snug against a gasket. These screws needed to be tightened. We handed Uncle Paul a screwdriver, he put it skilfully to work—and crack! the plate glass snapped. And it was precisely this glass that had delayed the completion of the case for three months, because the eight holes had been so hard to drill. Uncle Paul offered to put the thing to rights, but I decided to hurry to Mr. Steurer, the mechanic, who had made my first camera case.

I found him, and he promised me to do his very best. I was to come back next morning—this morning, that was to say. I was there at seven. Mr. Steurer, when he received me, was unshaven, with swollen, bloodshot eyes. Without a word he showed me the ruins of the aluminium case, so imposing the day before, and added a few not altogether flattering words about our Düsseldorf friends. He said the case was no good at all, all the gaskets were worthless, and it had been impossible to fix any part of it. My heart fell a foot. We were to leave in one day, and now we had no under-water camera!

But Mr. Steurer smiled, and when I saw this my hopes rose again. The good man had worked all night, and had actually created a new case. It did not look nearly so impressive, and, as before, you could work only the shutter release of the camera —but still it was a waterproof case, and the worst was over. Mr. Steurer yawned and rubbed his eyes. He said he had sent the cover to be cast this morning, and the glass had been promised for the afternoon. I was to come back at nine in the evening, and the case would be all ready.

So I came home in good spirits, and now the last blow fell. The long-awaited letter from the Dutch Foreign Ministry had arrived—on consultation with the *procureur général* of Curaçao they regretted to inform me that the intended trip could not be permitted at this time. There followed an explanation of the reasons, with excerpts from the letter of the *procureur général*.

So all I could do was to race up and down like a caged tiger. All was in vain, all our trouble for nothing! I looked at the ready-packed cases, and they looked sadly back at me—now they would stand here. Now we could not even try to get an entry permit for anywhere else: it was much too late for that.

We could not even go to Italy! Perhaps—if we were lucky—Lake Wolfgang.

But it was to come out differently.

I happened to think that we had one chance left. Nobody knew I had received the letter, and nobody need know. It might perfectly well have arrived two days later. Why not go ahead and chance it? Possibly we might somehow still get to Curaçao. What did one risk more or less mean anyhow?

So I said not a word to my companions, and we set out the following morning, laden with cases, harpoons, and blessings, as if everything had been in the best of order. At Hamburg they were not going to give us steamer tickets without visas, but I boldly asserted that the Vienna consul had inquired in Amsterdam, and had expressly told me no special visas were necessary in our case. This met with some doubt, but now Joerg and Alfred joined in the battle. Naturally they believed what I said, and their indignation was so genuine that the agent himself weakened, and finally gave in. If necessary we should simply have to come back by the next vessel, he reassured himself, and since we had already paid for the return trip the shipping line had no reason to care. With this we happily agreed.

We went aboard, and two hours before the vessel sailed two pairs of fins surprisingly arrived by air mail. Alfred volunteered that he did not mind swimming without fins, so that was all right too. And at last the great moment came. There was a screeching and tooting, people waved, some cried, as for me, I felt inexpressibly wonderful. All the worries of the past months fell from me like an old skin. The times of painful preparation were now past for good, and I need not waste another thought on them! Whatever I could do, I had done, and whatever I had forgotten I could not change now. Suddenly I was quite calm and confident. Once we were in America, the problem of the entry permit could be solved somehow. If not in Curaçao, then somewhere else.

46

In the Bay of Biscay, as was proper for a voyage by this route, a storm duly arose, emptying the dining saloon with panic speed. This was something the shipping line counted on to save the cost of a great many meals. In our case, however, the company had miscalculated—we ate as if years of starvation lay before us.

Off the Azores the sun came out again, and at the same time the passengers, pale as death, reappeared on deck, to spend their sad, enfeebled days occasionally sipping a little bouillon. Dolphins played around the ship, and the tiny pennant on the chart moved a little farther along each day. And then, after weeks, land came in sight again at last.

It has grown so hot (I wrote in a letter to my mother) *that the sweat is running down my pencil. Even so, people maintain it will be much worse in La Guaira. This morning we cast anchor in Barbados, a real South Sea island, rather flat, with palms and a white, shining beach. Black natives came paddling out in their canoes, and dived for coins that were tossed to them from the ship. From me they had a shiny trouser button, which caused the divers particular trouble. There was a white man among the mob too—possibly some stranded voyager.*

The next day we reached Trinidad, where we went through a tropical cloudburst that could be compared only to a water-fall. We were just lying in harbour at Port-of-Spain when, about noon, it became intolerably sultry, and thick clouds of vapour came down upon us. Gradually the abrupt, arsenic-green jungle mountains vanished from our view, then the city lying desolate in the paralysing heat, the harbour installations, and the three-masted schooner from Jamaica that was berthed beside us. Finally you could not see from one mast to the other on board. And then, suddenly, lightning let loose upon us. The water poured from the clouds as fiercely as if a sluice had opened right over our heads. Within an instant the decks turned to tiny lakes, whose level rose before our eyes.

And then in a moment all was over, as abruptly as it had begun. The clouds broke open, the air was now cool and clear, and before us, in the sparkling sunshine, lay Trinidad, one of the loveliest West Indian islands.

Another natural phenomenon came about midnight, as we were passing between the South American coast and the island of Tortuga. At first we had no idea what was going on. People hurried down the long passageways, whispering excitedly, and since nobody would answer our questions we hastily put on our trousers and ran after. Everyone poured towards the bow, and when we came out into the open air we saw the stern enshrouded in a magical gleam, against which the silhouettes of all the people crowding the rail stood out. Everybody was looking down at the sea, whence the light came glinting up. Sure enough—phosphorescence! I had read about it before. It was supposed to be at its most beautiful in the Strait of Malacca. . . .

But what does reading amount to? You read; think, Well, well, imagine that, and you read on. The reality is always different, more striking, much more impressive. No matter how bold our imagination, in the end it is always poor, because it can use only concepts that we have somehow gained before through sensory impressions. . . .

The ocean gleamed like molten silver. Every drop sparkled, and when the ship pounded, the bow waves splashed like sheaves of fire. Dainty strings of pearls drifted past, gold-gleaming chains, serpents glowing green. . . . And just ahead of the bow two big dolphins moved smoothly and placidly, their glassily glinting bodies like comets with luminous tails.

A girl with big, dark eyes stood beside me at the rail, and asked how this phosphorescence came about. I told her all sorts of stuff about the mysterious, minute, phosphorescent creatures of the sea, although I knew remarkably little about them myself at the time. Later I studied one of these tiny animals under the microscope; it was spherical, recalling the familiar illustrations of Mars with its canals. Only this Mars had a dainty curling tail with which it moved eagerly about in the water. Some nights millions of these creatures float about on the surface of the sea.

What produces the phosphorescence is even now among the great mysteries of nature. As with all other luminous animals (of which there are a great many, particularly in the deep sea), the light is cold, produced without warmth, and thus with a far smaller expenditure of energy. If it were possible to generate a similar cold light mechanically, man could save enormous amounts of money, time, and work.

Why these sea creatures shine is another problem still very much disputed. Some are infected with luminous bacteria, and thus shine whether they will or not; others attract prey by their light; others, in turn, use a suddenly dazzling light for protection. In most cases, however, the lights on the bodies of the sea creatures probably serve for reproduction. They are a wedding garment, by which male and female creatures recognize each other. So you might poetically describe the phosphorescence as an expression of love and yearning, and this was no doubt more or less what I told the dark-eyed girl.

When we put into Puerto Cabello and found that our vessel was to discharge cargo for a whole day, Alfred and I shouldered our harpoons and went off for an under-water hunt. Joerg gazed sadly after us. He had a bad infection on his foot and had to stay on board.

We went through the hot streets of the city and reached a magnificent sandy beach fringed as far as the eye could reach with tall coconut palms. A few dozen wretched fishermen's huts hid in the shade. Pot-bellied children played outside.

As we waded into the water with our spears, several natives came rushing up with loud shouts, making excited gestures to us. We paid no particular attention and slid into the water. As the beach was fairly flat, and the waves stirred up the sand, the water was very turbid. Alfred looked inquiringly at me, but said nothing, and we swam on. I did not feel altogether comfortable. In spite of myself I remembered Mitchell Hedges' tale of the child bitten in two. Besides, there was the ceaseless yelling of the natives, more and more dismayed and urgent. The bottom sank away gradually, and, being soon unable to see it, we took soundings with our harpoon shafts as we swam. It grew deeper and deeper, but the visibility did not improve at all. Alfred looked towards me again. As a matter of fact, what we were doing was simple madness. That there were sharks here was beyond question; we had no experience at all, could scarcely see six feet, and it was Alfred's first time with me. Dared I take the responsibility?

We swam a little farther, and then turned back. The natives pointed excitedly at the water, and we were glad when we got ashore unharmed. In the afternoon we tried on the other side, and found ourselves upon a broad, dried field of mud swarming with land crabs and begging children. The children ran along beside us like starving cats, persistently crying, "Money! Money! Money!" which was perfectly hopeless in our case, since we had none ourselves. Followed by this yelling throng, we crossed some muddy inlets on planks that lay ready, but soon realized that this path would not take us to the sea, and turned back. Now the children ran ahead of us, and when we got back to the inlets the planks had been taken away. On the far bank stood the jeering crowd of children, and round about us land crabs ran with menacingly uplifted claws.

47

Curaçao—which is said to signify "roast priest"—is about forty miles long, sausage-shaped, and rather flat; the few hills look like dirty grey shark fins. Because the Spaniards cut off the woods, and the goats they introduced kept nibbling away all the new tree shoots as fast as they grew up, the once fertile island is now dry and barren, awakening to life only once a year during a rainy season of two scant months. Then the soil greedily drinks up the rare moisture, and within a few days the island turns green. Grass sprouts everywhere, the dried hedges take on leaves, and before they are quite grown the first blossoms begin to unfold.

There was a similar sudden rain in the economic development of Curaçao too; it came from Venezuela, and its name was oil. When the great oil deposits near Maracaibo on the Venezuelan coast were discovered during World War I, Curaçao overnight became the focus of public interest. Maracaibo Bay is not navigable for large vessels, and furthermore it has a man-killing climate. For that reason—and also on political grounds—the Shell Company built its refineries on Curaçao (and the Standard Oil its own on the neighbouring island of Aruba). Oil tanks shot up out of the ground everywhere like ugly mushrooms, and were lovingly tended, for they brought money—any amount of money. Before dreamy Willemstad, with its old Dutch architecture, knew what was going on it had become one of the world's most important seaports. Ships went in and out every day, fetching oil and bringing goods and people. Dutch engineers under four-year contracts brought their wives and children along, and built a modern villa quarter with beautiful irrigated gardens. And more and more merchants, mostly Portuguese Jews, came from everywhere, opened their shops, and grew rich. For the tariffs were low, prices could be kept down accordingly, and so tourists were tempted in from the vicinity, and soon from parts of America as well.

There is one position, though, that Curaçao once had, then lost, and will never regain. Three hundred years ago the governor of Curaçao had charge, along with a few other small possessions of the Dutch in the Antilles, of the little town of New Amsterdam on the North American coast.

"Where are you going to live?" the official from the immigration service asked us when the ship docked at Willemstad.

"In the wilderness," I said, causing universal hilarity.

"Oh, I see." The official now looked at us very carefully.

"So *you're* the ones! We've heard about your plans. Come to the immigration office at twelve o'clock."

Then began one of the decisive battles of my life.

Public offices—I believe this is a piece of Chinese wisdom —are feminine, and have to be treated accordingly. No matter how often they say no, things are not too bad so long as you do not let yourself be put off. If you never contradict, and at the same time never give in, public offices and women weaken.

We arrived at the appointed time, and first argued for a while with a nice but subordinate official; then, after half an hour's wait, we were ushered into Mynheer Van de Croef, the head of the immigration service, a sinewy little man with piercing eyes. He greeted us with a curt nod, and informed us that we had received no permission to come to Curaçao, and that we must therefore go back to Hamburg by the same vessel. We did not contradict, but simply nodded sadly. It was dreadful, we said, but we had never got any letter. And now we had come such a long way. . . .

Mynheer Van de Croef remained quite unmoved. He repeated what he had said before, added a few words of regret and a few more of disapproval for the incorrect information of the Vienna consul, and made a definite gesture of dismissal. We didn't stir, but all three of us looked at him with deep sadness. He now added that the photography we had planned to do could not possibly be permitted on the island, and to this we did reply.

"But only under water!" we cried. "After all, we only want to photograph fish and coral . . ." And before he could say anything, I put the testimonials from the Museum of Natural History on his desk, and grouped around them under-water photographs from Dalmatia and magazines with illustrated articles about our work. He could hardly avoid looking at the pictures, and we improved this opportunity to tell him more about our hunting and our adventures so far. We kept taking turns; when one of us could think of nothing more, another would immediately carry on the story, so that there should never be any ominous pause. We kept hammering away at the same subject, never slackening, and slowly, very slowly, the "impossible" became a "perhaps".

"Please examine our baggage," was my last argument, "and then you can see for yourself what intentions brought us here." And this his dread eminence actually agreed to do, no doubt mostly because he had already had more than enough of us, and because we were, after all, in the tropics, where it is too hot for long arguments.

The baggage inspection took place the following morning. I carried out this fight to a finish alone. To my great delight, instead of Mynheer Van de Croef, the subordinate and much more approachable official came. I heaved a sigh of relief. To convince the man of our utter harmlessness, I did not wait until he began inspecting, but tumbled everything out of our bags myself, spilling much of it on the floor. The official reassured me and halted the exhibition. Then I showed him our under-water pictures, and explained to him the mechanism of our harpoons and cameras. He was interested in everything, and it turned out that he himself was a passionate fisherman. When we parted, it was with an agreement that we should go fishing together, and the "perhaps" had been replaced by a comforting "for the present".

48

You might have thought you were in the darkest Middle Ages. Joerg lay roped to a table, two men holding his legs, a third forcibly opening his mouth; in the hand of a fourth a knife gleamed. He dug in the point, cut, Joerg reared up, and a shrill cry rang through the room.

Then Joerg babbled: "Eighty-five . . . eighty-six . . . eighty-seven. I'll get to two hundred in no time!"

The poor victim did not know that actually all was over. The doctor cleaned the abscess and dressed the wound. The sailors let go of Joerg's legs, saluted, and went their way.

30. A plant-like growth made wholly by animals

31. Shoals of countless tiny fish whose forma-tions were reminiscent of astronomical spiral nebulae

32. And five deceased lobsters hung on our bag line

33. The stalks peering out of the coral cave were the feelers of a lobster

What a stroke of luck! When I got back from the baggage inspection, Joerg's leg was swollen up fat and blue. I first tried to wake Alfred, which, however, proved hopeless. He had celebrated a farewell until the departure of our ship at five in the morning, a very painful and obviously a very moist farewell, and now lay in bed like one dead. I let him lie, not altogether blessing him, and hurried into town, where I saw that another big German steamer had come in overnight. So I headed in that direction. I found the ship's doctor, a young Austrian from Graz, at breakfast. He finished eating his third egg, packed numerous instruments of torture in his bag, and came with me. When he saw Joerg's leg he shook his head gravely. At his request we managed to get Joerg aboard the ship, where the grisly scene took place in the officers' mess. Now, fortunately, all was over. The doctor patted the cheek of his patient, who was still plunged deep in anesthesia, and bade me good-bye. Within a fortnight things would undoubtedly have healed.

I still had any amount to do today. As soon as Joerg was back in his bed—and Alfred mercilessly flung out of his—we had to go to the Hamburg-Amerika agency about the rowing-boat they were to get for us, and then to the customs. We certainly hoped there would be no difficulty there about our stock of film. Joerg's guns were for it, surely. But the main thing was that we were here, and they had not sent us back right away, and above all that our money had arrived in good order.

The local representatives of the Hamburg-Amerika Line were touching in their solicitude. They had arranged immediately for us to sleep for a week aboard a small coastal steamer, which was just loading cargo; this would save us the price of a hotel. We could even eat there, which was very agreeable, particularly with Joerg ailing. Alfred and I were invited to go to the Spanish Water with a Mr. Evers of the chamber of commerce. Mr. Mannke of the Hamburg-Amerika, who had procured us this invitation, thought we could very well camp there. But the territory belonged to an English phosphate company, whose permission had to be got first. We would also have to buy provisions and anything else we needed. And then off into the wilderness!

Joerg had awakened meanwhile, and was rambling on about Pilsener beer and castles in the Vorarlberg. Suddenly he sat up and looked at me fixedly. "Ninety-two, ninety-three. I can still feel everything! . . . Ninety-four. I'll get to two hundred in no time!"

49

Mr. Evers called for us early in the morning with his car, and we drove out through a fairly dismal countryside to the Spanish Water, a many branched muddy inland sea in the eastern part of the island, connected to the open sea by a narrow channel. This channel, the so-called *boca*, was what we were heading for. Mr. Evers had a small boat with an outboard motor, in which we crossed the inland lake, and half an hour later we turned into the quiet, rather curving lagoon. The left bank was fringed with mangrove bushes, whose characteristic stilt feet projected far out into the water; beyond them lay a thicket of tropical trees, from which a constant screeching was heard. Mr. Evers informed us that these were parrots, and the somewhat higher cry came from a bright-coloured trupial. Then he indicated the right bank, which rose in an abrupt, rocky bluff. All I could see at the spot he indicated was one particularly shrivelled cactus among a great many other cacti, but Mr. Evers and Alfred both maintained that they could see a sleeping iguana there.

At the mouth of the *boca* we pulled up the boat on a little bright, sandy beach. We were now directly on the sea, which was comparatively calm. Only beyond the opening of the channel the waves broke in white spray. This was the starting point of a coral reef, which went out in a broad curve along the coast. On our side of the mouth there seemed to be no coral reefs, so we had first to cross the channel, whose water looked fairly turbid and muddy. Over at the reefs, however, it was clear; we could see that plainly by the blue colour. Another companion, who was following our hunting preparations attentively, mentioned that sharks very seldom came as far as the mouth of the *boca*. So much the better!

I slid into the water, and Alfred followed. Within a very few strokes of our fins the steeply shelving sand bottom vanished from our sight, and all was impenetrably grey around us, just as in Puerto Cabello. We kept close together, constantly peering in every direction. The disagreeable part was that in this water we could not judge how far we really saw. Nowhere was there a fish or any other indication of what distance a creature would appear at if it were coming towards us; very possibly it might suddenly take shape directly beside us! We hurried along, and could see plainly by the surface how far we still were from clear water. The dividing line must be very abrupt. The closer it came, the more excited we grew. And then the grey clouds did indeed flow away, and the dirty wall of fog remained behind us.

We paused.

There are pictures you never forget all your life; this was one. Before us, or rather diagonally below us, lay a most remarkable reddish forest, some of whose trees grew nearly up to the surface. (Illus. 16.) These trees did not in the least recall seaweed or such growing things as you see on land. They were perfectly rigid, and their gnawed, shovel-like branches thrust out in all directions like antlers. They were trees of stone—corals.

Stiff, motionless, and like a lunar landscape as this forest on the ocean floor seemed, the surface sunlight dancing upon it and the variegated life among the branches were all the gayer and livelier. Fish large and small whisked hither and thither everywhere, some of them so dainty and colourful that they reminded you more of butterflies than of water creatures. (Illus. 17.) As if in some blissful waltz they swung through the enchanted grove. Some of them appeared for only a moment, then vanished again in the uncertain shade of the branches; of others I never saw anything but the eyes, dancing like will-o'-the-wisps in the darkness of the wood.

And it was perfectly still in this forest. Over the whole

bright bustle there spread a mysterious, unearthly, Sleeping Beauty silence.

I caught my breath, and carefully glanced at the shore. There stood a few dry bushes, and beyond them dirty-grey cacti. A piebald bird was walking up and down along the beach, uttering loud, cawing cries. I slipped under again, and dived back into this other world.

I came close now to one of the coral trees, and touched a branch with my finger-tip. It was at once rough and slippery. So this was a coral branch! At that moment a monstrous head appeared below the branch. I clutched my harpoon tighter, but the head had already vanished, and in its stead there was a fat, radiantly blue fish, nibbling with yellowish teeth at one of the rust-red branches. This activity seemed to occupy his whole attention. Now and then he would swim backwards a little, as if to observe the spot he was gnawing at from a slightly greater distance; then he would suddenly rush forward again, and his teeth would rasp over the rough surface. I was about to aim my harpoon when I saw just above him a winged crab. Or could that be a fish too? Or perhaps two, embracing each other?

An involuntary motion on my part, and the mysterious creature was gone. Where to? It had suddenly dissolved into nothingness, like the reflections of the sun that danced about in the coral forest like many-coloured kobolds, appearing unexpectedly and as suddenly vanishing again. But wait! Over there was a gigantic fish. I could plainly see its tail fin jutting out behind a tree; it waved steadily to and fro, recalling a big, soft fan. With pounding heart and harpoon at the ready I sneaked around the tree. But instead of a fish I saw nothing but more fins of the same kind—they were some sort of fan-like coral growing up from the bottom like great leaves, not stiff, but swinging elastically to and fro in the swell.

I came up, and waited until Alfred, too, appeared on the surface again. But he did not even notice me. I only saw him gasp hastily for breath, then he was gone below the waves again, like a walrus or a dolphin, only surfacing briefly in all haste to catch another breath.

So I dived again, too, and swam on, peering attentively

116

into the darkness of the forest. Then I swam in among the trees, pursuing this and that fish, but I could never spear any, because before I got round to the thrust I was always distracted by some other creature. You would have had to wear blinkers to shut out the bewildering multiplicity. I came to an open spot covered over with the most remarkable corals. Some of them looked like flowers, others were a sort of hedge, others again recalled shed antlers. Among them, arranged in tufts, were yellow plates, along with blubbery, finger-like growths and big balls, some of which displayed the meandering pattern of a human brain.

I felt everything, and burned my fingers on the yellow plates. Strange, unknown creatures appeared, luring me on. I saw corals that I had never dreamed of, and wonderful, powerful fish passing by out yonder in the deeper water. Only sharks were not to be seen.

We encountered one fish that looked like the setting sun, and Alfred dived forthwith to harpoon it. But I followed after, and held him back by the leg. He was furious, and came to the surface flushing bright red—hunting fever had him in its clutches. But as he was telling me what he thought of me, I rejoiced, because far below I saw the rising sun vanishing. . . .

The following day we went to Piscadera Bay, where the Dutch have built a modern swimming place, protected from sharks by a steel grating. They had told us that there was some-one else there as crazy as we—a Dutch engineer who also swam around outside the barrier in the sea, hunting for fish under water with a catapult. Of course we wanted to meet the man.

We first hunted along the steel grating, and I harpooned two grey snappers and a mackerel in rapid succession; then we swam to the far end of a fairly long bay, where we occa-sionally saw a head appearing above water. That must be the man we were looking for.

As we approached, he swam towards us. We shook hands under water, and then looked at each other above water. Alfred and I mentioned our names, the blond man nodded politely, and replied: "Meyringh. Glad to know you." Then each party scrutinized the other's equipment.

Mr. Meyringh carried a home-made rather complicated catapult, with which he could fire off a metal arrow. On the arrow was a loose head, and both arrow and head had their own separate lines, wound up in such fashion that they unrolled of their own accord after the shot. Mr. Meyringh had no fins. At his belt hung one big and one small fish.

We swam on in company, and Mr. Meyringh told us that he, too, had originally hunted with a spear, but that he had found it too much trouble. With the catapult he could shoot six feet, which might perhaps not be quite so sporting but all the more profitable. I asked him what were the best places to fish around the island. He said he hunted almost entirely here in Piscadera Bay, because he thought it too dangerous alone elsewhere. He seemed to be very much pleased at our arrival, and immediately asked whether he might join us sometimes. Naturally we agreed with pleasure. We then shook hands again.

Suddenly Alfred gave me a nudge. "Look!" he whispered. "Over there. Now show him what you can do!"

Sure enough, there was a fish! It was fairly big, reddish-brown, with a broad head and dark stripes. Luckily Mr. Meyringh had not yet noticed anything. I called his attention, and dived cautiously, well aware that my reputation as well as that of the expedition was at stake. To be quite sure I went a fairly roundabout way, first diving perpendicularly to the flat bottom, about twenty-five feet down, and then stalking closer among the corals, just above the bottom. The fish did not stir; apparently it was asleep. I aimed very carefully, let a gentle current carry me still closer, then, in view of the pairs of eyes fixed upon me, tensed my body with somewhat exaggerated definiteness. Close beside me I heard a metallic clang in the water, and a glinting something flashed past me. The fish whirled around in a circle, and then fell, rigid, to the bottom. It was pierced through the middle by an arrow! Mr. Meyringh, who had swum close behind me, pulled his booty upwards on the line. As for me, I realized that I was still holding my body tense with somewhat exaggerated definiteness.

· · · · ·

Poor Joerg, meanwhile, lay in his bunk, sadly nursing his leg. I made his bed every morning, sprinkled a little water on the floor, and imagined myself a perfect nurse. In spite of this forced rest, Joerg occupied himself with under-water hunting. While in bed he practised the best way to hold one's breath, and developed an amazing method of doing so. He would first breathe very fast and as deeply as possible for two minutes, and then he could do without air for four whole minutes. We tried it, too, and achieved similar results.

"It is not a matter, as the layman might suppose," Joerg displayed his medical knowledge, "of saturating the blood with oxygen—no, not at all! Rather it is reduction of the carbon-dioxide content, putting the breathing centre in the spinal column out of action."

When we were finally through with the necessary preparations a week later, and moved bag and baggage to the *boca* of the Spanish Water, Joerg hopped down the gangway on his good leg, and was stowed away in the car among harpoons and bunches of bananas. During the trip he looked curiously out of the window, and saw for the first time the barren mountain slopes, the high cactus hedges along the roads, and the little windmills of the plantations, with whose help the ground was irrigated. As we approached the *boca*, the road grew so bad that the car finally could go no farther; Joerg had to hop the last bit on one leg. While we were pitching the tent, he devoted himself to the details, arranging photographic equipment, books, medicines, and the like in a trunk with a lock, putting up a string in the tent on which we were to hang our pyjamas in the future, and encouraging me to blow up the pneumatic mattresses, for which he was still far too frail, he said, while Alfred was to build a hearth as fast as possible, because he was already getting hungry. Finally he sent us both out to hunt under water.

When we came back two hours later with the desired "nutritious and digestible fish albumen" for our patient, not a sign of him was anywhere to be seen. Only parrots answered our shouts. We searched the vicinity, and finally found him on the bank of the *boca*, where his heavily bandaged leg was lovingly stowed among the stilt-like roots of the mangroves while the rest of Joerg was under water. When we pulled the leg, he came to the surface, puffing. He had his goggles on and was much excited.

"You have no idea," he cried, "how many fish there are in here among the roots! Tomorrow I'll take the harpoon along, and look after our supper myself!"

50

The first fish I harpooned was a red-patterned parrot fish. It came out unexpectedly from among the coral, and I hit it square, head on. It did not even switch its tail, so quickly was it dead.

The second fish that made unpleasant acquaintance with my harpoon also did not switch his tail—not, however, because I had hit him particularly neatly, or even at all, but because that is the usual habit of his species. He was a very peculiar character. I saw him floating slowly across the coral bottom, and as I approached I had leisure to observe him. He was almost three feet long, and so tightly compressed and flattened on the sides that he looked like a toy fish cut out of cardboard. Furthermore, he had quite unnaturally parchment-coloured skin, with blue and red spots, a snout prolonged like a trunk, at its outermost end a tiny mouth with even tinier projecting teeth, and on his brow a curved horn, which was always thoughtfully erected when the fish paused and looked at something. The tail of this preposterous creature was much too big for the body and trailed after it like an old-fashioned fan. It obviously served only for ornament—or perhaps for balance—but not for propulsion, which was accomplished entirely by a dainty fringe of fin along the back and belly line, undulating in tiny waves. The most remarkable thing about the creature was its eye, which had nothing reminiscent of a fish, but rather some thinking creature. When I approached, this eye looked into the distance, lost in thought, and observations of the surroundings—with occasional erection of the horn—seemed to go on rather mechanically and automatically; but the moment the creature became aware of me, unmistakable alarm glinted in its eye. With tail perfectly stiff and folded together in a bunch, the fish tried to flee. I thrust, but fell short, and barely jolted him in the side, which threw him into a panic. He now dashed quite aimlessly hither and thither among the coral, bumping into a branch, shrinking back with quivering fins, shooting in another direction, and bumping again. And all this with horn rising and collapsing, with nervously rolling eyes, and tail frantically thrust to the rear. The fish behaved in such scatterbrained fashion that it was less like an animal than like a human being. For animals in danger usually follow their sure instincts, whereas man, hampered by his power of thought, tends rather to indecision and bewilderment.

As I followed the fish I was suddenly stung in numerous parts of my body. First on the leg, then on the chest, then in the face. The different spots stung painfully, and yet there was no animal or other body to be seen anywhere in the water! I was groping with my hands for these invisible adversaries (they were tiny, transparent jellyfish), when one of the creatures accidentally got into a nostril. That gave me the finishing blow. I have seldom felt such a disagreeable sort of pain. I let the fish swim on unmolested, and groped back as fast as I could into normal, non-stinging water.

Determined to vent my ill temper somewhere, I stalked a few parrot fish that were grazing peaceably among the coral trees. But this injustice was not to be. As I approached from one side, there appeared from the other a long, very thin, grey-checked, in short very remarkable creature, which, instead of a normal fish mouth, had a trumpetlike trunk. This trumpet fish, as I privately baptized him (and as indeed he is actually called), shot straight at one of the parrot fish, and laid himself along its back, to its obvious surprise and uneasiness. And in this position he stayed. The parrot fish, a rather portly citizen, rolled its eyes and started off with pronounced displeasure

The trumpet fish followed, staying in position. This was too much for the parrot fish. It angrily bumped along among the coral trees, trying to shake off the intruder by quick turns. But the latter hung on like a skilled rider on a shying horse. And so the two disappeared in the distance. (Illus. 53, 54, 55.) What the thing meant I did not find out until much later; at the time I took it for an erotic perversion on the part of the trumpet fish.

As I was still looking after the two, my eye fell on a coral tree, under whose branches floated a big, gelatinous body. At a closer glance this supposed body turned into a school of several hundred little copper-coloured fish, poised close together and rocking to and fro *en masse* in the swell. For the fun of it I scared them apart, and in so doing I discovered two wide, shining eyes in a cave to the rear. A grouper, I thought, and at the same moment my harpoon shot forward. I could feel plainly that I had hit. Like a flash I yanked the harpoon back, but too late; the line was already caught. Probably the creature had jammed itself in the hole in the familiar way. I fumbled along the line into the cave, and found it was caught between two corals. With a certain amount of patience I managed to undo it, but then I was out of air, so I shot to the surface as fast as I could go.

As I was swimming upwards I could feel the resistance slackening and the creature being pulled out of the hole, but what was on my line I did not see until I had got a lungful of air. It was anything but a grouper. Basically the creature I had harpooned consisted entirely of a gigantic square head with pop eyes and a small tail fastened to the rear end of this head. Not so much as a hint of a body existed. At least not at that moment. Even while I was pulling this monstrosity up to me, a strange transformation began: the fish started swallowing water through its thick-lipped mouth, eagerly and greedily, swallowing and swallowing, and before my eyes its body swelled up more and more; spines that hitherto had lain unseen along the skin thrust out in all directions, and when the creature reached me it had turned into a spherical ball of spines. Tiny tail and eyes now peeped out from among the prickles. (Illus. 22.)

122

The creature struck me as somehow familiar. Where could I have seen one? Then I remembered: it was in Hamburg, in a bar, when we were wandering around the evening before sailing. We were sitting about a round table with numerous bottles, and over our heads dangled the spiny skin of a hedgehog fish. "That one's from Helmut's day," one of the girls had said; "he brought it to us from Java."

51

During our first days in the tent all kinds of things were stolen. First chocolate—we looked at one another with mutual suspicion—then spoons and forks. "It can't be Negroes," Joerg observed, "because they eat with their hands." So our suspicions fell upon the policeman from the phosphate company, who had brought us vegetables and mangoes. But the man was innocent. The real culprits sat hidden underground by day; we discovered them one night when they were just stuffing themselves on our carrots. They were big land crabs that lived in deep holes, where we found the vanished things—not, however, the chocolate.

Another creature that considerably disturbed the peace of our tent was a kid that I once caught during an unsuccessful lizard hunt. We christened it Joschi, and proposed to tame it. Alfred spent hours trying to replace its mother's milk with a Coca-Cola bottle and a linen rag, but Joschi's only reply was struggles and constant attempts to escape. The kid bleated so pitifully that it went to our hearts. We sat over our Sunday dessert practically without any appetite at all, and Joerg and Alfred upbraided me earnestly for having caught the kid. All night it bleated almost incessantly; in the morning it was hoarse, but had succeeded in persuading me to let it go. The little animal disappeared joyfully in the bushes, but within a few minutes it was bleating from afar more pitifully than ever. Alfred vanished like greased lightning into the bushes; when he came back, he was carrying Joschi in his arms and giving me most reproachful looks. The kid's outcry had attracted a bird of prey, which had attacked it and chewed it up badly. Alfred had barely managed to save it. Of course it was my fault, because I simply shouldn't have caught the poor kid in the first place. But this experience had suddenly tamed Joschi, who allowed himself to be bandaged without resistance, and no longer scorned the Coca-Cola breast. The little animal now skipped around the tent, bleating joyfully, and stayed with us without being tied. This idyll lasted two days, and then, during the third night, we suddenly heard a bleating dialogue. That was a load off my mind—the mamma had arrived to fetch Joschi! At last I could sleep again without feeling guilty!

We led an idyllic life. By day colourful humming-birds whirred in the trees, and at night, when we bathed for fun, the sea gleamed as we moved. As soon as darkness descended (which goes so fast in the tropics that you have to light the lamp immediately after sundown) we would sit down around a fire where the mosquitoes could do us the least harm, and each of us would tell what observations he had made during the day. Alfred, who now had charge of the kitchen, would prepare fried, baked, or steamed fish, and with it there would be fried, baked, or steamed bananas. Since shaving, of course, was out of the question now, we raised beards, and soon entered on a fierce competition. Alfred quickly dropped out, because his hair grew unevenly; the decision between Joerg and me, on the other hand, was a close one. Joerg's hair did grow somewhat faster, as we established definitely by measuring; but mine was far easier to see. My beard was strikingly black, whereas Joerg's was blond and curly, twining about his face so inconspicuously that he merely seemed to have somewhat fatter cheeks. We carried on long arguments as to whether the length of the hair or its colour was the more important, and finally the decision came all unexpected. That day we had gone to Willemstad for some shopping, and took occasion to visit our helpful friends at the Hamburg-Amerika Line. When we went into the office, my beard attracted great attention, and I was stared at from all sides.

Then one of the ladies turned to the patiently waiting Joerg. "How about you," she asked; "aren't you growing one?"

52

On many tropical coasts the barracuda, a pike, is no less dreaded than the shark. It does not grow nearly so big as the shark—only five to six and a half feet long—nor is it able, like the shark, to bite a man's arms or legs clean off, but there are plenty of cases known in which barracudas have attacked bathers and torn the flesh piecemeal from their bodies. (Illus. 49, 50.)

The first barracuda we met was floating motionless above the tops of the coral trees. Since precaution, as the German proverb has it, is the mother of all wisdom, we began by keeping some distance away. When nothing happened and the predatory fish only glanced contemptuously past us, we swam closer, and arrived just in time to see an unusual spectacle. A fish as long as your finger suddenly appeared in an opening; because of its powerful teeth we christened the species "biter". Well, this biter appeared outside the coral tree, which he obviously inhabited, and, when he saw the barracuda coming, rushed at it without a moment's hesitation. He swam straight up to its tail fin, which was considerably bigger than himself, and bit into it several times with considerable force. At first the barracuda did not react at all. Then, when the biting continued, it made a little indignant motion, as if so insignificant a trifle were beneath its dignity. But the biter did not give up. He kept biting again and again, harder and harder, and at length actually got the colossus, easily fifteen times his size, to start moving. The biter immediately followed, and did not give up until the barracuda was out of sight of his coral dwelling. Then he swam back satisfied, and at a window of the coral cave, proud and arrogant, appeared Mrs. Biter!

53

At last Joerg's leg was well. It was a great day for us. We formally introduced Joerg to the reefs, showing him each hiding place, and acquainting him with the fish, many of which he already knew from the frying pan. Since a huge number of the tiny stinging jellyfish also gathered to greet him, and it was rather stormy besides, we soon had to turn back. Not until later in the afternoon did it grow somewhat calmer, and we now tried the other side of the *boca*, where, as already mentioned, there are no coral reefs.

Alfred had hurt himself in the morning, so this time I was alone with Joerg. Things were just as they had been at Lopud and Cavtat: Joerg was on the right, I on the left, and in front of our harpoons, adventure. We swam across a flat, tiresome bottom, with merely some spherical coral shapes sprinkled among green and grey plants, and then reached a sharp edge thirty or thirty-five feet down, along which the bottom fell away abruptly. As it was already fairly late, the scene under water was sombre and uncanny. We looked around frequently; I had a vague feeling that a shark was bound to turn up suddenly somewhere. It was strange enough that we had not met a single one as yet.

Suddenly Joerg pointed downwards. A broad, dark shape had appeared in the distance and came swimming along the pitch just above the bottom—a big ray, beating the water with its winglike sides. Like a ghost in the night it fluttered along the bottom, its long, whiplike tail behind it. On this

126

tail the creature has a poisonous spine, provided with such a dreadful barb that it can be removed only in the direction it was driven in. If you are struck in the leg—says Brehm's famous book on animals—you have to pierce a hole from the opposite side of the leg, and pull the spine out straight through. What you are to do if you get a spine in the stomach the author does not say.

I did not dawdle, but dived to meet the ray. He took no notice of me, going calmly on his way. Even when I drove the harpoon with great force into his body, he paid no attention. It was several seconds before he noticed what had happened. Then, indeed, he quickened his pace, and headed directly for deep water. As so often before, I clutched the harpoon shaft, and tried to check the creature's speed. But the ray was considerably the stronger, and easily pulled me after him. What had become of Joerg? We kept going down and down, and I was quite out of breath.

I looked round, but Joerg was nowhere to be seen. Then, all at once, I noticed he was beside me. He reached for the rope, I let go, and he was pulled away below me. I caught a flash of him bracing himself with desperate strokes of his fins against the water, then I shot to the surface as fast as I could go.

When, after a few deep breaths, I stared downwards again, I saw a trail of mud leading across the bottom far below me. Joerg and the ray were almost out of sight. I raced frantically after, and when I finally overtook draft animal and driver, Joerg was already at the end of his strength. I took over the rope, and he shot upwards. Then he came back, and I shot upwards. We went up and down several times; we passed the rope to each other like the baton in a relay race. And slowly it turned out that the ray was tiring. His movements grew heavier, the pull weaker, he flapped around in circles, lashing his tail, and after half an hour we had the great creature in shallow water, and pulled it ashore fairly exhausted. As the ray was still lashing around, we threw the harpoon across its tail, pressed it to the ground, and Joerg cut it off. Not until then could we kill the brute.

As Joerg was slightly put out that he had not harpooned

127

the ray, we swam out again immediately, although by now it was very dark and uncanny indeed. Sure enough, we met a second ray, even bigger, even darker, fiercer-looking. Joerg harpooned it with a delight that made it plainly evident how eagerly he had longed for this moment, and for safety's sake I drove my harpoon into the creature's back as well. Thus we were able to hold on by two ropes. But this ray was too strong for us. It pulled us with irresistible force down the slope into the depths, and there was nothing for it but to cut the lines, so that we lost two heads at once. (Illus. 24, 25.)

When native fishermen came past in their boats, and saw us swimming around among the reefs, they usually rowed over to warn us against the "tribon", the shark. But day after day passed without our seeing a single one. We ventured farther and farther out into deep water, and our excitement kept growing, until finally the great moment really came.

There were three of us, just turning a reef, when a big body materialized out of the distance and came towards us with calm, steady movements. By the blue colour we could see that it was a blue shark—a man-eater. How often I had studied its picture in Brehm's *Animal Life*.

This was it.

I don't know what got into me. From everything I knew about sharks I should really have been afraid. But this creature was so handsome, so graceful, looked so unlike a bloodthirsty man-killer, that for the moment I could think only how fine a photograph of it would be. I forgot I had not even a knife on me, and I swam towards the shark, armed only with the camera. I had not the slightest misgivings; the voice of reason was completely silenced.

Every detail I saw in those seconds stamped itself indelibly upon me. To this moment I can see the plump body fairly exuding power, the sharp pectoral fins, thrusting forward on both sides like the fins of a bomb. I see the big, crescent tail fin, almost imperceptibly beating the water, and the dorsal fin, curved backwards—the dreaded "black triangle above the waves". The shark's body was perfectly streamlined in shape; as the creature was swimming between me and deep water, it

128

34. Alfred with a savoury catch—two soup turtles

35. A living being? When I touched it with my finger, the finger passed through without resistance

36. The queen's trigger fish, one of the loveliest West Indian species

37. The two black angel fish that did not want to be photographed

38. Joerg, every muscle tensed, stalked the sleeping shark

39. The wounded creature pulled the boat, Bernardo and all, along after it

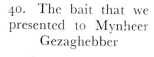

40. The bait that we presented to Mynheer Gezaghebber

41. The bottom was fairly flat, overgrown with tall, bushy sea whips

stood out in the round against the background; its outlines were bathed in sunlight.

Abominable beast? No! Without doubt it was the most beautiful of all living animals!

The shark came closer; strangely enough, I did not see its eyes. They must have been too small, hidden somewhere between the pointed nose and the five sharply marked gill openings in the shadow. I could make out the maw below. Twenty feet. . . . Fifteen feet. . . . Closer and closer the shark came!

When the thirteen-foot creature was within what my companions judged to be eight feet of me, its massive body gave a sudden jerk. With a cat-like suppleness quite incompatible with the calm majesty of its previous movements, the shark spun around almost on the spot. A few quick fin strokes vibrated audibly through the water, then it was out of sight.

Not until we got to the surface did we really take in what had just happened. The shark, the king of the sea, had fled before a small, unarmed human being. How could that be?

Actually the explanation was obvious enough. The shark is accustomed to having all creatures flee before him; it has always been so since time immemorial. And now, suddenly, it had met a strange creature that had shown no fear, but actually swam at it as if to attack. This must have been most unusual to the shark. Was the simple-minded creature not bound to think that this strange being was stronger than it?

After this we often met sharks, and always with the same result: no matter whether they were large or small, blue, grey, or the light-grey ones especially feared on some coasts, they all fled when we swam towards them, just as if we, not they, were the dreaded tigers of the sea. This reached such a point that I had real difficulty in getting good shark photographs. I soon discovered that one seldom comes as close as had been the case in our first encounter; usually the creatures turned away at a distance of fifty or sixty feet. Once, when, as usual, I was vainly trying to photograph a shark, Joerg summoned me to him for some reason or other. I left the creature behind, hurried towards Joerg, and found that the shark, so timid but a moment ago, now came after me in a most interested fashion. The faster I tried to get away, the faster it followed. This discovery led me to a method that may be classed with applied animal psychology. Henceforth if I wanted to photograph a shark I pretended to flee as conspicuously as possible, thus awakening the instinct in every beast of prey to chase what tries to escape. And I actually succeeded thus in luring sharks after me. When I saw that they were close enough, I would suddenly spin and swim towards them with camera at the ready. And before the creatures had recovered from their surprise and turned away in disgust I already had their image on film.

I must admit that some months later, when we were hunting on the stormy north coast of Curaçao, it turned out that sharks are not always so good-natured. Once, after a successful stalking hunt, we were swimming back to the coast, and since I had a lot of fish with me, I lagged behind my companions. Suddenly I noticed that two sharks had appeared behind me. They followed, looking like twin brothers. Both were equally big, equally grey, both approached simultaneously, both turned away simultaneously when I hit out in their direction with my fins. Obviously the blood of the dead fish was what attracted them. They kept coming back, and since I felt perfectly safe, I even let them get close to the fish several times, and then snatched them away from in front of the sharks' noses. I never dreamed for a moment that the situation might grow dangerous. And yet it did. As a strong surf was running, the water was turbid for some distance from shore; besides, it was just ebb tide, and muddy water was coming out of the neighbouring cove, whence the current carried it along the coast. In short, about a hundred and fifty feet from shore I got into muddy water that lay like a wall of cloud between me and the coast. I had to get through this dark zone. I strove to scare away the sharks, but now they seemed more interested in my company than ever. Giving up the fish was obviously out of the question. There was nothing for it but to swim into the foggy water despite the sharks, relying on the creatures' cowardice. But at the moment when I could see nothing, and thus lost my own assurance, the timidity of the twins vanished. The two of them now appeared unexpectedly behind me, beside me, below me, and finally even in front of me, always close together, with wily, wicked eyes. I pulled my fish close to me, swivelled my head frantically in all directions, and swam as fast as my fins would carry me. But I grew so nervous that I finally thought I saw the sharks even where they were not. I hit about me with the fins like a madman. The more scared I got, the saucier grew the twins.

It was a hundred and fifty feet to the coast, and then another hundred to the place where one got out of the water —a short, and yet, I can assure you, extraordinarily long, distance!

54

I have described the course of our Curaçao expedition in another book. Years have passed since then, and I have gained a little more perspective on our experiences. Some things I then thought worth telling now strike me as meaningless, and other things that I scarcely mentioned then have acquired importance since. Thus in my first book I ended the section about our hunting the Spanish Water with the remark that the beautiful reef grew more deserted every day, because—I said— the bigger fish probably told one another about our machinations. I didn't dream of the real connection between our activity and the conspicuous disappearance of fish.

Five years before we went to the Caribbean, the well-known Munich biologist Professor von Frisch spent his summer holiday on Lake Wolfgang. He spent the time studying the little silvery minnows, which he watched and fed from the boat. Once one of the creatures was injured, and swam off, bleeding. Thereupon the others grew increasingly uneasy, and in a short time all were gone. The sprinkled food remained untouched.

This observation led Professor von Frisch to investigate more carefully, and it turned out that the skin of the minnows (and of many other fish) contains a chemical that spreads through the water if the fish is injured, and is perceived, even when diluted, by others of the same species. The psychological significance of this "warning substance", as Professor von Frisch called it, is obvious. If some predatory fish is up to mischief anywhere, the warning substance spreads through the neighbourhood, and members of the species involved are warned against swimming in that direction.

On the Spanish Water reef we were the ones who killed the fish, whereupon they shunned the vicinity. Afterwards, too, we often discovered that places where we had hunted successfully were considerably less populous the day after. This indicates that the discovery made on Lake Wolfgang probably holds good in the Caribbean as well.

55

If you imagine a midwife's bag with pop eyes, devil's horns, and dainty fins, you will have an idea of the appearance of a trunkfish. (Illus. 29.) Two kinds occur near Curaçao: small creatures with black-and-white patterned bodies, and larger ones, distinguished by a remarkable change of colour. They are usually green and brown, but the moment you scare them they turn radiant blue. This appears to be a sign of excitement in general, because the same change takes place on their bridal night. At Jan Thiel, our second camp on Curaçao, I myself saw the love play of two trunkfish. There they were, dancing across the ocean bottom—imagine the comic spectacle of two blue dancing midwives' bags! Then the creatures came shooting perpendicularly upwards, their fins vibrating yearningly, and kept circling around each other with the greatest

132

excitement. They felt each other with their lips along head and belly, and turned such a luminous blue that light seemed to be coming through blue glass. Their motions completely blended; like two leaves in an autumn wind they spun upwards, constantly circling about each other. Not until they had reached the surface of the water did they stop. Now their motions slackened, and while their bodies resumed their normal greenish colour, they slid back, exhausted, towards the bottom. But there the dance began anew, and I hurried ashore as fast as I could go, because naturally I did not have my camera with me when I needed it. I simply had to have a picture of this love dance.

In the shallow water I stumbled over my fins, and fell full length into a field of sea urchins. I rose, cursing, and immediately fell again, this time bottom side down. Then I reached the bank, hurried to the tent, quickly put a colour film in the camera, and hastened back into the sea. But when I reached the spot again, nothing more was to be seen of the trunkfish anywhere. No doubt of it, they had gone on their honeymoon.

Anyone who has never sat down on a tropical sea urchin may consider himself lucky, because it is not a pleasing experience. These delightful little creatures cannot be compared in any way with their harmless relatives in the Mediterranean. Their spines are a good four inches long, very thin, brittle as glass, and poisonous, each one stinging on its own account. In a word, they interfere with sitting down.

Jan Thiel was a pretty camping place, and we could get milk, cheese, and fruit from a neighbouring plantation, but the wretched sea urchins caused us a good deal of trouble. They dominated the shallow regions of the beach, through which we had to pass several times a day; they would settle in broad, black fields, and each time it was an acrobatic feat to get through uninjured. The first day we tried to clear a path through this barrier of spines, but the blood bath we caused in the process was vain. By next morning the space we had swept clear was paved with newly immigrated sea urchins, strolling merrily about on their spiny legs to find as cosy a spot as they could for themselves and posterity.

Finally Joerg has pulled the last spine out of me, and we set off to hunt. Alfred "locks" the tent, Joerg stows away his instruments of torture in the medicine chest, and we wade cautiously through the sea-urchin zone. As soon as we are knee-deep in water, we ease ourselves in, and swim with tiny, propeller-like fin strokes just barely over the beds of spines. When the surface dips once for a moment I have to pull in my stomach, in absolute terror of being jabbed again. But then we are in deeper water, and I can heave a sigh of relief.

Once we have crossed the reefs, we keep to the right. This time we want to follow the coast westward, where a wreck lies a mile or so away, in whose hull, according to the fishermen, a gigantic fish is supposed to be hiding. We have our eye on this fish.

The sea floor grows flatter, and changes its appearance. As far as we can see, green and silver-grey plants cover the bottom, bushes whose branches wave like ostrich plumes in the swell. Seeing these growths for the first time you would take them for seaweed. (Illus. 30.) Actually they are not plants, but animal colonies, likewise coral, distinguished from rock coral only in that the tiny polyps which build up the structure secrete no calcium, but an elastic, horny substance. The German name for these *gorgonidae* is, in fact, horn coral. It is remarkable that there are very few plants on the tropical ocean floor; almost all the growths that look like plants are actually coral. All the more confusing, then, when the few seaweeds that do occur are not in the least like plants, but like coral. They are spherical calcium formations, almost indistinguishable from rock coral.

We dive.

Among the coral shrubbery Joerg has discovered a porcupine fish, which we want to photograph puffing itself up. As it is in the shadow, Joerg and Alfred get at it from the other side, and drive it out into the sunlight. In the process they nudge it with the harpoon heads, and the obedient creature actually starts blowing itself up without further attempt to escape. It swallows water, and grows fatter and fatter; nevertheless no picture is taken. Can I believe my eyes? Or is it only a shadow? Behind the porcupine fish, in a cleft under a big rock, is a sickle-shaped shadow. Without attending further to the inflated creature, I swim closer. Sure enough, in the hollow below the rock is the tail of a shark. The rest of the creature must be hidden in the rear part of the cave, where I can't see in. Judging by the size of the tail, this shark must be a good six or seven feet long.

"Want me to show you how to harpoon a shark?" I ask my companions on the surface.

I borrow Joerg's harpoon, swim close to the cleft, aim in leisurely fashion, and thrust. But alas! The skin is much too hard; the head doesn't penetrate at all. But the shark is awakened from his noon nap. There is a violent turmoil in the cave, and I am barely able to squeeze to one side when the creature appears in daylight. I can hardly believe my eyes— surely that is no shark! Or else it is a shark monstrosity. The beast has a blunt, broad head, short, fat body, and looks exactly as if it had swum head on into a cliff, hard, in its youth. Aft of this hammered-down head is the quite preposterously large tail fin. And since the creature swims close past me, I also see it has a pitifully small mouth, with short, thick strings of moustache hanging down on both sides after the fashion of a great catfish.

With joyful shouts we pursue this peculiar character, but his big tail gives him a head start, and he soon vanishes into deep water. Probably he will start looking around down there for a quiet spot to continue his nap. Joerg informs us that this was a nurse shark; he has seen one in a museum. Round about the cleft from which the nurse shark rushed out so tempestuously large and small fish have gathered, obviously lured from their hiding places by the noise. Among them, belly upwards, floats the porcupine fish, which has already grown slender again and is now inflating itself anew. Joerg and Alfred harpoon one fish each, and then we go on.

The wreck, unfortunately, is a disappointment. Here we find nothing like grisly cabins and dead men's corridors, but a completely hollow, rusty iron hulk, only a small part of it under water at all. Naturally there is nothing to be seen of any particularly large fish. Only swarms of countless tiny fish are swimming around here—swarms whose arrangement recalls cosmic spiral nebulae.

We go ashore, and warm ourselves in the sun. Then I open a watertight container at my belt in which matches and a spare film are kept. While I load the new film into the camera, Alfred and Joerg get a fire blazing and roast their fish on the ends of their harpoons. The fish get somewhat charred, but they taste good anyway. With them we eat oranges, which we have also brought along, without any special container, since they are naturally waterproof.

While we are swimming back, Joerg suddenly pauses and calls our attention to a coral hole, from which two long, thin stalks peer out. We have seen such stalks often before, and have always taken them for some form of coral; but these stalks move as arbitrarily as if they belonged to some animal. Joerg dives and takes a closer look. Then he comes back to the surface with every sign of excitement.

"A *langouste*!" he cried. "Those are the feelers of a langouste!"

In a moment all three of us are below, and Joerg takes command. So that the creature shall not escape, we are to approach from three different directions. The langouste is no fool either. Discovering the superior force with which it has to contend, it takes its leave through an emergency exit on the fourth side. We are hot after it at once, and a wild chase through the coral begins. The langouste dashes from one bit of coral to another, a grotesque spectacle, because it swims tail forward, pulling the long feelers after it. At the same time it twists one of its stalk eyes forward to see where it is swimming, and the other backwards, to dodge our harpoon thrusts. Since this gives it only one eye for a lookout in each direction, so that it has no depth perception, it misses its aim several times, and soon ends its promising career on Joerg's harpoon.

Having grown curious, we now search the neighbouring caves as well, and encounter the dependents of the recently assassinated langouste. The briefest consideration suffices to show that the grief of the survivors can best be ameliorated by killing them all, and a terrific slaughter begins. Fifteen minutes later five deceased crabs hang on our bag line and five full-grown langoustes—a supper such as we have not had for a long time. (Illus. 32.)

We stay no longer, leave the fish to their own devices, and hurry back to our camp. As we are swimming past a steep cliff, suddenly a shout is heard above us. On the cliff appears a Negro with a catapult in his hand, and at the same moment a large body splashes into the water directly in front of Alfred. Alfred jumps, and when the spray has died down somewhat we see that a dragon-like creature about three feet long is floating in the water right in front of us. It is an iguana. Green, with a saw-toothed comb, it hangs easily in the water, staring at Alfred with eyes as surprised as Alfred's own. Then both recover themselves. Alfred raises his harpoon, but the iguana is quicker. It dives and shoots straight between Alfred's legs. Then it is back on the cliffs, where it clambers up into a cleft and vanishes. And we and the man with the catapult are left gaping.

Too bad! The tail of the iguana is supposed to taste as good as chicken. That would not have been bad—first langoustes, then chicken!

Back at our tent, we discover that we lack a suitable festive board. Langoustes carry an obligation. Since we are cold anyway, we start right to work, lugging coral fragments large and small up the little rise to the tent floor, and each of us tries to create a special architectural work of art. By the time twilight falls, everything is ready. A big coral slab serves as a table, round it stand three massive coral armchairs, and over it our little spirit lamp hangs from a branch. Alfred has brought fresh bread, Joerg is stirring mayonnaise. The langoustes are already boiled and red, and I am in the act of dividing them impartially into three equal shares. Then the meal begins. Each of the many langouste legs is cracked and sucked dry with great relish; what is left is thrown over our shoulders to the rear, where it is already awaited by pocket crabs as big as your fist, even more avid than the land crabs.

137

Evening descends upon us. Now the sun is racing across the sky somewhere between Panama and Australia. In a leisurely fashion the moon rises, and the stillness about us grows even stiller. Each of us lies back in his armchair, Joerg and Alfred puffing at their pipes. I alone am not quite happy. Unfortunately the traces of the sea urchin's spines are still quite plainly perceptible.

56

No other biological sphere of the earth has created such delicate, transparent animals as the deep sea, where no current mars their fragile forms. Among the salpas and jellyfish, and above all among the glass ropes of the deep sea, are shapes that could hardly be daintier. And at that, the most delicate forms are certainly not yet known; mere contact with a net or any other device annihilates them. Only now and then, when gentle upward currents prevail in the sea, they are carried up unharmed to daylight.

The day after our langouste banquet we followed the coast eastward, and swam as far as the lighthouse on the cape at Caracas Bay, where Alfred discovered a large, gelatinous body floating just below the surface. It was a good five feet long and eighteen inches thick, in the shape of a spiralled cylinder. The formation was so transparent that you could see it only against the light. There was not the slightest sign of any organ. I tried to touch it with my finger, but the finger passed through almost without resistance. If this was in fact a living being—and what else could it be?—it had no more reality than the teleplasm of a spirit materialization. (Illus. 35.)

We photographed the formation, then a wave broke, shattering the enigmatic shape. Had it really lived? Was it dead now? What did life and death mean in this case—or in any other?

57

One day Mr. Meyringh came to see us. He brought a new and even better shooting harpoon, which he wanted to show us, and also a letter that we had been most eagerly awaiting. It was the answer of a Dutch veterinarian named Dr. Diemont, who was living on the neighbouring island of Bonaire at the time, and had been described to us as a very helpful man, interested in all matters of fishing. As we wanted to move to Bonaire, we had written to him, and his reply was most cordial. We should come over as soon as we could, he was most curious, and would be entirely at our disposal.

"You're sure to see jewfish in Bonaire," said Mr. Meyringh, when he heard of our plans. He said these were gigantic, extra-ordinarily fat groupers, sometimes nearly eight feet long, that frequented only one particular place. Just recently one of the monsters had lain for weeks next to the net in Piscadera Bay. But the fishermen had not been able to catch it.

"Why didn't you harpoon it?" we cried with one voice.

"Harpoon it?" was his reply. "Wait till you meet a jewfish, and then you can try it for yourselves!"

As we were preparing for the hunt, Mr. Meyringh explained a new method of his. He said he had noticed that mackerel were interested in shiny objects, so he had polished his harpoon heads quite bright. It was a very simple matter. With one hand he would hang on to the net in Piscadera Bay, with the other he would stick the catapult into the water. Mackerel would always turn up in a very short time to get a closer look at the harpoon head, and then he would simply let fly.

We now went into the water, and matched ourselves as hunters against Mr. Meyringh. All at once a gigantic hammer-head shark appeared, easily sixteen or seventeen feet long, of terrifying appearance. Fat as a steam roller, massive, dark, monotonously swinging its hammer-shaped head to and fro

139

as it swam, the monster came on. Luckily I had the camera with me.

I dived.

Back and forth the hammer-shaped head swung, as if the giant saw but badly with his tiny eyes on the outer ends of the hammer. I got within twenty feet of him without his discovering me. Like a locomotive the creature whizzed past below me, going straight and impervious on its way, then vanished in the distance, still monotonously swinging its head back and forth—something, incidentally, that I never saw but that once.

When I surfaced again Mr. Meyringh stared at me in blank astonishment. "That makes us all square," he snorted, "or are you tired of life?"

58

Two days later, bag and baggage, we were on our way to Bonaire. We had entrusted ourselves to a Venezuelan sailing cutter and were paying five guilders a head, for which price the captain also served us salt fish.

Unfortunately the sea was fairly active, so that the voyage lost a good deal of its charm. Along with us there were a few Boy Scouts on board, who, depending on how they felt at the moment, sang either very merry or very melancholy songs.

First Willemstad vanished from our sight, then the lights of Jan Thiel and, barely hinted in outline, the dark mouth of the Spanish Water moved past us. "Tomorrow," said the captain, "if the wind will have it so, we shall be in Bonaire."

And if Neptune will have it so, I thought, we shall meet a jewfish there.

Anyone who describes Kralendijk as a godforsaken dump need have no fear of being sued for libel. Kralendijk is the capital of Bonaire, the headquarters of the almighty Mynheer

Gezaghebber, the representative of the Dutch Crown; that aside, it is a tumbledown village comprising a few dozen pale houses, which lie carelessly and at random along the coast, and among which Mynheer Gezaghebber's two-storey house looks like a swollen and ailing member. Scattered along the beach lie the skeletons of a few half-finished ships, which will undoubtedly still be unfinished next year.

The road passing among these skeletons and through the worm of houses is desolate and dusty, quite deserted most of the day. If, God forbid, you want to buy something in Kralendijk, you find the astonished shopkeeper at home in bed. He resignedly puts on his slippers, unlocks the shop without a word, then, after you have been able to determine that nothing of what you need is on hand, he goes straight back to bed. Only chamber pots exist in Kralendijk at reasonable prices and in any desired quantity; they were once sold here by a particularly accomplished salesman, and the supply is surely adequate for some decades, no matter how brisk the demand.

When our ship moored at the pier in Kralendijk, a gaping throng gathered. The children squeaked at our beards, and the customs official shook his head portentously at the sight of our baggage. Of course once again there was something not right about our papers. It was suggested that we had better go straight back by the same vessel.

Since this time we actually knew we were in the right, we became recalcitrant. We insisted on a telegraphic inquiry at the immigration service in Curaçao. A long, perspiring confabulation ensued, during which we made the acquaintance of Mynheer Gezaghebber, with whom we immediately found a point in common; namely, mutual dislike at first sight.

Finally the dispatch of the telegram had been argued and accomplished, and the gentlemen withdrew to their *siestas*. We went out in search of Dr. Diemont, and found him by the torso of a half-finished ship—his new ship, as he assured us with a sigh. Dr. Diemont was a slender man in his mid-thirties, with clear, quick eyes and a curved, enterprising nose. We told him about the unkindly reception we had had, and thenceforth we scarcely needed to lift a finger. We had barely finished our tale when he was off to Mynheer Gezaghebber to plead our cause, and to the customs man, and they practically came to blows. He invited us all to dinner, after which he organized a pleasure trip in the schoolteacher's boat, which had a small outboard motor. Whenever I think back to those hours and all the others that we spent with Dr. Diemont, I am filled with a warm sense of gratitude. We have him to thank not only for the great help he gave us, but for being an example of how helpful a person can be.

Our little cruise took us to a place called Punt Vierkant, where we found conditions worthy of paradise prevailing on the ocean floor. For some reason or other the natives of Bonaire believe that the fish at Punt Vierkant are poisonous, and have not fished in that region since time immemorial. The fish, which were correspondingly plentiful, were so unsuspecting here that we could actually touch some of them with our fingers. Alas that the customs man had not yet released our harpoons—ostensibly because weapons were forbidden! But we discovered in the boat a short spear, whose wobbly head was something like that of a halberd. We might just as well have chased the fish with a pointed broomstick, but it worked even so; each of the three of us took a fish, and Dr. Diemont was enchanted. When we got back to the pier, he told everybody in great detail what miraculous things we had performed. The harpooned fish and a langouste that we had also taken passed from hand to hand. Dr. Diemont spoke in the local Papiamento, so we could only gather from his gestures what he was saying. At any rate he managed to turn the general feeling in our favour. The customs man released the harpoons, and Mynheer Gezaghebber, who had probably had an answer from Curaçao meanwhile, did not appear, which we took as permission to stay.

After considerable conversation with Dr. Diemont we decided to set up our first camp on Little Bonaire, a small, completely uninhabited island not far from Kralendijk. As we wanted to move over that very evening, we hastened to buy the necessary provisions. Dr. Diemont, meanwhile, set about finding a boat suitable for our purposes. He haggled for a good hour with an old, white-haired Negro, who wriggled like a cat, and kept raising his arms imploringly to heaven from time to time. Finally we settled on fifty guilders a week, for which Bernardo, a son of the old man, was also to be our servant, starting the next morning.

Just before sunset all the preparations were made at last, and Dr. Diemont took us in the heavily laden motor-boat to Little Bonaire. He helped actively in the unloading, which was not easy in the prevailing darkness. Only when he had made sure we had everything we needed did he go back to Kralendijk. He said he would come again the following morning with the rest of the baggage and a water barrel.

59

On 23 July, 1939, I wrote in my diary: "First day on the island. Spent cold, windy night wrapped in blankets in the shelter of some bushes. Bernardo arrived at seven in the morning. Alfred was supposed to instruct him in dish-washing. Alfred found this unpleasant. . . ."

Insignificant as this note is, it indicates a problem that made its first appearance and kept troubling us thenceforth —the problem of authority. Among the three of us there had not been any such problem because we had been friends for many years, belonged to the same social group, and were pursuing the same object in our expedition. I was the leader of the enterprise, of course, but this scarcely ever became apparent. If one of us wanted another to do some job, he would say, "You know, we really ought to . . ." or, "Maybe you'd . . ." and the other would understand. Towards the boy, naturally, this was not a suitable way to behave. Only, in spite of the fact that we were paying him plenty, we had inhibitions about giving him orders. It seemed to us much easier to turn to for ourselves than to sit back and give orders. This was something none of the three of us liked to do.

Nevertheless, with united forces we managed to utter the repugnant words. Bernardo now busily washed dishes, then got our breakfast, and went with us in the boat when we were hunting. This last was particularly helpful to us. If we had a fish on the line, we simply yelled for Bernardo, and at the same time he would pass us a fresh harpoon, so that the hunt could go on without interruption.

At noon we ate fish with bananas. Bernardo cooked and served, but did not partake of the meal himself. He gave us to understand that only poor people in these parts ate fish and bananas. Then he took meat and bread from his bag.

60

Murky night, the campfire has gone out, and hypnotic snores come from both sides of me. Joerg lies to my right; Alfred, whose snoring is somewhat more melodious, on the left. As for myself, I sit between them on my rubber mattress, sweating because I am shrouded in a thick blanket, and cursing because the night seems endless. In the triple darkness of night, tent, and the blanket, I am winding the films we have taken in the last few days out of their cartridges. My motions are slow and precise, for fear a single drop of sweat shall fall on the film. It is not very entertaining work, the same thing over and over again: open the cartridge, wind out the film, then pack it carefully in tinfoil, put it to the left, and reach for the next cartridge on the right.

We have been on the island three days now, and what experiences we have had! Almost each hour brought something new. Even now, this evening, something was still going on. It is hardly two hours since there was a terrible yelling

42. The grouper tried to flee into the depths, but Joerg was
hot on his trail

43. The jewfish knew we were after him, but stayed quietly just outside his cave

44. Joerg signed to him that he must come up at once

45. The moray bared
its teeth in a photo-
graphically admirable
way

46 and 47. The low point of our underwater activity; we found a weir basket in which a fish had got caught. Joerg dived and stole it from the basket

from the sea. We rushed down, and found Alfred in a state of great excitement, yelling, His kingdom for a harpoon. He had started to take an evening bath in a natural tub among the rocks, and had come within an ace of sitting down on a sting ray. The ray's tail had happened to twist above water, allowing him to discover at the last moment that the tub was already occupied. We harpooned the ray at once. Its spine was a good four inches long. Alfred uses it now to clean his pipe.

It is a regular Robinson Crusoe's isle we live on here. At least to the extent that we are the only inhabitants of the island —aside from a few wild goats and donkeys, who wake us at six o'clock every morning by galloping heavy-footed past our tent. Otherwise, however, this islet is not at all like Crusoe's. The tree under which our tent stands is the only one far and wide. For nearly three-quarters of a mile stretches a dismal plain, with nothing but brush and withered cactus. It is said to rain here only once a year. The animals drink out of a hole filled with brackish water on the other side of the island; we passed by there our first day as we were lugging the baggage across. It is a little puddle twelve feet below the plateau, with matted seaweed and skaters on the surface. But anyone with a real thirst does not fool around long. We pushed weed and skaters to one side, and drank.

What an abominable job of lugging! We had to carry our things for almost two miles half round the island. At the same time the sun burned as if to transform us, too, into cactus. The cactus jabbed back wherever you put your foot. Where the cactus did not happen to prick you, the horseflies saw their opening. It was not a pleasant walk. We were able to transport only the diving helmet and the water barrel by boat; the wind was so strong that the boat did not arrive until an hour after us. Dr. Diemont was always in the lead. Naturally he had taken the biggest load, the tent, and a bag besides. At the same time he kept telling stories, conversing, and urging us on.

Our camp is ideally situated; there are very beautiful corals here, and fish in plenty. Within an hour we saw our first. After the tent was pitched, I went straight out with Dr. Diemont to reconnoitre the neighbouring sea. I fitted him with a pair of goggles, to please him. And indeed he was as pleased as a child when he went into the water with me. Unfortunately we had picked a poor spot; the bottom was covered far and wide with monotonous coral hedges, and not a single fish to be seen. Only farther offshore, where the bottom suddenly falls away as in Curaçao, there were fish enough. We first observed a big queen's triggerfish, and then encountered two comical black angelfish, which behaved like a fussy old married couple. (Illus. 36, 37.) I dived immediately. At first the two would not be photographed on any account. They kept turning to and fro, and whatever one did, the other immediately imitated. But as they were not only timid but extremely curious, I succeeded in outwitting them. I dived, rested quietly just above the bottom, and made slow, circling motions with my left arm. The fish were a comical spectacle enough. The two of them would keep coming a little closer, then suddenly turn away in fright, but immediately peer back at me, then turn again, and come still a bit closer. Finally, overcome with curiosity, they came quite close, and I snapped them, which outraged them, earning me a highly indignant stare.

When I swam to the surface again I found poor Dr. Diemont quite pale and quaking. "I was trembling very much for you," he burst out in his Dutch-German. "The whole time while you were taking pictures down below, a blue shark was lying in wait very angrily just behind you!"

And so it went. There was always something going on. Once Joerg was pursued by a pack of half-grown barracudas, then Alfred discovered a big, snakelike creature deep down among the coral, and then the affair of the great rudder . . .

If I ever grow old and become a grandpa, I shall tell my grandchildren the story, and make their hair stand on end— just as mine did. How did it happen? I was chasing a barracuda. The water was turbid, and the brute kept swimming down and down into the depths. I followed, and suddenly the barracuda was gone. I saw nothing beyond a big movement in the water, but the barracuda was nowhere to be seen. Instead I saw a big rudder, a perpendicular plate at least eight feet high, moving slowly in the water. With the poor visibility I could tell no more. At first I actually thought it was the rudder of a ship. I was even silly enough to surface and look round. Of course there was no ship. Instead, some distance away, I saw a big, black movement below the waves. And then it dawned on me. My hair stood on end. Now I realized! What I had taken for a rudder was actually the tail fin of a gigantic shark. The shark had dined upon the barracuda before my very eyes, and then turned slowly to one side. Because of the turbid water I could just barely make out his tail fin. I cast another glance below water—the rudder was still there. But the shark did not seem to have noticed me. Probably the barracuda had saved my life. Quite slowly and softly I sneaked away, and then made for shore pell-mell as fast as I could go. If ever knees trembled, they were mine when I felt solid ground under my feet again. How long that shark was I dare not even guess.

"Aren't you through yet?" comes a grunt from my left.

Then Joerg rolls noisily over, and goes on snoring. But now I am finished, thank heaven, and before long I, too, am asleep; the trio is complete again.

61

The experience that awaited us the next morning makes sense only if you know the rumours current about our activities at the time.

Actually you couldn't blame people. At a moment of great tension, with the outbreak of the war just ahead, suddenly three youths from Vienna appeared, for no other reason, they insisted, than to go swimming among sharks. They had cameras with them, wanted to live in solitude, and pitched their first camp at the *boca* of the Spanish Water—less than a mile from the oil tanks of Caracas Bay. Surely this must mean something, after all?

One day a detective called—to spend his day off with us, he said; actually to search the tent and its vicinity during our absence. Then at Jan Thiel we saw a man with field glasses sitting behind a cactus. And these were further reasons why we moved to Bonaire, where there are no oil refineries yet.

Meanwhile, however, the rumours continued to circulate. The news was published in Panama that "under-water agents were active" in Curaçao, "holding secret conferences on the sea bottom with German U-boats." This story and others like it were picked up by the North American Press as well.

The morning after—I take this passage fairly verbatim from an earlier book of mine—the goats awakened me as always. I went sleepily outdoors, looked at the barren island, at the calm sea, and at our Bernardo. He was crouching not far from the tent at a fire, where he was preparing the *repa*— a cake of sugar, water, and flour—as he did every morning. At the same time, while waiting with restless eyes for the tea water to boil, he kept slapping his thighs with a steady beat, obviously for no reason except to create a rhythm, which he needed for any action he performed.

Suddenly he pointed towards the sea.

A big motor-boat came snarling up, and cast anchor directly offshore from our camping ground. We watched a man in a white suit clamber into the tender and be rowed ashore by a native servant. A few minutes later he appeared at our tent. He was short and spare, had a serious, squinting expression, and in fact seemed generally inclined to a pessimistic view of life. The Dutchman greeted us with conspicuous amiability and a smile that froze on his face: Mynheer Gezaghebber was out in the boat, Mynheer Gezaghebber wanted to speak to us, would we please go to Mynheer Gezaghebber.

Even from afar the spare man had looked to me like a detective; now that he lured us so adroitly away from our tent, my suspicion became a certainty. We were eager to know what this exalted visitor signified, and were soon to find out. Mynheer Gezaghebber greeted us with exaggerated cordiality, told us he had happened to come by with friends on a fishing trip, but the bait had got left at home, and it had occurred to him that we might be able to dive with our harpoons and fetch him up a few fish for bait.

Aha! So that was the way the wind blew! Mynheer Gezaghebber wanted to put us to the test and see whether we could catch any fish at all. All right, he should have his bait!

So off we went to hunt. Joerg swam to the left, Alfred to the right, and I fished right in front of camp. And as always happens when you need a fish, you don't catch any. Half an hour passed, and Mynheer Gezaghebber was already observing us with a malicious smile. Then I heard a yell from the rocks. Joerg had climbed ashore a few hundred yards from camp and now came bounding with incredible speed across the rocks, waving and yelling wildly. I hustled out of the water just in time to meet Joerg. He told me hurriedly, in great excitement, that he had discovered a sleeping shark.

Now there was a lively turmoil. I raced to the tent to fetch the camera, and remembered in the process that I needed to put in a new film. Joerg, who was pelting along beside me, panted out as he ran that he would instruct Bernardo to get the boat ready. We would tie the harpoon head to a long line, the other end of which we would fasten to the boat. In that way we could tire and land the shark from the boat, if we should harpoon him.

Everything went pell-mell. Bernardo rushed to the boat, Joerg after him, and finally I had my camera ready. We were not the only ones excited, though, for Mynheer Gezaghebber could not understand what had suddenly got into us. He stood up in his boat, and shouted across. He wanted to know what all this meant. But we had no time to answer; we even forgot that Alfred was not with us, and pushed off hurriedly from shore. As soon as we approached the spot Joerg indicated, we pulled our oars slowly and as noiselessly as possible, so as not to awaken the sleeping brute.

This was supposed to be it, here, where the sea was perhaps thirty feet deep.

With exaggerated care Joerg entered the water first, looked down searchingly, then swam ahead of the boat. We followed him, but suddenly he turned, and by his excited gestures I saw

149

that he had rediscovered the sleeping shark. He was quite grave with excitement, quite pale in the face, for this was the opportunity we had long been awaiting. I, too, quickly slid into watthe er with the camera.

Sure enough, there was the shark indeed! He rested between tall green coral chunks on a sandy spot, and his form stood out very clearly against the dark background. It was a beautiful creature sleeping there, easily six and a half feet long. The shark was completely motionless except the gills, which slowly widened and then narrowed again. That was how he breathed.

I forced myself to be calm, crept up, keeping just behind Joerg, to within fourteen or fifteen feet, and arranged things so that Joerg was between me and the shark. Joerg did not thrust yet. He set to work with infinite patience—even, it seemed to me, in my agonizing expectation, with too much caution. I kept my eyes fixed on the shark; he did not stir, he noticed nothing, he was asleep. It was an incredible picture that I saw through my view finder: the shark, standing out against the bright sand, and the luminous brown figure of Joerg, who, sweeping the creature with his eyes, every muscle tense, swam up to the attack. Now, at last, he was at the right level; now he thrust like a flash and with all his might. (Illus. 38.)

Within a matter of seconds the water, so clear up till now, was muddied. In his savage pain the shark plunged off, exerting his strength to the utmost. His body lashed the water furiously. Joerg, holding harpoon and line, was pulled along. The shark now wound himself around a big coral stalk, which, however, broke into many pieces. Then he raced on in a wild zigzag, still dragging Joerg after him. Joerg was flung hither and thither, banged hard into various coral masses, and, thank heaven, realized it was hopeless to try to pull the shark to the surface, so he let go and floated to the top, completely exhausted.

I, too, had arrived meanwhile. I took a deep breath, and my first glance went to the boat. I saw something spooky: the boat, to which the harpoon line was made fast, suddenly

150

turned, as if seized by an invisible force, and hurtled off. Bernardo yelled, whether with delight or terror we could not tell at the moment. Anyhow, he was standing in the boat, which rocked alarmingly, and was dragged away by the shark. (Illus. 39.)

We followed as fast as we could, and Mynheer Gezaghebber's boat soon arrived also. Mynheer Gezaghebber had turned pale. He probably could not imagine what strange and highly suspicious things were going on here, and perhaps thought that another submarine was involved. But we ignored his yells, because we had to act fast, or the shark would snap the harpoon line on one of the sharp coral banks. The boat turned a sharp curve—Bernardo almost fell overboard—and then came heading straight for us. But just before it got to us its pace slackened. I reached quickly into the boat and grabbed my long, sharp hunting knife. A glance below the surface had shown me that the shark was wound up with the harpoon line among the coral chunks at a considerable depth—more than forty-five feet. As I took breath, I unexpectedly saw Mynheer Gezaghebber's pale face close above me. He had come racing up towards the whole mysterious occurrence and was leaning forward in the boat, staring down at me.

With a yell I swung the flashing knife over my head. He instantly sprang back in alarm. Then, the better to swim, I took it in my mouth, and plunged to the bottom. Nearly fifty feet is a long way to dive. The water pressure squeezed the goggles painfully against my eyes, I felt as if I could scarcely bear the pressure in my ears, but I saw the shark below me, and that gave me strength. He was close beside the coral around which the long line was wound, lashing his tail wildly. I clung to his belly with my left hand, pressing my body to his back, and stabbed the shark several times from the side and from below.

Then, when the shark's blood stained the water, I let go and grabbed the line. I was scarcely able to act at all, since I had no breath left, but I did just manage to undo the line from the coral chunks, and not until then did I shoot upwards as fast as I could go to the longed-for air. I had a fierce headache

151

from the pressure in the depths. I lay on the water, resting.

When I opened my eyes I saw Joerg and Bernardo just pulling the shark into the boat. Mynheer Gezaghebber was still standing speechless at the gunwhale. Casually, as if all this were nothing at all, I called to him, "Your bait, Mynheer Gezaghebber!" (Illus. 40.)

62

While we were still camping at Jan Thiel, Curaçao, I once harpooned a fish that fled into the nearest cleft in the coral and literally stuck there. Only its tail projected from the hole. I tugged at it, and also at the line, but I could not get the fish out. I looked to see whether it had wedged itself in after the fashion of the grouper, but this was not the answer either.

So I braced my feet right and left against the coral, and this time tugged quite violently at the tail. Sure enough, the creature emerged inch by inch. But when I relaxed for a second it promptly snapped back to its former position. Yet the fish was stiff and lifeless—a complete mystery. The brute seemed to have a rubber band fastened to its head, keeping it in the hole.

I tugged again, and again the fish snapped back. But this time I saw why it was: a great snake, hidden in the cleft, was holding my fish by the nose and pulling it back each time. This snake-like creature—a fish, actually—had the most malignant eyes I had ever seen.

It was a moray.

The first time I ever saw a moray was in the pictures, when I was a small boy. It was for Adults Only, and I had sneaked in with an old hat of my father's. The film was a rather sexy affair laid in ancient Rome, in which we saw a banquet with lavish courses and exceedingly voluptuous dancing girls.

During the dinner the morays were also fed. Hundreds of serpentine shapes boiled on the surface of a pond; sharp, poisonous teeth sparkled in avidly gaping maws, and then some slaves were tossed into the pond. Human flesh to fatten the morays! The corpulent Romans hooted, the slaves struggled, and the voluptuous girls danced. The scene was very gruesome; the director had done himself proud. And yet he forgot the most effective bit of all. He should have shown the morays' eyes, incomparably cold and malignant, the way I once saw them. . . .

It was the day after Mynheer Gezaghebber's visit. I was fishing alone on the north shore of our islet, fairly late in the afternoon. The reefs rose dark and silhouette-like from the ocean floor. I was swimming twenty-five feet under, intending just to go as far as the corner of this particular reef and then return to shore with the two fish I already had, when I saw something I shall never forget.

A big snapper, weighing easily thirty pounds, which had swum rather slowly up from the depths, suddenly whipped the water with a frightened blow of its fins and raced off with every sign of terror. At the spot where it had just been there gaped the yawning jaws of a giant moray whose body rose erect from a cleft in the reef, a ghostly silhouette with the light behind it.

Before I realized what I was doing I had driven my harpoon through the monster's fat green throat. That very instant the harpoon was snatched from my hand to go dancing off among the coral masses. Then all was still again, and I saw the harpoon cord now leading into a hole from which a thin thread of blood curled up.

I struggled to get the creature out of its hiding place, but an hour passed without bringing me the slightest success. My nose was beginning to bleed from constant diving, and the sun sank ever closer to the horizon. Finally I gave one last yank, with redoubled fury, at the harpoon line, and suddenly the whole coral mass exploded as if by dynamite, and the moray, which had produced this blast with its own frenzied power, shot out of the ruins straight at me.

153

Not until now did I realize what a monster I had tangled with. The moray was as tall as I am.

It rushed me at once; I parried with the harpoon shaft. And so began a regular duel. Again and again the brute tried to get at me by every imaginable feint. For instance, several times the moray shot perpendicularly down, dragging me after it, then turned like a flash and shot straight up again, at me. It came from every quarter, squirming through the water like a snake, with venomous eyes and wide-open jaws. I defended myself with the harpoon shaft, and toiled to drag the raging creature towards shore.

Twice the moray got quite close to me, and then, finally, I had it up to the reef, and flung it over into the shallow water of the lagoon. Unfortunately I now discovered that the lagoon bottom, like that at Jan Thiel, was paved with thousands of sea urchins. How was I to get across with the savage moray?

Since the sun was already approaching the horizon, I had little time for reflection. I was determined not to give up the moray; Joerg and Alfred simply must see it. I looked across the lagoon again, hunting some possible way over the grisly black fields, and resolved to try it in spite of all. I wound the harpoon line as often as I could around the shaft, to give the moray less play, and off I started on my arduous journey.

For a while I managed, then I reached a spot where there seemed to be no clear space at all among the sea urchins. Just one little round ball of coal arose from the bed of spines. I stepped cautiously upon it, shifted my weight, and then my foot skidded off the slippery surface, and I lost my balance. To break my fall and shield face and body from the spines, I flung my arms forward; they were impaled in twenty places. At the same time I involuntarily pulled back the harpoon, and this gave the moray a chance to get at me.

As I opened my eyes wide with pain in the water, I saw slavering jaws and wicked, venomous eyes just in front of my face.

Somehow I managed to stretch my arm away, and so to pull the creature back by the harpoon shaft at the last moment. I still wonder how I did it. The eyes of that moray I shall never forget. Their expression was so evil, so hateful, that it would be hard to imagine anything more fiendish. I believe there are only two other living things capable of such a look—the fabled sea serpent and man.

At Nauru Island, in the South Seas, morays are caught with a noose. The natives dive down into the reefs, put the open noose before the moray's cavern with one hand and with the other dangle a juicy piece of bait outside the entrance. When Alfred, in the course of his favourite under-water "cave hunting", discovered a medium-sized moray in a reef, we decided to take films of a South Seas hunt. We fastened a wire noose and a bit of meat each to a stick, and Joerg at once began to practice using the new implement.

But this did not suit Alfred at all. "I can't see why Joerg should get the job again," he said. "He harpooned the shark too. Besides, it's my moray."

"Oh, don't mind me!" said Joerg touchily. "By all means go ahead and try!" And then, turning to me, he added in a stage whisper: "If he doesn't bring it off, you can get a scene of me showing him how it ought to be done. In fact, it might be a nice final shot of me patting him on the shoulder under water afterwards."

Alfred said not another word. So we left him to play the part of a South Sea Islander.

The reef where the moray held forth was fairly close to shore, so I went down from there in the diving helmet, while Bernardo sat on the rocky shore with the pump. I was tossed around a bit by the surf at first, and fumbled rather helplessly in the shallow, foaming water, but then, luckily, I fell into a deep channel where the water was calm and clear. Alfred brought me the camera, and after encouraging Bernardo, at a signal from me, to pump somewhat more vigorously, he led me to the scene of action.

The moray was an obliging creature. Scarcely had I approached its dwelling and unsheathed my camera when it appeared, absolutely on cue, at the mouth of its den, baring its teeth in a pictorially admirable snarl. (Illus. 45.)

155

I took two very nice close-ups, and then sat down on a block of coal about twenty-five feet away. High above me floated Alfred, who seemed to have a touch of stage fright; beside him was Joerg, a silent onlooker. After one last look at the focus of the camera and a brief pressure on the button to test the drive spring, I raised the camera into position and gave the prearranged signal.

Alfred dived down with powerful strokes. He moved as if he knew nothing about the moray, as if he were just happening by. Then he checked himself, noticed the coral mass, the hole where the moray was, seemed to see something there, cautiously moved back, took the two sticks from his belt, examined noose and bait—I was going to cut in a close-up here—seemed satisfied, took one stick in his left hand and one in his right, looked searchingly at the hole again, then stalked very cautiously and agilely along the cliff, closer to the cavern, carefully slid the noose over the entrance, waited a few seconds, dangled the bait invitingly beyond the noose—and practised patience.

He waited, I waited, Joerg waited; and so did the moray. When nothing happened I cut the camera to save film, but kept it still ready at my eye. Too bad I had not loaded it with colour film: Alfred grew slowly redder, like a tomato with advancing summer. At the same time he kept on dangling the bait with inflexible determination before the hole, occasionally introducing a few particularly inviting capers. I caught myself holding my breath too—probably in sympathy. When I glanced upward, I saw Joerg grinning until his ears wiggled. Finally Alfred couldn't hold out any longer, and shot upwards after one last angry caper.

The course of events was the same in the second and third scenes, with the one difference that Alfred's face now turned from red to purple to blue-black, like a ripening blackberry.

At the fourth attempt Alfred was so groggy that he simply moved the bait dully to and fro outside the hole. This time the moray decided that the moment had come. Just before Alfred was ready to give up again, it shot unexpectedly out of the hole and through the noose, grabbed the bait, snatched it

156

nimbly back, and when Alfred finally noticed and gave a yank, instead of the moray he caught his own stick. He cursed so savagely that a whole flock of bubbles went gurgling out of his mouth. And similar bubbles poured from Joerg's mouth above.

But Alfred did not give up. I saw him, with gritted teeth, preparing another bait, and he tried several times more—approached casually, checked himself, looked, swam back, tested noose and bait, crept forward, put the noose over the hole, and dangled the bait invitingly.

The moray's appetite, however, was satisfied; it watched the periodic goings on with complete equanimity. By now I was quite stiff from supporting the camera, and besides, my footage was almost used up. To get some cinematic good out of the situation, I gestured to Alfred to harpoon the moray. But the poor fellow was too weak for that; he jabbed into the hole twice, missing both times.

There followed a brief and apparently rather brisk interchange on the surface, after which Joerg took over the harpoon. My film was now completely exhausted, and so was the moray's patience. At the very moment when Joerg came whizzing down, the moray finally decided to move out. It left the hole and moved surfacewards on the point of Joerg's harpoon.

"Gosh, I did want to pat him on the shoulder," Joerg whispered to me afterwards. But this time he spoke low enough so that Alfred could not overhear.

63

A fish was swimming along the shore, weeping. True, it was not shedding any tears, but its emotions were so unmistakably sad that one was justified in assuming it was weeping.

The party responsible for this anguish, if you pursued the chain of cause and effect back to the beginning, was none other than Mynheer Gezaghebber. He had asked us for the bait, for his sake we had gone fishing, and so Joerg had discovered the shark, inflicting on it so awful an awakening that the poor shark died and the still poorer remora lost his good big friend. For three years he had lived with the shark, always fastening his sucker to its skin as they swam—and the skin had been so delightfully rough!—and had shared each of its meals —and it had shared so generously! And now? Now one was suddenly all alone in the world; every muscle ached from this frightful having to swim for oneself. As for meals—where were regular meals to come from now? The world had become a very dismal place. And responsible for it all was Mynheer Gezaghebber!

I slipped unsuspectingly into the water and swam on my accustomed morning stalk, when I suddenly had a vague feeling of being no longer alone. I looked round in every direction—obviously I was. And yet I would have sworn something was moving behind my back. So I turned suddenly again on my longer axis and found my suspicion confirmed. Close beside me swam a very dainty black-and-white fish, about six inches long, with a large suction disc on his head. He behaved perfectly trustingly, and now inspected my stomach, obviously to see whether it would do as a place for him to travel on. When I reached for him he slipped away from me, and returned to my back. There he stayed, and we carried on our hunt together.

The world is a sad place indeed! The remora was swimming frantically along shore again. He had scarcely found another big friend, who was slow and very smooth-skinned, but otherwise a fairly likable fellow, and everything had started off so well, when suddenly he goes and dives up into the air of his own accord, and doesn't come back! What kind of business was that?

64

The three of us are wandering across the island. We are
naked, as always when we are not actually photographing one
another, but not stark naked. Each of us wears a sun helmet,
and also a knife on a belt. Our harpoons we have shouldered;
our fins dangle from Joerg's harpoon. As we are to leave our
little Crusoe's isle tomorrow we are winding up with a visit to
the south coast, the only part where we have not yet been.
The road thither leads across a red-hot field of dried coral.
Once upon a time fish swam about here inside a little atoll,
which rose in the course of many centuries and became land.
It is desperately hot; a good thing we are not wearing trunks.

Finally we are there. We split up, as we now usually do,
and each of us goes into the water at a different spot. Unfortunately the water is so warm that it offers no refreshment. I
hurry to get across the shallow reefs, and then dive down to
thirty-five or forty feet, where the cooler layers of water begin.
Here I take a closer look at the vicinity. The bottom is flat,
overgrown with tall, bushy *gorgonidae*, or sea whips (Illus. 41.)
It teems with gay parrot fish, gold-gilled snappers, perch, and
all kinds of triggerfish. There are so many porcupine fish here
that they look as if they were holding a convention.

At a spot where a barracuda sleeps among the bushes we
three happen to meet again. The fact that this barracuda is
asleep we can tell by the dark transverse stripes, which always
become visible on his body in a state of repose. If the creature
awakes, they disappear. (Illus. 49.)

As Joerg has at his back the light current prevailing down
here, we signal to him to take the lead. He dives almost perpendicularly, and drifts just above the bottom towards the fish,
which still hangs unsuspecting and lost in dreams. A few
moments later he brings it proudly to the surface; this is the
first barracuda any of us has taken. Alfred maintains that Joerg
owes this entirely to us, because we distracted the attention of

the barracuda, but Joerg protests vigorously. May he hang the fish to my belt? he asks, but I am unwilling. The barracuda has a terrible set of teeth, and we have often enough observed that fish long since dead would still bite viciously.

Our argument is cut short by a blue-and-red angelfish, which swims past below us. I follow it in the direction of shore, and it leads me to the shallow reefs, over which I swam heedlessly before, and thus to a gigantic head with pop eyes, peering out from amid the coral trees. That head must belong to a thirty-five-pound grouper. What can the fellow be doing here in shallow water? I wonder, at the same moment driving the harpoon into him. But that very instant it is in pieces. The fish snaps the iron shaft with a single motion, and breaks the line as well. Bleeding, it rushes past me, and vanishes among the reefs.

I call for Joerg and Alfred, and we hunt together. We do not find the individual we are looking for, but we do find a number of other groupers, likewise very large. One tries to flee into the depths, but Joerg is right after him, and he is the first to pay the penalty. (Illus, 42.)

In ten minutes the battle is over. Along the reefs hangs a cloud of blood, mostly from the groupers, of which we have overpowered no less than six, but partly also from us. The creatures were so powerful that they twisted the iron shafts of Joerg's and Alfred's harpoons into corkscrews. They dragged us after them through the coral thickets, so that the branches shattered off, converting our skins into a colourful map of scratches and abrasions. Alfred bagged the last grouper with my broken harpoon shaft; it was the same one that had first escaped from me. He discovered the fellow in a remote coral hole, from which a thick stream of blood poured out. He could see only the tail, and harpooned from the rear with such force that he pierced the whole fish lengthwise, and the tip came out at the head.

Exhausted, we swim ashore, where we lay out the fish according to size. It is all very pleasing that we have taken this many, the more so since Dr. Diemont had asked us for fish to salt down, but how to get them all home is another question. It is, after all, a load of one hundred and fifty or one hundred and seventy-five pounds, and a hot, laborious trip.

48. Every day we took great catches, which were sold on the
sly to restaurants

49. When asleep the barracuda displays dark cross stripes

50. The barracuda is no less feared on many coasts than the shark

51. We could often watch trumpet fish hanging head down, stiff, motionless among the coral

52. If an unsuspecting parrot fish swims past, the trumpet fish darts towards him . . .

53. The parrot fish does not welcome this approach

54. But the trumpet fish climbs on his back all the same!

55. And he follows every movement like a rider on a bucking horse

But they can't be left behind. We string them through the gills on two harpoon shafts, which two of us support, walking one behind the other, one harpoon on each shoulder. The third man walks alongside, singing rousing patriotic songs, which makes the lugging very much easier. From time to time we change round. The shafts bend and dip, the tails of the largest two fish brush the ground. "At Mantua in shackles the faithful Hofer lay . . ." The sun is high overhead, it is frightfully hot, and a lucky thing we didn't put on bathing trunks!

65

The sea was fairly rough when we sailed away from Little Bonaire the next morning. With foaming bow and bellying sails we passed across the deep blue, white-capped waves. We looked mournfully. For the last time we saw the parched, barren plain with the lonely tree under which our tent had stood; the coast, whose every nook we knew; the little hollow where Alfred and the sting ray had tried to bathe together; and the thicket beyond our camp that Mynheer Gezaghebber's detective had searched so eagerly for a short-wave transmitter, but had found only rotten fish heads.

The island grew smaller and smaller. Then this part of our expedition, too, lay behind us. I was a little bit sad, yet glad also that something new was coming. Above all I was glad that we had a ship of our own at last. We owed it to the efforts of Dr. Diemont, who had negotiated once more on our behalf with the old white-haired Negro. The price was a hundred and twenty guilders a week, for which not only Bernardo but also his elder brother Leonardo, as "captain", was now in our service. This was not cheap, but thus far we had lived so economically that we could afford the luxury now. Besides, it was absolutely essential for our expedition to be a little more mobile.

I liked Leonardo much better than Bernardo. He did not

sit around dreamily, merely patting his thighs rhythmically now and then, but immediately displayed a will to work, and even thought for himself. Furthermore, he called me "Chief". On his advice we had picked out a little fishing settlement named Lac, on the east coast of Bonaire, for our first goal. He maintained we would find an abundance of every fish we could possibly desire—sharks, rays, turtles, langoustes; everything the sea had to offer was there. I was rather dubious, because I considered Leonardo a great slyboots, who wanted only to steer us to the fishing village because he had a cutie there. But as aforesaid he called me "Chief"—and this flattery I was helpless to withstand.

Lac is a sea inlet running for a mile or two into the country and cut off by a straight coral reef from the open sea. Only at one end of the reef is an opening, through which the water pours out of the bay at ebb tide and streams back at high tide. Through this gate, a channel some one hundred and thirty feet wide, we sailed into the sheltered water of Lac early in the morning.

I woke up, because the boat had suddenly stopped rocking, and went on deck. It was not yet sunrise. The water of the big bay lay glassy as a lake; above the tall mangroves whose jungle fringed the banks hung a delicate bluish haze. We pitched anchor beside some fishing boats. On shore I saw a dozen primitive huts, made entirely of branches, some of them partly hidden by great piles of oyster shells. On one of these piles lay the dried head of a hammerhead shark. As there was no sign of life anywhere, I crawled back into my berth and went to sleep again.

We breakfasted about eight, which gave rise to a vigorous difference of opinion among the three of us. Dr. Diemont had told us about the head of an unknown sea creature washed up on shore not far from the fishing village, a head of extraordinary size and highly mysterious origin, which we must not fail to look at. According to Dr. Diemont's description we were agreed that this could only be the head of the mythical sea serpent; what we disagreed about was to whom the head should belong. I argued for the Natural History Museum,

162

towards which we had already fallen far behind in our collections anyway; Joerg and Alfred wanted to have at least part of the head for themselves. As no agreement was reached, each of us armed himself with a sharp knife, and we set out together.

That the head actually lay where it was alleged to was plain even from some distance by a pestilential stink. Dr. Diemont had not exaggerated: the head was actually very big and very strange. If we had not been absolutely certain that this could be only the head of the sea serpent, we might perhaps have taken it for that of an unusually large sea cow. Clenching our teeth, we set to work removing the rotting flesh from the bones. When, with great difficulty, we finally punched a hole at one spot through the stony elephant-like skin, such an abominable corruption poured out that we took to our heels. No matter if it remained undiscovered, we wanted nothing further to do with the head. We hurried back on board and recuperated over a second, once more perfectly harmonious, breakfast.

In the forenoon we set a new record. We harpooned thirteen langoustes, one after the other, ate them likewise one after the other, and went right back into the water.

At first we did not feel at all bad. We swam into the aforementioned channel, where we hunted tarpon and unusually large parrot fish, not noticing in the excitement that the ebb tide had come and a strong current was setting out of the channel, sweeping us with increasing force towards the open sea. When we finally did notice, the current was already so strong that we could not swim against it. We shouted at the top of our lungs, but the fishermen, who led a rather more regular life than we, were just having their noon naps, so that our shouts were unheard. In addition, the water pouring out from the sandy bay was quite milky and opaque. We now remembered with a slight start the tale of one of the fishermen that tiger and hammerhead sharks cruised in large numbers off the mouth of the channel after the turn of the tide.

We swam as hard as we could, but the langoustes lay like lead on our stomachs. The current kept carrying us farther and farther out. I expected every moment to see the dorsal fin of a tiger shark appearing near me. Alfred, who had no fins, and was being driven even harder as a result, suddenly turned white, and shouted to us that he was feeling sick, and could not go on.

But finally we did get out of the main current, and slowly, very slowly, came back in a wide sweep towards the reefs. The water was pouring out among the coral there, too, but not nearly so swiftly as in the channel. Now, too, we could see to the bottom again, where there was an unusual spectacle. Just above the floor the current was so strong that even the fish could not withstand it; hundreds of them hung in the lee of the coral trees, huddling anxiously together and swaying to and fro in concert like a bright flag.

In spite of this strong undercurrent, high waves were rolling along the surface towards the reefs, producing breakers in the shallow water that made swimming even harder. We were carried forward on the crest of the wave, snatched back by the current in the trough, and whirled about by the following breaker till we were stunned. The only possible way to get ahead in this turmoil was to use the forward motion of the waves as much as possible, then dive and cling to some coral formation, waiting until undertow and breakers were past, and then to surface, take breath, and swim on with the next wave. In the shallow water we used our harpoons to brace ourselves against the current, and covered the last hundred feet riding the breakers like hobbyhorses. Here we were overtaken by Alfred, who now seemed quite restored and full of fight. As he confessed later, he had "abandoned" the langoustes in deep water.

66

Here also we found and tackled the promised jewfish, with the following result:

After we had failed either to harpoon him, or to cut a hole in his skin with a knife (in order to drive in the harpoon), or to put a noose round his tail, while the natives were still urging us on to kill their old arch-enemy, I finally had a glorious idea. For some reason or other the jewfish kept opening his mouth from time to time. Why not harpoon him through the mouth from in front? Surely he must be vulnerable in the throat.

No sooner said than done.

We dived, and the three of us gathered in front of the jewfish's mouth and waited for it to open. But the jewfish was not going to do us that favour. His mouth remained hermetically sealed, and he merely looked at us contemptuously. Finally we were out of breath, and had to surface again.

Thereupon we posted a sentry. One of us had to stand guard in front of the mouth, to see if it would not open, while the others were getting breath. Then we took turns. And at length the jewfish did get tired of it. Suddenly his great mouth opened like a gate, and the next moment he had the harpoon deep in his throat. He tossed us aside with one furious flip of a fin, and charged off, grumbling loudly, simply dragging the boat with Leonardo and the fishermen after him.

Finally he caught and snapped the line, and that was that.

67

Leafing through my diary of the Curaçao expedition after the first ten days, you will find encounters with sharks mentioned on almost every page. First described in detail, then only fleetingly noticed—but sharks were always there. They passed by in the distance or circled around us or popped up unexpectedly among the reefs; but since they did not threaten us, and we could do nothing with them unless they happened to be asleep, we soon stopped paying any particular attention to their presence.

After our battle with the jewfish we were still hunting

165

every evening at a short distance from the spot where the head had been washed up. For some unknown reason—algae, perhaps—the water was coloured a luminous yellow, which gave the undersea landscape special vividness. Its colours were quite unreal in their richness and brilliance, just as if you were looking through a yellow photographic filter. It was fairly late by then, and I had a disagreeable premonition, but swam out into deep water nevertheless. There I met a sea bass that was obviously too big for me to bring up alone. I don't know what induced me to harpoon him just the same; at all events he was so strong that he snapped the iron head of the harpoon right in two before my eyes, and then dragged me downward like child's play by the short line. With an odd sort of resignation I recalled the similar situation near Drammond, when the big grouper was towing me, but I did not let go; I fought back against the pull, hopeless as it was. Not until I felt myself fainting did I finally draw my knife and cut the line.

"I remember vaguely that two sharks were beside me as I swam up," says my diary in conclusion, without further comment. Today, with more experience of sharks, I wonder whether many situations that we then risked without a thought might not just as well have ended differently.

"Have an amusing new game," says the next page of the diary. "Joerg was out with Alfred, seized a sleeping shark by the tail, and let himself be towed. I hear he was very much surprised, the shark, I mean."

68

One evening—we had sailed to Kralendijk to get our harpoon heads repaired—a motor-boat suddenly came alongside of us. Two men boarded us, and in spite of the darkness I had a definite feeling that I had already met one of them somewhere. He had piercing eyes, and barked at us, asking where we had been all day, and what doing. At the same time the other clambered agilely down the hatch into the hull of the vessel which he carefully searched. This obviously not having led to the result he hoped for, we were ordered to report to Mynheer Gezaghebber the next morning. Then the two disappeared in the darkness. Somewhat later shouts were heard from shore. We recognized Dr. Diemont's voice, and hastened to fetch him with the boat. He was rather pale, and we found out later what had happened.

Germany had marched into Poland!

Next morning, at Mynheer Gezaghebber's, I recognized the man with the piercing eyes. He was none other than Mr. Van de Croef of the immigration service at Curaçao, with whom we had fought the battle of our residence permits. He informed us that we were now to report to Mynheer Gezaghebber's at twelve o'clock noon daily, and we would receive further instructions from Curaçao.

Slowly we walked along the street of Kralendijk back to our ship. In two weeks we were to have started our homeward voyage; now there was no telling whether any German vessel would cross the Atlantic at all. "We may have a new world war today or tomorrow," Mr. Van de Croef had said. What would become of us then?

We counted up the money we still had after paying for the ship: it amounted to three hundred guilders. This would still carry us through several months if we were careful. We immediately gave up the ship, and pitched our tents at Punt Vierkant, where we had seen so many fish on our walk the first day. Naturally Dr. Diemont put his best efforts at our disposal, and the other people were very nice also. Even the white-haired old Negro whom we had found such a keen trader now showed himself a man with a heart. When we settled up with him, he volunteered to let us go on using the rowing-boat for nothing.

The same day war was officially declared, Leonardo offered, if we would instruct him in the art of under-water fishing, to keep on coming with the ship every day, and sail us to Kralendijk to report to Mynheer Gezaghebber. Naturally we accepted with delight. Leonardo was outfitted with goggles, harpoon, and much good advice, but proved to be too fat for the sport. He floated on the surface like a gob of grease on soup, and when he tried to dive, his legs first kicked three feet above the water, so that all the fish around were quite aware Leonardo was coming. Nevertheless, as a point of honour, he bagged one fish—a plaice. It did not fall until the seventh blow, and when he finally had it, it looked like a butcher's chopping-block, but this did not in the least diminish Leonardo's pride. He insisted on my immortalizing him with his prey in a photograph.

When Leonardo realized that he was too well fed for an under-water huntsman he switched to another form of fishing, where his portliness actually did him good. He would float on the surface, looking under water, holding a line and fish-hook in his right hand. Through the watertight goggles he could see exactly where the fish were near the bottom, and would dangle the bait right in front of their noses. Very few could resist this temptation, and thus Leonardo became the pioneer of under-water angling.

69

It is evening; we are sitting around the campfire, eating. There is fried fish—oil is cheap—and with it polenta made of corn meal, which is also reasonable. For dessert each of us takes a spoonful of sugar, which costs practically nothing here.

While Alfred lights a cigarette, I suddenly realize how incredibly brown we all are. Each of us is in tiptop physical shape. We have grown completely accustomed to the amphibious way of life; even my early sinus troubles have disappeared. Only Alfred's ears are not as they should be; he no longer hears well. "No wonder," says our expedition doctor, Joerg, "most pearl divers go deaf sooner or later. And most of them die of emphysema of the lungs," he adds, "but so far, luckily, there has been no sign of that."

Each of us got his mail today, and each has his mind somewhere else.

"Our dachsund's had pups," says Alfred with a melancholy smile; "five at once!"

"Sure," Joerg nods, "and Litzi has got married too. I wish I knew whether she was blonde or brunette now."

Thereupon, by way of celebrating the occasion, we each allow ourselves another spoonful of sugar.

Your picture in the beard (Mother writes to me) *is unspeakably ghastly; Father can't bear to look at it. I put it on his desk for a joke. . . . Your new room is going to be where the dining-room used to be. You'll find it very pretty and cosy when you come back.* (When, indeed, when I come back!) *Do write soon about what you're doing and about fishing and how you cook and eat and sleep, about the vicinity where your tent is, if you're living under palms, and if you're well, how you stand the climate and in fact how everything is.*

Well, we hope the mails will still go through!

When the fire has burned low and each of us knows the others' letters by heart, we lie down side by side in the tent, and can't get to sleep.

"Just imagine—a real roast goose with red cabbage," says Alfred ecstatically.

And after a pause Joerg adds, "Or walking barefoot through a very cool, soft forest meadow."

70

As you look at a bottle of soda water, the liquid in it appears just like ordinary water. If you take off the cap, little gas bubbles fizz up, and the drink foams. Why?

Soda water is ordinary tap water with carbonic acid gas under added pressure. Under pressure any liquid will absorb gases in solution. If you take off the bottle cap the pressure is released, the water can no longer hold the gas, and it bubbles out.

Something similar took place in Alfred's blood when we were taking films near the Punt Vierkant lighthouse, and he very nearly died of it.

"Did you realize that this was an anniversary?" said Alfred, the morning of that day. "We arrived in Curaçao fifty days ago today!"

We decided to take films in the morning along the reefs near our camping grounds. Alfred was to be the cameraman. He went down to the bottom in the helmet and took a few scenes of me diving with a spear and swimming away across the coral bottom. Joerg, meanwhile, was at the pump in the boat. Just as we were getting along splendidly, it turned out that we would have to stop work at once. As Leonardo had failed us, we had to set out on foot the long walk to Kralendijk so as not to be late for our daily report.

Sweating and very much exasperated, we hurried through heat, thickets, and cacti. We had already asked Mynheer Gezaghebber several times to change our report to another hour of the day, because the noon sun was best suited for our films, but he had always taken refuge behind Mr. Van de Croef's instructions, and had steadfastly refused to make another inquiry on the subject in Curaçao. He obviously enjoyed making us walk two hours through the midday sun every day simply to report to him, "Here we are", whereupon he would say with a lofty gesture and an ironical smile, "That's fine, you can go now."

This time, however, we were fairly saucy to his High Mightiness. We insisted that he must telegraph Curaçao about us again. Then we went back to camp, feeling a good deal better for the fiery flush that had come over Mynheer Gezaghebber's face.

After a brief lunch we resumed our film-making, and that was when the accident happened.

Alfred, in the diving helmet, was at a depth of nearly fifty feet; Joerg, who was actor this time, was to dive down to him and break off a coral. I was above in the boat, pumping and sweating, and cursing because matters made no progress. Alfred had been down more than half an hour, and Joerg came up only occasionally to get breath. I was just thinking out a speech that I would deliver to Mynheer Gezaghebber tomorrow when suddenly the pump failed. The piston no longer had any suction. It gave at a touch when I pushed. Obviously the packing had dried out. And I had no oil with me!

On impulse I held the pump under water to make it air-tight again, but this did not work as I intended. Alfred told us later how surprised he was to get an unexpected warm shower in his helmet.

Nevertheless Alfred was not to be put off. He had a rare fish in front of the camera, and went placidly on taking films. Even when I sent down Joerg, who made frantic signals that he was to come to the surface immediately, Alfred remained calmly at his post. He made equally frantic signs to Joerg not to disturb him and not to scare the fish. Joerg surfaced in desperation. (Illus. 44.)

But Alfred finally did get short of air. We saw him moving at first slowly, then faster and faster, then bounding across the bottom. But by now it was too late. He had not enough air left to get to the rope and climb up it. We saw him fling off the helmet and swim frantically upwards. Then he appeared on the surface, pale as death, and groaning heart-rendingly.

And this brings me back to the matter of the soda water: if a diver works for any length of time at a depth of more than forty feet the water pressure dissolves the nitrogen

171

from the air he breathes in his blood, and he must not come up again too fast, or else the gas in the blood will bubble out—just as the carbonic acid does in soda water—and an air embolism, the dreaded bends, will result. Tiny bubbles of nitrogen stop up the blood vessels; pain in the joints, dizziness, cramps, and paralysis are the result. Not infrequently the outcome is yet worse, because even a bubble the size of a pea getting into the heart may bring instant death. For this reason the diver must come back to the surface only very gradually, sticking to an exact schedule in the process. If, for instance, he has worked for fifteen minutes at a depth of one hundred and fifteen feet, on his way up he must stop for five minutes at thirty feet, another five minutes at twenty feet, and ten full minutes at ten feet, so that it will take him longer getting to the surface than his entire work down below. If this rule is not followed, and an embolism is the result, the diver must be put under pressure again at the first possible moment, because this will dissolve the bubbles in the blood again, after which he can be slowly and properly depressurised. In experiments where frogs were subjected to extreme variations of air pressure, and their arteries were observed under the microscope, the creation and disappearance of these bubbles could be clearly seen. When fish are brought up from the deep sea, the swift, huge change of pressure makes gas form in their circulatory fluid to such an extent that the creatures explode by the time they reach the surface.

About all this I knew very little at the time when we dragged the half-paralysed Alfred into the boat. Even so, his pale, distorted features, and the sounds that came from his throat instead of words, told me well enough how matters stood. We rowed ashore as fast as we could, and Alfred began hobbling around in a circle, in terrible pain. He was completely awkward about it. His arms dangled, apparently quite useless. They had no more feeling than rubber, he groaned.

We dragged him to the tent, and there at last it proved that Joerg's father had not made his son study medicine for nothing.

"He'll be better in a minute," said Joerg, and sat down

172

on Alfred's chest. With all his weight, at that. And Alfred actually did groan with relief. So I promptly followed suit and sat down also.

And that was the end of our anniversary.

Alfred was in a bad way that night. He moaned about insupportable pains around his neck, and his arms kept going numb in turn. If you put your ear to his chest, you heard a definite gurgling around his heart. We lay sleepless beside him, racking our brains to think what we should do. But we could do nothing. We had already made a tight compress with a sheet, and had gradually loosened it, but it had not helped much. A better way would have been to take him down to the bottom in the diving helmet and then bring him up again at the proper slow rate, but because of the ruined pump and his alarming condition this was impossible. Joerg was graver than I had ever seen him before. And Dr. Diemont, who happened to come in the evening with some more letters, ordered Alfred under all circumstances to lie quietly on his back, lest the bubbles get into his heart.

By morning his condition had improved. The pains and the paralysis had more or less disappeared, but there was still a gurgling around the heart. Dr. Diemont came back in the morning to keep watch. As Joerg had blisters on his feet and Leonardo was missing again, I walked in alone to Mynheer Gezaghebber's this time. Naturally he did not believe a word I said, and excitedly threatened to send the police boat and investigate at once. I told him I really wished he would, because then I should not have to walk back, whereupon he quieted down and finally decided not to send the police boat after all.

As Alfred's condition continued to improve, and we had to think of our food supplies, we left him alone in the afternoon, and went into the water near our tent. Just as we were harpooning a big ray, which dragged the skiff and Dr. Diemont along after it, Mynheer Gezaghebber appeared in the police boat. He had some guests with him who took films of us harpooning the ray. He himself glared in a way that boded ill

173

for Joerg, who I had said was also sick. Then they disappeared again.

On the way back to the tent Dr. Diemont hurried ahead, and met us halfway.

"Oh, dear, Alfred has gone and been terribly foolish!" he cried out. "He got up and went swimming and even caught a fish."

We rushed to the tent, and saw with our own eyes. It had been insufferably hot. Alfred declared he had only wanted to cool off a little, and had just taken along the harpoon to lean on. And then in the water he had stumbled and slipped, and the stupid fish had swum straight into the harpoon head.

Mynheer Gezaghebber, luckily, had not seen him.

Events the next day followed one another pell-mell. First, early in the morning, Dr. Diemont appeared with the doctor from Bonaire.

"I didn't tell him to come," Dr. Diemont assured us, for he hated nothing so much as a word of thanks. "He found out himself about Alfred's accident, and he insisted on coming."

On examination the doctor declared that Alfred's condition was very serious. He had an air embolism and hæmorrhages of the spinal cord. He must lie absolutely quiet on his back, or there was no answering for his life. And he must not dive for a year.

At noon I appeared alone once more before Mynheer Gezaghebber, who received me at once with a tart remark about Joerg's "injured feet".

That didn't mean anything, I retorted fairly boldly, you didn't need to wear shoes in swimming. And incidentally the doctor . . .

"*Incidentally*, Mr. Hass," I was interrupted, and Mynheer Gezaghebber straightened up impressively, "incidentally, I had an official communication from Curaçao today concerning you."

There was a long pause, whose effect he savoured thoroughly.

"Well, Mr. Hass." he went on finally, "you and your

accomplices are to leave this island at once and return to Curaçao. For *internment!*"

Wham! In the first shock, and to gain time, I said nothing at all. I rushed to Dr. Diemont, who immediately invited me to dinner, and boiled with indignation when he heard the news. "Wait here, and I'll try something right now," he said, and dashed off, leaving me alone at dinner. When he came back he said he had talked to the doctor. They would try everything; I was to come back later. So I hurried to camp where we held a serious council of war. Then I raced to Kralendijk again.

Dr. Diemont was in despair. The doctor, he said, was very ready to help, but could do little, because he himself was dependent on Mynheer Gezaghebber. Still, if Alfred inclined towards seasickness, transportation by ship would be at the risk of his life, and the doctor could not approve it.

Naturally Alfred inclined towards seasickness.

I hurried once more to Mynheer Gezaghebber, with whom I had a fairly heated exchange of words. All three of us would leave Bonaire tomorrow morning, he bellowed, or he would have us arrested and locked up. Finally we agreed that Joerg and I would leave. Alfred was to be fetched by the police and taken to the hospital, where he would stay until he was fit to be moved. This still left us a little hope of going back to Bonaire. In Curaçao we would ask permission to fetch our ailing companion, and this might perhaps give us an opportunity for a brief excursion to Lac. For this was our greatest desire. Joerg was still on fire to finish off the jewfish that had snatched the barracuda and the harpoon from him, and to earn the ten dollars the fishermen had put on the creature's head. If the jewfish was still alive, he would come back sooner or later to his old stamping ground, we were sure of that.

Next morning our sad departure took place. Alfred was removed by the black-skinned police, and where the tent had stood there remained a bleak spot which now presented a remarkably empty spectacle, although it had always looked exactly like that.

At the vessel we took leave of Dr. Diemont. He told us

175

how sorry people in Kralendijk were about our leaving. Particularly Leonardo, Bernardo, and their father, the white-haired Negro. Just before the ship cast off Dr. Diemont hurried to the captain, to whom he talked emphatically, pointing several times at us. As far as we could understand, he was urging him to feed us as well as possible. "They like a lot of coffee!" we heard him say.

71

In Willemstad there was no sign of war as yet. Everything was going on in its accustomed way. Possibly the little newspaper boy on the corner yelled a little louder and made a little more money than usual; possibly the refreshment bars and some of the girls did a little poorer business, because the sailors from the Dutch cruiser were not getting any shore leave at the moment; and possibly the chemist looked a little bit graver than usual, because he was wondering whether he could still get medicines from Germany. But in the outer appearances of the little town nothing had changed. Countless straw hats billowed as ever through the Dutch alleys of the inner town, perched on both white and pitch-black heads; among the white linen suits of the men, as ever, gleamed the gay silk dresses of the young Negro, mestizo, and mulatto girls, whose teeth shone as brightly as their eyes, and whose red lips were as striking as their perfume; as ever, gigantic American sedans pushed through the turmoil of the people, fruit stands, garbage cans, and open clothing stores—slowly and phlegmatically if perspiring Europeans were aboard, or like hornets gone mad if a Negro gentleman or an American tourist was at the wheel.

Our looks attracted some attention. Skin tanned brown, hair much too long, beards as long, and shorts all the shorter,

56. What I saw were not individuals, but groups of three
dolphins, nestling close together

57. Coral towers and
sea whips—some grow
only on certain coasts.
Why is it?

58. A great day in my life when I found a shark willing to be photographed

59. Trembling in every limb, camera pressed to my eye, I swam from one shark to the other, and had the great pleasure of finding each willing to be photographed

we lounged casually through the streets, and a train of yelling children followed us. Joerg, who soon got sick of this, gave in and had his beard shaved off. I stood fast, and had my reward. While I was waiting outside the barber-shop, a young American girl spoke to me. Would I mind having my picture taken with her? Since she was pretty, and willing to accept a drink afterwards, I had no objection. She showed me some pictures that she had already collected on her trip. The first showed her with a chimpanzee, the second with a crocodile, and the third with an unusually prickly cactus.

After the picture was taken, the drink drunk, and Joerg's face transformed into a baby's pink behind, we headed for the immigration service. We did not see Mr. Van de Croef this time, but were informed in his name that henceforth we were to live aboard one of the German vessels in the harbour. By day we could come ashore at pleasure, and could also go on with our work under water at certain places to be determined later. The Hamburg-Amerika Line would have to pay our keep aboard ship, because in spite of our having return tickets the line could not take us back to Germany. All in all, people were much nicer to us than we had expected. They also approved the intended trip to Bonaire, to fetch Alfred.

We made a few calls in town, and then went out for lunch to the German vessels, of which no less than nine, more than 30,000 gross registered tons altogether, had taken refuge in the neutral port. They now lay lashed into a little island in the middle of the Schottegat, the spacious natural harbour of Willemstad. Twice a day a ferry plied from this ship island to the town, but the other Germans had only limited permission to go ashore, and in most cases no Dutch money anyway. They were feeling correspondingly depressed. We, on the other hand, were delighted with the cabins assigned to us, the clean beds, and the regular meals. For the time being we were satisfied with our lot.

In the afternoon we went ashore again. As we loafed along the quay, where the bright-coloured Venezuelan sailing cutters were selling their cargos of bananas, I happened to hear one dealer say to another that the Germans were scoundrels, the Dutch boobies, and the English wretched cowards.

For the sake of my anthropological education, I asked the man why this was so.

"Why?" snorted the old man, scanning me mistrustfully from head to foot. Then he picked up a rotting banana, of which there seemed to be plenty aboard his ship, and pointed accusingly at the German ships. One of those scoundrelly tubs had no less than ninety thousand stalks of bananas in her damned belly, which were all ripening now and being flung on the market for a song. Whether the honest traders starved in the process did not matter in the least to the Dutch, those boobies. And the English submarine that had been around for several days, the cowardly cockroaches, could easily have sneaked into the harbour long since and sunk the whole lot of them.

"We don't think much of war, my dear sir," the banana trader wound up his speech.

72

It is usually maintained, with justice, that fish, unlike crabs, swim head first; but in particular cases the opposite does occur. Without being Baron Munchausen, I have seen fish swim past me tail first, so fast that it was by no means easy to hit them with the harpoon. This happened in Bonaire the day we fetched Alfred.

Joerg and I had guilty consciences as we drew near the familiar pier of Kralendijk aboard a banana-laden cutter. Since our departure from Bonaire almost three weeks had passed—three very jolly weeks, incidentally. But Alfred did not mind our long absence. He received us, fat and beaming, at the dock. The Negro nursing nuns in the hospital had spoiled him and stuffed him until he had gained nearly eighteen pounds. One of them had even passed him secret love letters. In return he had drawn crosses, goblets, and monstrances, which were now on exhibition in all the rooms of the hospital. Once, when he amused himself by drawing a map of Bonaire, Mynheer Gezaghebber appeared and confiscated it. Such were his experiences, and he was completely recovered.

Without stopping to ask if we might, we rented a car and drove the country road to Lac with Dr. Diemont. Unfortunately a heavy surf was running, and the water in the channel was so dirty that we could not tell whether the jewfish was at home again. The fishermen had seen nothing of him.

As the water in the entire region of Lac was turbid, we walked along the coast a way, and went hunting inside some reefs where the visibility was better. The surf was so strong here that it simply washed the fish through the opening among the coral plants, once towards shore, and then back towards open water. This gave me the idea of a new technique in under-water hunting. I clung to the inner edge of the reef, and lay in wait with harpoon at the ready before one of the bigger openings. When the fish—which always headed into the current—were swept through the reefs, one fish after another would come right past my harpoon head, each one tail first.

We spent the night with the fishermen at Lac, and were fetched by the police next day. Mynheer Gezaghebber was beside himself, they said—it was the same old story.

As the ship that was to take us finally back to Curaçao did not leave until evening, we found occasion during the forenoon to go back to our camping ground at Punt Vierkant, where we had left some of our trophies and collections: salted shark skins, which we intended to have made into leather coats; dried ray tails with brightly polished sting; flexible riding quirts made from the backbones of sharks; the shell of a sea turtle that Joerg had killed with a splendid thrust through the neck; the dried head of a young hammerhead; the inflated skins of some porcupine fish; bright-coloured shells; snails; mounted fish heads, and, last but not least, the collections for the Natural History Museum—two tin canisters of small coral fish in formalin and some dozens of different kinds of coral, which we had bleached in the sun, and which looked like flowers carved out of ivory. We packed it all together now, put it aboard, and took it along.

In the afternoon, as I was strolling up and down the flat beach outside Kralendijk, I noticed thousands of dried films sticking to the stones. Looking more closely, I discovered that they were the sad remains of innumerable jellyfish. The sea had washed them ashore, and they had dried out in the tropical sun.

I got into the water, and could see that the ocean was full of jellyfish far and wide. Carefully, in order to avoid touching the dangerous filaments, I swam out among them, so far that the bottom vanished from my sight. It was a really fabulous spectacle. As far as I could look in every direction and into the depths, glassy, opalescent bells, shimmering in a hundred tones, filled the deep blue space. They all moved in the same beat with rhythmically pulsing motions of their discs, and bright-coloured little fish danced to and fro unharmed among the dangling, poisonous tentacles. I swam closer, and watched the confident motions of these little guests. While the jellyfish mercilessly embraces, stings, paralyses, and drags to its greedy mouth all other fish, these little favourites enjoy its protection, although the jellyfish hardly gains any advantage from it. Can it be that these fish in the course of their lives have grown so used to the venom that the jellyfish can do them no harm? Or is it really possible that this creature, among the lowest forms of life with more than one cell, consisting of more than 97 per cent water, and drying up in the sun to a wretched little film of organic substance—can this creature distinguish and prefer, can it have impulses comparable to those we call liking?

Highly puzzling forms of animal companionship are known. In the tropical Pacific lives a big sea anemone on whose oral disc gaudy-coloured little fish often stay. When darkness falls the fish lie down on the disc, and sleep safe and untroubled in the shelter of the poisonous tentacles. Next morning, in return, they clean dirt and parasites off the sea anemone. If danger threatens, they flee into the intestinal cavity of the sea anemone, and find, where others are digested, a refuge well provided with food. It has been found that these fish cannot be kept at all in aquariums except with sea anemones; without sea anemones the predatory fish soon devour them. And the grateful fish know their duty. If you offer them an angleworm, they take it—to the sea anemone.

73

Weeks have passed, weeks in which very little has happened. Our life of the past few months had left us fairly well exhausted. After all, we spent almost six hours of every day in the water. And sometimes eight. A thing like that leaves its mark, particularly if you eat as little as we did. When we came back from the hunt we were too tired to spend much time cooking and too chilled to be hungry. And in the morning we would eat even less, on account of the diving. We were correspondingly emaciated, and needed rest.

Besides, we have time now, all the time we want. Before, every day had to be used to the utmost, because we had a bare sixty days for our expedition; now we may have to stay here for months. Furthermore, there is a war going on, everything is changed, and who knows what will happen? What's the use of being in a hurry? And there's the heat. We were always in the water before, and scarcely noticed that we were close to the equator. Now we toss naked in our cabins, with the fan turned straight on us, perspiring in every part that the stream of air does not hit at the moment. Somebody did say that it was not healthy to keep the fan going all night, because it gave you rheumatism, but what of it? And then there is the regular and abundant food. We are exhausted after every meal. And when we have recuperated from this effort, we are hungry again. The ship's crews have to keep busily polishing and chipping rust, and when they are through at one end, they start over again at the other. To keep them from getting ideas, the captain says. Rust, he says, you can always chip; it hardly does the vessel any harm at all. Luckily we don't need to work, because we are carried as passengers. The Hamburg-Amerika has to keep us until it can bring us home. If the war should last the rest of our lives, the line would have to feed us the rest of our lives—while sailors chipped rust outside.

And then there are the detective stories, available on board in great variety. Detective stories are just the right reading matter for the tropics. You stretch and gape under the fan, thinking. Marvellous to think of them all working so hard!

However, I did pull myself together at last. Something had to be done, or I would rot alive. So I started playing the piano—a very pretty piano in the saloon opposite our cabin, a black piano with nice, smooth white keys, inviting to the touch. Much less inviting in every way, however, were Joerg and Alfred, who displayed not a trace of human understanding for my music. But by now they have got used to it. In the tropics you get used to everything. Because if you don't, you sweat, so it's easier to get used to it. Only the barber in the cabin next to ours does not seem to mind the heat at all. It's amazing: he entertains a new girl almost every day. Yesterday he asked us whether he shouldn't send one over. But the noises from next door are enough for us. Some time we may possibly bore a hole in the wall. But that is the limit of our exertions.

That, then, is our situation at present. Joerg is reading an Edgar Wallace, Alfred a Tarzan. Sometimes we read a paper or a letter, and occasionally I play the piano. That is to say, in the past week or so I have somehow had a renewed fit of energy. I am now repairing my unfortunate camera. The poor thing was in oil—like a sardine. Its light went out almost immediately after Joerg and I came to Curaçao from Bonaire; we were invited to a picnic at Santa Cruz Bay. I was taking a picture of some coral fairly far out when I noticed that the watertight case was full of water, and my camera was taking a bath inside. The rubber gasket had wrinkled in closing. I tried to clamber up on a rock, but the stone overhung in every direction, and I kept tumbling back into the water. So I gave it up, and swam back to shore. By now it didn't make much difference anyway whether the camera was in salt water for ten or for twenty minutes. On shore I washed it out with fresh water, and put it in oil, where it lay for weeks.

Now that I finally summoned the energy to take it apart, and penetrated to its vitals, with a screwdriver, a pocket-knife, and two old hairpins, a pitiful sight met my eye: a jumble of rusty little wheels and springs, encrusted with the lacquer that had softened and come off everywhere.

So, going to work with a deep sigh, I cautiously extracted one little wheel after the other. All at once a tiny spring jumped into my face. I had not the faintest notion where it came from. You probably have no idea how complicated the mechanism of a modern miniature camera is, particularly the clockwork that regulates the various shutter speeds. As I went on taking the thing to pieces I made careful sketches. When at last all two hundred little parts were cleaned and neatly ranged on the table, a gust of wind blew open the window, and I had to search every crack in the floor for my component parts. This time I was really panic-stricken. Unless I could manage to bring order out of this chaos, to replace the rusted springs and get all the wheels together in their proper places, my photography was finished. I simply had to solve the secret of this mechanism, had to discover what each tiny cogwheel meant. Before me lay a detective mystery more exciting than any I had read in the past few days.

I shut the door and windows tight, even let Joerg and Alfred go alone to dinner, worked until late at night, again from morning till evening the next day, and at last I had done it. The camera worked again. There was still the question, however, of whether replacing the springs had not altered

183

the exposure times. And how was I to check on that? Once again Sherlock Holmes retired into his corner, without a burning pipe, but burning the more brightly with the fires of genius. Then I borrowed the barber's gramophone, the ship's engineer's stopwatch, and a tiny torch from the cook. I fastened the torch to the turntable of the gramophone, carefully timed a single revolution of the turn-table, and photographed the torch on the revolving turn-table from above. Sure enough, the film, which I developed myself in the cold-storage compartment, showed the path of the lamp as a bright curved line, from whose length I could calculate the exposure time.

It turned out as I had feared, that they were all completely different. One was too long by half, another far too short. And now the really ticklish part of the job had just begun. I filed, exchanged cogwheels, photographing and developing now and then, and finally—now I have done the trick! I have just discovered that both the hundredth and the fiftieth of a second are correct again. Even so the other times are completely out of kilter. But since I don't use them under water anyway, I can let them go. It is now eleven o'clock at night, and I am honestly exhausted. Wild horses will not get me out of bed in the next few days. Now, though, by way of celebration, let me play the piano a bit. A few variations from the great triumphal march in *Aïda*.

74

Every Saturday afternoon we had an invitation to the Tischers', the family of a prosperous Hamburg businessman who had a shop downtown and liked to play ping-pong on Saturday afternoons. He had lost his business and his entire property in World War I, and then industriously built them all up again. The same fate was in store for him now, but of course he did not dream of it then. We played ping-pong until it practically brought down the house, ate Mother Tischer's *apfeltorte*, which seemed to be better each Saturday than the Saturday before, and positively snatched the German magazines from one another. Usually there were also friends of the daughter of the house present, among them a young Spanish girl in whose deep, gleaming eyes even a good swimmer might easily have drowned. I did drown, and laid my heart at her feet with Spanish fire; but unfortunately her feelings towards me were less tempestuous. "Well, if you didn't have that beard . . ." she once hinted to me, and, self-sacrificing as men in that state are, I promptly had it shaved off. The following Saturday I arrived with a smooth chin and great hopes, and now the girl confessed—that she had liked me better with the whiskers!

75

"Well, now, would you look at that!" said Mr. Fischer with a strong Austrian accent, and we looked, and unfortunately did not see much.

Mr. Fischer, a Viennese photographer who ran a flourishing photographic business in Willemstad, developed my films. He tried everything—special fine-grain developers, intensifiers, everything; but it's hard to make something from nothing. Terrible yet true: almost all the pictures were out of focus or wrongly exposed. One film after the other came out of the developing tank, one after the other with the same dismal results. The hammerhead shark—completely blurred. Shots of the jewfish—four times under-exposed. The pictures from Punt Vierkant—completely out of focus.

Mr. Fischer, who seemed surprised that you could take

pictures under water at all, praised the few good shots, and made enlargements of them. But my heart bled. How many glorious opportunities had I wasted! But for the war, if we had gone home according to plan, this would have been our entire photographic take. A complete flop! For the first time I was glad of our predicament since, after all, it gave me a chance to make good my mistakes. Starting today, I would carry on my under-water photography in a very different way. I would make careful experiments and develop each film immediately, learn from my mistakes, and avoid them the next time. And the watertight case had simply got to be improved; this fixed-focus business was quite hopeless. Not until I could set range and aperture from outside would I get sharp, properly exposed pictures. Undoubtedly the ship's mechanic would help me solder two new packing glands to the brass case. Then two cog-wheels, cut corresponding teeth in the lens, mount a pointer, scale, and window outside. . . .

"Well, would you look at that!" said Mr. Fischer, and the drama marched inexorably on. . . .

"Something most disagreeable has happened!" said Joerg when I came back on board.

"What's that?"

Joerg sighed, from over in his bunk.

"The detective stories are all finished," he said. "I'm afraid there's nothing for it now but to go fishing again."

So the three of us set out, but with mixed fortune. I was successful enough, bagging fifty fish in one day—with the camera. Joerg and Alfred, meanwhile, missed every thrust so that it was a pleasure to see—for the fish. As for the others, the two had been living too well. They had grown fat and easy-going, but what they said was that the fault lay with the poor fishing grounds here near town. We should have bicycles, they felt. So we looked around and actually found some at a possible price—two men's size and one child's. Since Alfred is the smallest of us—and also the strongest, as we hastened to point out—he had to make do with the child's model, which relieved him of a good part of his newly acquired beef. The gear ratio of his wheel was so low that he had to pedal twice while we pedalled once. While we would amble through the countryside at any easy pace, he would pelt along beside us, pumping like a racer in the home stretch.

For the overture of this new wheeled era in our hunting we took a day's trip to Hato, a place on the north coast of Curaçao, which offers the only spring and the only airport on the island, otherwise only sparsely vegetated rocky fields and surf dashing high. For ten months a year the constant north-west trades send towering waves upon the deeply cracked and split north coast of Curaçao: consequently the fishermen with their little boats cannot put out there, so the waters are practically unfished. We had long hankered to hunt in that region, but we had been warned on all sides. People said the breakers, eddies, and currents were so strong you could not possibly swim back to shore. Even a Dutch swimming champion had recently drowned there.

We pedalled straight across the island, at first on the good road, then on narrower and narrower, poorer and poorer paths, and when we could get no farther with our bicycles we hid them in a streamlined bush. (Since the wind blows from the same quarter year in, year out, the bushes along the north coast have taken on the shape of least resistance.) The last bit of our way led us across a flat, extraordinarily jagged rocky area that plainly betrayed having once been ocean floor. Then we were standing close by the shore cliff, looking down upon the wildly foaming sea at our feet, which would sink away, bubbling and hissing, for five or ten feet, and seconds later would hurl breakers at the rocks again.

Alfred being exhausted and bathed in sweat, Joerg and I were the first to venture the plunge into the unknown. We waited for a few slighter waves, and then jumped as far out from the rocky edge as possible so as not to land on some hidden reef. Here we were immediately plunged into the middle of an eddying, boiling mass that clutched and spun us mightily. I pressed my goggles to my eyes with my left hand lest they be snatched off, but the water was so full of bubbles that I could not possibly see anything. I waited to catch a quick breath between two breakers, and then let

187

myself sink so as to reach calmer, clear water. Clouds of foam went almost to the bottom.

When I reached it, I was washed along a rock slab with only a few bushy seaweeds on it. I clung to one bush, and waited until the fog of foam lifted slightly. Now I could see sixty or seventy feet. The heavy surf had scoured the bottom quite flat; not a trace of fish anywhere. Suddenly a large form materialized out of the foamy sky—Joerg, also seeking refuge in the depths. We saluted each other, but already there were more grumbles, and a cloud of foam reaching to the very bottom obscured our vision. I pushed quickly off from the floor, and got back into the roaring, foaming turmoil. As the mountainous waves did not run straight but diagonally to the cliff, they were flung back at an angle, causing them to crisscross and form wave cones that skipped irregularly.

"This is no happy hunting ground!" Joerg cried to me, and we swam back to the cliffs.

But people had not been so wrong. Regaining dry land was no child's play. Currents and eddies kept pulling us away from the rock wall again and again, and the breakers would come thundering down upon us in between. The cliff itself had been so hollowed out by the surf that its upper edge overhung like a balcony. Sometimes this balcony would be high out of reach above us, and then again a wave would lift us up level with it. That was the moment when you had to grab the edge—no easy trick when you had to keep the camera from smashing. Twice I caught hold of the sharp jag of rock, and both times I tumbled down again when the wave sank away. Each time I would fall into the grinding mill of the next breaker, and undercurrents would pull me away from the cliff. Meanwhile Alfred stood on the balcony, laughing his head off.

When we finally made the top, flayed alive, he told us the thing had to be gone about quite differently. He said he had been carefully studying the movement of the waves, and would now show us the correct method.

He thereupon went into the water, and vanished, as we had done, in the whirl of the breakers. Then, at a signal, he

188

started on the way back. His method consisted of suiting himself to the rhythm of the waves. It is well known that a big wave is always followed by two or three smaller ones, after which comes another big one. Alfred waited for some unusually small waves, and swam along with them as fast as he could towards the cliff. Here he arrived just in time to be swept up by the next big wave to the edge. He grabbed the sharp rocks like a flash, and swung himself on to the parapet as the wave sank away.

The method was sound, and everything would have gone beautifully if this wave had not permitted itself an extra flourish. Sixty or seventy feet from Alfred it had broken with particular force in a notch in the cliff, so that a torrent had climbed up the rocks. Since the waves broke, as aforesaid, not perpendicularly but diagonally on the cliff, this mass of water described a curve, and flowed back into the sea just where Alfred was swinging himself over the parapet. For this the poor fellow was not prepared. When the flood suddenly surprised him from above instead of from below, he lost his balance, and tumbled down from the balcony. At this moment, however, the trough of the waves had just sunk to its lowest point, so that he fell a good fifteen feet, turning an involuntary somersault.

"A very pretty method," Joerg observed to me, and this time it was we who grinned from ear to ear.

In January 1913 a pearl diver by the name of Treckle was taken to the hospital in the Prince of Wales Islands, Torres Straits, with terrible wounds. This unfortunate man had dived from a ship into the sea, and had landed head first in the open maw of a hammerhead shark. The shark shut its mouth but could not bite through Mr. Treckle's hard skull. Amazingly, the islander kept his wits about him. While his own eyes were enjoying the rare opportunity of studying the interior view of a live shark's gullet, his fingers goped for the eyes of the brute. He found them at the ends of the hammers, and put one out, whereupon the shark let go. Treckle, streaming with blood, was pulled into a boat, and went on living, while some days later the hammerhead bit on a hook, and thus ended its one-eyed existence.

A similar fate might have awaited us during our days on the north coast. As we discovered later, there were plenty of large sharks here who came directly up to the cliffs and were by no means so bashful as those on the south coast. To practice Alfred's method, we jumped at least a dozen times off the cliffs into the boiling water. Not head first, like Mr. Treckle, but still with our legs. . . .

76

Strong principles are something that can make life difficult. If we ever showed principle, it was in our absolute rejection of Mr. Meyringh's shooting instrument. Even though he did catch more fish, we would be true to our simple harpoon all the same. Only with it did under-water hunting strike us as fair. A catapult represented a mechanical advantage that would deprive our sport of its sporting element. No, we would be true to the harpoon!

If you go along the coast of Willemstad to Piscadera Bay, at about the halfway point you come to a tower-like lime kiln. If you go into the water—which involves getting your feet dirty, because the constantly passing tankers have left a crust like pitch all over the beach—and then swim out until you can't see the bottom, and a little bit farther, you reach a place where the word Caribbean takes on a special meaning for you. Between forty-five and sixty feet down is a flat coral bank, well known to the fishermen, which we happened to discover for ourselves.

Joerg pointed to a few dark spots on the sea bottom. Were they coral shrubs?

They were not coral shrubs, they were hundreds and

hundreds of grey snappers, floating quietly in close-packed schools above the sand bottom. Each one of these fish must have weighed from two to five pounds, and among them swam big, striped silver perch, easily from twenty-five to thirty-five pounds. Staring down, we were carried along by the rather strong current. Suddenly about a hundred gleaming fish heads materialized from the depths and came swimming towards us with big, staring eyes. In the lead a vanguard of particularly powerful creatures, then the rest, actually in rank and file. They were jacks, which we christened Prussian fish because of their military behaviour. They came straight at us, with every appearance of wanting to attack. But it was not an attack, it was a parade. Hardly six feet from the tip of Joerg's harpoon the vanguard suddenly swung about, and at the same moment all the others turned likewise—all in the same direction, as if at the word of command. And they vanished again in the depths as regularly as they had come. Their steadily beating tails were the last we saw of them.

"You could have shot them like anything with Meyringh's catapult," sighed Joerg, as we swam back against the current.

When we reached the coral bank a second time, the parade of the Prussian fish was repeated. This time Joerg followed them down to the bottom (Frontispiece), where I saw him, very tiny, among the supposed coral shrubs, which literally flew apart when he suddenly thrust into the middle of them. A glinting in the water indicated that he had made a hit: one of the big silver perch was flapping on his line.

As he was struggling to pull the darting creature upwards, so many things suddenly happened all at once that we could not even reconstruct events until later, when we were back on shore. Whole regiments of Prussian fish appeared from the depths and circled around Joerg, in concert with snappers and silver perch. At the same time several dozen big blue mackerel appeared from the open sea, darting hither and thither with frantic speed through the turmoil. Then, swimming even faster, there came a shark, closely followed by a second, and along with these two a jewfish also appeared, mingling casually with the rout. It was a scene such as I have never seen before nor since. In the centre Joerg with the silver perch, which was fighting hard and glinting brightly at each turn; hundreds of fish, gone completely crazy, in a silver merry-go-round, plus the two sharks, which twice whisked past, almost grazing him, and the jewfish, slowly following the whole crowd upward.

Back on shore, Joerg's eyes were melancholy. "We mustn't tell Meyringh about that place on any account," he said. "He's perfectly capable of shooting those nice Prussian fish by the dozen."

The next Sunday we went with Mr. Meyringh in his car to the Boca Vacao, one of the few bays on the north coast. The weather was calm for once. We first fished in the bay, where there were a lot of langoustes among the stones, and then swam out to the left headland, where we suddenly found ourselves surrounded by big, silvery fish. They were tarpon, and in a second Joerg and Alfred had each harpooned one. Upon this brief pleasure followed an immediate double cry of disappointment. On each harpoon head was a scale, half pierced; the fish were on their way. The creatures' scales proved so hard that we could not pierce them with our harpoons. Joerg harpooned another, with the same unsatisfactory result.

Meanwhile we had lost sight of Mr. Meyringh. Now, when we saw him again, he was being towed through the water with every sign of excitement. Ahead of him leaped a gleaming tarpon, and we saw at once that this tarpon was on the line. We rushed to help him overpower the creature; it weighed thirty-eight pounds. The slim arrowhead of the catapult had gone straight through the fish's scales. Joerg and Alfred looked at each other meaningly. . . .

Nevertheless we remained steadfastly true to our sporting principles. This cost us more and more of a struggle every day, simply because all of a sudden we did not catch any more fish. Heaven knows why it was, but our every thrust went wrong. Each day we went to a different part of the coast, we even discovered some excellent fishing grounds, and yet we usually came home with an almost empty bag.

192

60. To earn money for our trip home, we swam in search of specially handsome coral

61 and 62. Joerg managed to catch a turtle by hand

We reached the low point of this period once when the Tischers asked us for a fish for Sunday dinner. The three of us set forth, and went spearing around ten or twenty thousand times among the reefs—missing every time. Finally, exhausted and resigned, we swam back towards the coast. Then our eyes fell upon a trap put out by some fishermen, in which an easily thirteen-pound fish had got caught. We looked at one another under water in silence, then Joerg dived and stole the fish out of the basket. (Illus. 46, 47.)

I delivered the unlucky fish to the Tischers, and came back aboard towards evening. I found Joerg and Alfred highly animated over a bottle of whisky. And beside them stood a harpoon catapult! Good old Mr. Meyringh, who was just returning to Holland, had made us a farewell present of his catapult. This was a ticklish situation indeed!

"Really, you know, we've got our future to think of," Joerg greeted me. "We can't stay here in the West Indies forever."

"We've decided," Alfred added, "that we can very easily get home by way of North America, Japan, and Russia."

"How about the money?"

"We'll earn it!" was the triumphant reply. "We'll simply sell fish. What matters now is not sport, but making as much money as possible."

"With the harpoon catapult, then?" I finished, and they both beamed as only people can beam who are turning unprincipled on principle. "Yes, with the harpoon catapult!"

77

A barracuda comes swimming straight at me. He weighs a good dozen pounds. His number is up.

With the catapult in my right hand I swim slowly towards him. It is my first attempt with this instrument, and also the last, because I have firmly resolved to hunt only with the camera in future. But I have arranged with Joerg and Alfred for this first hunt with Meyringh's catapult. I am alone, facing a barracuda whom I know well, because I have often photographed him. This character is so shy that I have never been able to get anywhere near him with the harpoon. Today his number is up.

One last glance of inspection at the complicated weapon in my right hand: it is a tube which expels a metal arrow by means of strong rubber bands. At the end of the arrow is a loose head, fastened, like the arrow itself, to a line. Both lines are neatly coiled so as to come loose without resistance when the arrow is fired. The whole thing is fairly complicated, but well planned. A brief squeeze on the trigger will be enough, and the barracuda will be done for.

The barracuda has now come within six or seven feet of me, and is turning slowly away. His mouth is somewhat open, his eyes wear a superior expression. He knows me, and knows by experience that no harm can befall him at this distance. But this time he is wrong. I need only stretch my arm a little forward with the catapult, aim straight at the head—so that in case he should try to dodge I will hit him in the middle of the body—and then I squeeze.

The arrow is so swift that the barracuda has no time to dodge. A clicking noise in the water, and at that very moment his head is pierced through the middle. The arrow has gone straight through the hard bones, and projects equally far on both sides of the head. The barracuda has just time to give one twitch of regret with his tail, and he is dead.

A pity about him. He did not die an honourable death.

Mr. Meyringh's present brought a noticeable increase in our hunting activity. Joerg and Alfred now took a big catch every day (Illus. 48), which we sold secretly to restaurants—secretly, because as foreigners we were not allowed to work for pay. Our profits were so good that we soon had a second harpoon catapult made. I went along with the camera, and took pains to get good hunting pictures.

At first I would stay close behind the hunter, but pictures taken that way were not very satisfactory; they showed part of the hunter large in the foreground, whereas the fish, beyond the harpoon head, looked preternaturally small in perspective. For effective pictures the fish had to be in the foreground, which, however, was possible only if hunter and cameraman stalked forward from opposite directions. Now it is hard enough to get close to a fish unnoticed from one side; if you approach from two sides, however, the result may be an occasional good picture, but the fish positively will not let itself be harpooned. After a few such attempts Joerg and Alfred refused to sacrifice their best chances to my camera craze any more. Our budget for the voyage home was much more important, they insisted. So I left them alone, and turned to photographing fish and coral. I decided, if possible, to get a few good pictures of each kind of fish, and this was no simple job. There are more than a hundred different kinds in the reefs of Curaçao, many so timid that I had to struggle for weeks before I succeeded in outwitting them. Being thus compelled to acquaint myself thoroughly with the occurrence of the various species, their way of living, their habits, and traits of character, I came in much more intimate contact with the creatures than before. Each new species became for me a new problem requiring to be solved. I gathered experience, and became aware of many interconnections that I had previously never noticed.

Gradually I began to take an interest in scientific questions. Some fish occurred only near particular kinds of coral, many corals grew only on certain definite parts of the coast. Why was it so and not otherwise? And in general why had one fish this form and another that? What connections were there between inanimate and animate nature?

At first I had hunted with the harpoon, and looked for bigger and bigger fish. Then I had become a camera huntsman, looking for the most artistic shots. Now the creatures themselves began to interest me, and I discovered with regret how little I knew. How much many a scholar must envy me this opportunity to observe the creatures in their natural surroundings, and how little I could profit from it as yet myself! I lacked all knowledge of the scientific problems. I could do no more than keep my eyes open, so that later perhaps I might draw upon these observations. Suddenly I had opened my eyes, and realized how blind I was; for man sees not with his eyes, but with his mind, with the grey cells of his cortex.

Why, I wondered, do you find such luxuriant coral reefs at some spots along the coast, while quite near by the ocean bottom is completely bare? For instance, the *boca* of the Spanish Water: to the right of the mouth, glorious forests of coral, stretching in deep ranks for many hundreds of yards along the coast; to the left, not a single coral bush. Chance? Or had this coral growth some connection with the nature of the bottom? Were the polyps better fed there? Or did some other animals or plants live there upon whose occurrence the corals for some reason were dependent?

As yet I could not answer those questions; later some of the connections became clear to me.

What is coral, anyway?

To begin with, the coral I am talking of here, which builds up reefs, atolls, and, when elevated, even whole mountain chains (such as probably the Dolomites), has nothing to do with the fine coral that ladies hang round their necks. Whereas the latter is fetched up from depths between one hundred and sixty-five and six hundred and fifty feet in the Mediterranean and around the Cape Verde Islands (as well as in Japanese waters), reef-building coral occurs exclusively in tropical seas, and scarcely ever more than one hundred and thirty feet down. Furthermore, the reef coral has not a red but a snow-white limestone skeleton; the only coloured part is the creatures themselves, tiny polyps that sit on the surface of the limestone mass they have secreted and multiply like plants by budding.

According to the development of the limestone skeleton, hemispherical, mushroom-shaped, star-shaped, and branching tree-like corals grow up, but sometimes the same species will make different shapes in different localities. Coral grows best

196

in surf, because the water keeps throwing up bits of food and is particularly rich in oxygen. This growth in one particular direction leads to the formation of reefs, which lie like natural breakwaters offshore and surround islands in a ring. If one of these islands sink into the sea (which occurs not infrequently because of seismic movements), the circular reef continues to grow upwards, and when the island has quite disappeared below the surface it becomes a so-called atoll, a reef ring, on which coconut palms sprout and in the middle of which is a sheltered lagoon.

An atoll that formed over a sinking volcanic mountain chain once formed the south-east part of Curaçao. Later this atoll, along with other north-westerly reefs, rose bit by bit out of the sea, forming a basin encircled by low mountains. Water once more penetrated this basin at several places (for instance at the *boca* of the Spanish Water), thus creating many-branched inlets, several of which lie along the south coast of Curaçao.

Whereas coral could not thrive in the muddy water of these inlets, highly luxuriant reefs have formed at their mouths, but always on the western side alone. This has to do with the steady north-east trades. As I said before, they blow the waves diagonally against the north coast of Curaçao, producing an east-to-west current along the south coast. When the ebb tide carries the turbid water from the inlets, abounding in nourishment, out into the ocean, this east-west current washes it along the western shore like a grey flag, thus forming the aforementioned reefs there.

Both large and small effects are marvellously interconnected in nature. The shape of the islands is explained by seismic movements and the growth of coral according to regular laws. The current along the south coast is a result of the north-east trades, whose direction, in turn, is established entirely by the diversionary force of the earth's revolution. Nothing in nature happens "accidentally", and nothing happens "alone". The great variety into which our mind divides the world is in reality one great unity. If the earth did not revolve from east to west, the coral forests at the *boca* of the Spanish Water in Curaçao would not grow exclusively on the right-hand side.

Another question: Why are parrot fish so conspicuously coloured?

The gay dress may be advantageous to the small coral fish, because it makes the creatures invisible in the gaudy confusion of the corals, but this does not hold good for the parrot fish. Their blue, red, or green colouration is so luminous and so conspicuous that you see them at once among the reefs. Surely this festive garb must be most inconvenient, because, after all, it shows any predatory fish from afar that a tasty dinner awaits him.

But actually it is otherwise. The chain of cause and effect begins with the fact that the tentacles of the little coral polyps have most unusual arms. There are spherical bladders in the skin, which end with a tiny projecting point and look perfectly innocent. But if the coral polyp seizes some creature with its tentacles, and the points are touched, these commonplace-looking infernal machines immediately go to work. A bunch of spears shoots out of the bladder, pierces the body of the prey, tears open the wound, gives way to a tube that pours in paralysing venom, and then thrusts itself in to stick fast and immediately start digesting. To this complicated equipment the corals owe the fact that all fish treat them respectfully.

An exception are the parrot fish, which treat the coral with no respect at all, actually grazing off the polyps with relish. In the process these fish take in so much venom that their own flesh is inedible to other creatures. And for that reason their conspicuous colour is highly practical. It tells the predatory fish at first glance, Look out! this is a parrot fish, one of those nasty-tasting characters! And the predatory fish curbs his appetite and looks elsewhere for a victim.

The gleaming colour of the parrot fish, again, has something to do with the peculiar behaviour of the trumpet fish that had struck me during our first days at the Spanish Water.

Again and again we saw the same scene: a parrot fish would be swimming unsuspectingly along, when suddenly a trumpet fish would shoot at it and lay itself along its back, so close that its thin, stick-shaped body looked like the parrot fish's dorsal fin. The parrot fish did not seem to care for this at all; it would try hard to shake off the interloper by quick dashes hither and thither. The trumpet fish would follow every movement, and stay on its back like a rider on a shying horse. So the two would go swimming together through the coral.

I racked my brains for a long time over what the trumpet fish meant by this behaviour; at first we thought of some erotic perversion of our lanky friend. But we probably did him an injustice. The strange creature obviously has another and quite prosaic aim in view which causes his even stranger behaviour.

The trumpet fish is a freebooter who plies his trade in a most crafty manner. He saves laborious stalking by using his long, stick-shaped figure so skilfully that his prey positively swims into his mouth. Often enough we would see trumpet fish hanging stiff, head downward, as motionless among the coral as if they were part of it. (Illus. 51.) If some unsuspecting fish came darting along, the trumpet-shaped mouth would suddenly open, and in a flash the little fish was devoured.

Actually the riding on the parrot fish was a simpler but even wilier dodge. As aforesaid, the parrot fish live on the tiny coral polyps; they do no harm to other fish. Accordingly the small reef fish show no fear at the approach of a parrot fish; they recognize him from afar by his conspicuous colouration and let him come as close as he pleases. And that is evidently the reason why the trumpet fish "rides" on the parrot fish. Snuggling close to the body of his "horse", the robber creeps up on the small reef fish unnoticed, and then suddenly shoots forward from his hiding place and makes a meal of some innocent.

To get a better understanding of this amazing process, I investigated to see whether similar behaviour had been observed with other animals. And indeed the animal kingdom offers examples enough of one creature's using another for some selfish purpose of its own. Thus there is a crab in the Indian Ocean that usually carries a sea anemone in each of its front claws, and holds them out to the attacker at moments of danger as a living shield. Whereas this is a fairly brutal enslavement, the reverse sometimes occurs in the Pacific: a sea anemone that catches on the leg of passing crabs, crawls up on their backs, and uses them for transportation. Along with these two cases we have the well-known symbiosis of hermit crabs and sea anemones, which is reciprocally advantageous, since the crab is protected by the stinging tentacles of the sea anemone, while the anemone has free haulage and a share in the crab's meals. If the hermit crab changes the snail shell in which he hides his soft posterior, he strokes his sea anemone tenderly with his claw, whereupon it good-naturedly allows itself to be detached and transplanted to the new dwelling. A yet higher degree of friendship binds the hermit crab *eupagurus* to a sea anemone of the genus *adamsia*, of which he always carries just a single one on his shell. And the *adamsia* takes particularly good care of him. It embraces him so lovingly that only his head peers out from its clutch, and it spares the toils and perils of moving house, secreting horn to enlarge the snail shell whenever it becomes too small.

78

Once upon a time a young lady went down to the ocean bottom. She had a diving helmet on her head, an easel in her hand, a pretty figure, and the idea of painting a coral landscape. First her brush floated off. When it was sent back down to her, weighted with a stone, some fish turned up and ate the red and yellow paint off her palette—no doubt female fish, wanting to change the colour of their scales for spring. Nevertheless the young lady finished her work of art. She gave a signal to haul it up, and then rose to the surface, puffed with pride. But much as people usually admired her art, this time she was received with a supercilious smile. And when she saw the picture herself, she sat down in despair. It was completely transformed—an utterly non-representational daub, with each colour swearing at all the rest.

And the answer to the puzzle? Owing to the way water absorbs light, the colours she had used for her painting forty feet down had looked completely different. In order to regain her reputation, all the young lady could do was to invite her supercilious critics to look at the painting forty feet below the surface.

79

In scientific description of tropical fish you encounter the difficulty that most of them change colour. Whereas usually only the depth of pigmentation varies in the fish of northern seas, in tropical varieties you may observe the most amazing shifts of colour. One that you saw a moment ago in a brilliant yellow will shortly reappear stained violet; another suddenly loses his pattern, and new marks come out on his body. You ask yourself, which one is the natural, or rather the normal colour and pattern?

It would be more correct to ask which is the normal mood of the fish, because usually the creatures' colouration is closely connected with their state of mind. I have already mentioned that trunkfish turn luminous blue on their bridal night; many other fish change colour no less vividly during the mating season. Some also change colour when you frighten or chase them. I once noticed a barbel, whose silvery body bears three sharply marked black triangles, rooting through the sand in search of food; every time it found a morsel, the black triangles disappeared, and instead dark transverse stripes appeared on a pink background. Many fish also take on similar transverse stripes when asleep (Illus. 49), which leads us to the cases where the change of colour is not only the expression of mood but also serves some useful purpose. Thus I have seen a sleeping "tobacco pipe" (a relative of the trumpet fish) hanging just above the bottom and rocking steadily to and fro in the swell; blue dots and dark transverse stripes kept appearing in turn on its body, and disappearing again, so that in its rhythmically moving surroundings the fish was extremely difficult to make out. And just as there are some human beings who have their moods in control, or even simulate anyone they please, there are actors among the sea creatures that use their change of colour in masterly fashion to hide or dissemble. The plaice adapts himself with great skill to the colour of the bottom, but is outdone by the polyps that can, it is alleged, live on the borderline between a sandy and a spotted stretch of bottom, and appear half sandy and half spotted.

All marine animals change their colours by means of tiny colour organs in their skin, which expand or contract, either by order of the brain through the nerves or by way of the circulatory system through hormones. If you hit the centre line of a fish with a harpoon, and injure the nerve that lies there, the control in the rear part of the fish ceases, the colour organs expand of themselves, and the whole section turns black. The results are similar if a fish goes blind, because then it can no longer see the bottom, and hence can no longer adapt its colouration. In death many fish become particularly colourful; some even don the wedding dress again on this occasion.

For all these reasons the colour illustrations of tropical fish that you see presented with loving care in scientific works are largely wrong or else unnatural. Almost always the models are dead or captured creatures, not ones in their accustomed surroundings and normal frame of mind. Here the underwater photographer can do valuable scientific work; the only pity is that colour film is not exempt from the light-absorptive effect of water. Even at thirty feet the red, and shortly thereafter the yellow, rays disappear from the spectrum, and pictures taken at a greater depth register nothing but blue and green.

To get really true colour pictures of fish you would have

to use an under-water flash that did not falsify the tones. But even then you would still have to keep in mind how old the creature was (because the colours often fade with age), the season (it might happen to be the mating period), and also the time of day (because many creatures have different colours at night). In addition you would have to consider the nature of the bottom and the temperature of the water, which may also affect colouration, and last but not least the momentary mood of the fish, hungry or satisfied, tired or scared. Probably one would discover that many fish have no such thing as a "normal" colouration, but that their colouring simply reflects the conditions they live under, just as facial expression and mannerisms do with people.

80

On the one hundred and tenth and one hundred and thirteenth day of our expedition we had two unusual experiences.

The first began with me swearing most blasphemously. For one thing because the dorado-like fish I was labouring over could not be made to see that picture-taking is a perfectly innocent pastime; and for another, because each time I did manage, with great difficulty, to get within snapping distance of the fish, a cloud would invariably pass over the sun. That day turned me into a meteorologist. Shivering and squinting upwards, I marked the formation and movement of the clouds in detail, longingly following the passage of the little blue holes among them. Whenever I saw one of these holes moving towards the fiery ball of sun that shone behind the clouds, I would take a deep breath, dive, and creep up, in order to snap the shutter if the seascape turned bright and sunny for a moment. Mostly, however, these holes missed the sun, or the fish would just be vanishing in a coral crack, showing me nothing but their hastily disappearing tail fins. An easy job it was not.

Suddenly I noticed out in the deep sea a peculiar three-pointed dorsal fin, almost motionless above the waves. Little as I know of zoology, I did know that there is no creature with a three-pointed dorsal fin. So what could it be? The jagged comb of a gigantic lizard? Possibly the sea serpent?

Joerg and Alfred were nowhere to be seen, so I ventured out alone. It was a long trip across bottomless water, which seemed doubly far to me because my heart was pounding twice as fast as usual. Once the three-pointed hat upon the waves disappeared, and I was afraid my curiosity was not going to be satisfied, but then, luckily, it bobbed up again. Finally came the eagerly awaited moment when the first delicate outlines stood out under water in the distance. I stared ahead. Why, there was not one three-pointed creature swimming there, but two others as well, completely under water. Each, in addition to its three-pointed dorsal fin, had also a three-pointed fin on its tail! (Illus. 56.)

After a moment's blank amazement I realized what was what. It was not individual creatures I saw, but groups of three dolphins each, snuggling so close together that a group looked like a single creature. And these dolphins moved so evenly that they seemed to be glued side to side. Not until the click of my camera cut the silence did the groups suddenly break up and the creatures shoot perpendicularly into the depths, where the blue-black abyss swallowed them within a matter of seconds. Some time later they reappeared, enormously swift and supple, and came straight up towards me. At the same time I heard a definite squeaking in the water, rather like the cries of young pigs.

The second experience began at midnight with a curse from Joerg. Someone had burst into our cabin, turned on the light, and waked us out of a sound sleep. He was a member of the ship's crew. Could we keep quiet? he asked us. When Joerg, instead of keeping quiet, began to bellow, he asked whether we wanted to make ten guilders.

That was another matter. To us ten guilders was the same as catching, lugging, and selling thirty-five pounds of fish. Joerg fell silent.

Fifteen minutes later, in beach robes, and carrying spears, we left the ship, which was then lashed alongside the pier to discharge cargo. The customs official who was standing guard at the gangway blankly looked at us and then after us, but as we were considered crazy anyway, he thought it quite possible that we might be going fishing at midnight. So he only shook his head, relaxed, and went back to sleep.

It was a matter of smuggling. Our nocturnal visitor had tried to smuggle paint ashore from the ship, and his little skiff had tipped over, sinking to the bottom of the harbour along with the heavy paint cans. But it happened that he had collected an advance payment of half the price for his goods and had already turned the advance into alchohol. First he had gone to a native diver, who, however, demanded sixty guilders. So the man reflected that the Viennese students would undoubtedly do it cheaper. And, as you see, he was right as rain.

It was perfectly dark, without a star; only a few lanterns burned on the far side of the pier. We groped for a while through the darkness, then the man stopped on the edge of the pier. This was the place, he whispered. The paint cans, he said, were about thirty-five feet out; the water was about thirty feet deep. The fact that a half-inch scum of oil lay on top of the water the man chose not to mention; I soon discovered it, with little or no satisfaction, when I started swimming, as I usually do, with my mouth open. I had volunteered for the first attempt, and regretted it even before I dived. The water below me was perfectly black. What might not be lying or prowling on the bottom of the harbour? What would be the first thing I touched when I got below?

The fellow called from the shore in an undertone that I was exactly over the spot. I waved my arms irresolutely in the water, causing it to gleam brightly around me, because the sea was phosphorescent that night.

Getting a grip on myself, I dived with a quick turn. The

farther I went into that black soup, where only a tiny dot of light flashed here and there, the slower grew my movements. Suppose something were to touch my face? I groped cautiously ahead with my hands. And suddenly I was startled as one almost never is. All grew suddenly bright around me! I had expected anything, but not that. Whence came this glow? Here, in the pitch-black night, twenty-five feet down in the black harbour water?

I could see plainly all about me for twenty-five or thirty feet. Just below lay the flat, sandy bottom, and close ahead of me three paint cans. I quickly grabbed two in my right hand and the third in my left hand, and pushed off from the bottom with all my might. The brightness fell away below me, and I rose again into the murk. But the very next moment I was in brightness again. I had expected too much of myself; all three cans at once were too heavy. They pulled me straight down again. So I dropped one of them, and pushed off again.

This time the darkness held me. I swam upwards, swam as hard as I could, swam, swam—and suddenly realized that I could not tell whether I was moving up at all. Above and below and round about me lay uniform pitch blackness. Everywhere the water had the same disgusting smell, and everywhere the same tiny creatures gleamed. But only so briefly that I could form no idea of my motion. I could not even tell by the pressure in my ears whether I was moving up, because my ears were already roaring and whistling from want of breath. Now there was an uncanny ringing about me, and I wondered briefly why I did not drop the paint cans. Then the ringing grew louder.

When I regained consciousness, I was lying on the pier, and Joerg was working over me. I had a revolting oily taste in my throat—obviously I had swallowed water. Joerg told me that after an absolutely endless absence I had come to the surface for just a moment, and had then sunk away again, gurgling. He had jumped in after me and pulled me out. Along with the two paint cans, which I still clutched rigidly. They weighed nearly sixty pounds.

Then Joerg went down for the third paint can, and saw the same strange brightness. Where might it come from? We do not really know. Presumably the light of the innumerable little luminous animals in the water, reflected in all directions by the sandy bottom, creates a faintly lit zone. But perhaps it was the ghost lanterns of drowned pirates, wanting to give me a good view of the paint cans and then drown me in the attempt.

81

Ernst Vogel's first name in German means "earnest", but he did nothing to deserve the title. He was a sailor aboard one of the German ships, and wanted to join us. As we needed someone to carry the fish anyhow, and did not belong to the intolerant party that objected to his queer speech, we took him along.

Ernst turned out admirably. Our very first stalking hunt led us to the north coast, where he nearly drowned in exemplary performance of duty. The next day he defended himself stoutly when sharks tried to eat the fish he was carrying. Everything turned out well. Ernst was afraid of nothing, did his share in everything, and was soon diving to twenty-five and thirty feet.

A week later, while we were resting from a hunt, he casually tossed off a confession. "You know," he said, "as a matter of fact the doctor really strictly forbade me to do any diving at all. You see I have no ear-drum at all in one ear, and the other has several holes, and pus comes out every day . . ."

Through Ernst we got acquainted with Pepe Schemel, who soon made up to us what we had lost in the incomparable Dr. Diemont. Pepe was of German and Colombian extraction; he showed the German side in his great fondness for music and alcohol, the Colombian in his truly Spanish hospitality. Pepe's possessions were few—a refreshment-bar, a car, and a little back room with a piano; but what he had he shared with us. This meant that we could consume as many ice creams, Coca-Colas, Pilsener beers, and whisky-and-sodas as we chose, that I could play the piano all I liked in the back room (though this permission was revoked after my very first renderings), and, above all, that the car and Antonio, the chauffeur, were at our disposal. We now drove out regularly on Sundays with Pepe to the remote parts of the island; the trunk compartment on the way out would be full of innumerable ice creams, beers, and whisky-and-sodas, which would gradually vanish in the course of the day, to be replaced by our catch of fish and langoustes.

In this fashion we went, among other places, to Ronde Klip, a remote plantation on the north coast, which belongs to "Nigger Arnold", one of the most remarkable and maddest people of the West Indies. When we arrived, the man greeted us by firing a shotgun just over our heads, and then, in our honour, sang several folk songs that he presented in an enormous voice with an active dancing background—songs that I cannot imagine are sung anywhere except on this plantation. Then we ate his coconuts and he drank our whisky. So we made friends with this remarkable coal-black man, who seemed to know the whole world, and had, in his lucid moments, an amazing store of knowledge.

The hunting grounds of Ronde Klip were to surprise us no less than the behaviour of its owner. This was the first time we really came to know the north coast at all. At first we hunted in a shallow bay along the cliffs, but here the surf made the water much too dirty for photography, so I let my companions swim on by themselves, and kept Pepe company.

When Joerg, Alfred, and Ernst reappeared on shore an hour later, I could see at once that something unusual had happened.

"You have no idea what you missed!" Alfred shouted towards me. "You could have photographed as many sharks as you felt like today. We were way out, the water turns perfectly clear out there."

63. One of us gave a piercing yell into the water—with an amazing result

64. The shark was almost as scared as we had been by his
tempestuous approach

After a rest very much abbreviated by my importunity all four of us went back into the water, and as we vanished in the boiling surf Pepe looked after us anxiously.

If you want the principles of Einstein's theory of relativity vividly demonstrated before your very eyes, try diving along the north coast of Curaçao.

I dived down through the foam of the surf and went almost to the bottom. I could see it plainly below me—a flat floor covered with matted seaweed. Down here there was no current at all; I floated quite still above the carpet of seaweed.

What was that?

A rock whose point peered out through the carpet of seaweed suddenly moved off. It rushed faster and faster along under the seaweed (yes, *under* the seaweed), plainly visible all the time by its jutting point. Then, after travelling a hundred feet or so, it slowed down, stopped, and hurried back to its original location.

I was completely bewildered. A boulder running on its own power under the seaweed! Not rolling, no. Standing up quite stiff, its point always jutting and cleaving the seaweed like a ship—that was how it rushed to and fro!

At first I could not believe my senses, but then a light dawned.

What I saw below me was not, as I had supposed, the weed-covered sea bottom itself, but a carpet of dead and derelict seaweed floating just above the actual bottom, swinging to and fro in the surf at the same pace as I myself. From the real, invisible bottom below only one pointed rock stuck up, cleaving the layer of seaweed as it moved to and fro. So not I and the carpet were motionless, but the stone, whose peculiar "travels" had so amazed me. We and not it were swaying to and fro—here was the solution to the puzzle.

"You think the stone is in repose?" smiles Einstein. "How can it be in repose when it's on the surface of the earth, and the earth revolves once a day, swinging once a year around the sun, and in addition is rushing, along with the sun, at enormous speed towards the nebula of Andromeda? Or is that flying towards us? But if so, what's the difference?"

Yes, movement and repose are relative. You can never be in repose except with relation to another body. Just as I had been in apparent repose along with the swaying blanket of seaweed.

But who had really been moving? Was it really I and the seaweed below me that swayed? Or was it not, after all, the stone and with it the bottom, the shore, the island, the earth, and the whole firmament that moved?

Joerg and Alfred swim ahead, Ernst and I follow, he with the big net for our catch and I with the camera. The turbid water of the surf is behind us. We have moved a couple of hundred yards offshore from the jagged, shattered cliffs and their clouds of spray rising constantly skywards, and are now swimming still farther out. The bottom is twenty-five or thirty feet down; it is perfectly flat, an endless rock terrace, over-grown with only a few little dirty-green seaweeds. The constant heavy surf has scoured everything smooth, preventing any coral from growing. Consequently there is not a fish in sight.

Not until we have swum another fifty yards or so does the appearance of the sea floor begin to change. The terrace sprouts humps, and isolated coral appears here and there. Then comes a zone fairly thickly grown with little yellow stinging coral, then another fifty-foot strip of tall staghorn coral. Then there is a sharp edge, and the bottom plunges off suddenly. There is just such a plunge on the south coast of Curaçao as well, but there it is fringed with big coral spheres. Here on the north coast the yellow stinging coral and the staghorn coral, both usually to be found in shallow waters only, have retired to these deeper regions. This likewise has to do with the heavy surf, and thus indirectly with the north-east trades.

Joerg dives.

He has his eye on one of the large groupers that lie every-where among the coral trees down here, goggling up at us with big eyes. This is a particularly fat character, and Joerg harpoons him just at the moment when he is turning heavily around. The grouper charges off, and before Joerg has time to do anything about it a good fifty feet of the line has unwound from the reel, leading hither and thither among the coral. Joerg makes one last effort to free the line again, but is out of breath, so he puts the catapult down on a coral branch and swims upwards with hurried leg strokes.

Meanwhile Alfred and I have dived. But we have not got to the place when a small shark and then two big sharks appear in rapid succession, circling in a mad whirl around the coral. As soon as they notice us, their circles grow larger and their motions slower. So we need not worry any more about them. We are now at the coral, and together we untangle the line, which is far from simple, because we first have to thread it through several narrow passages in the coral. Finally it leads us to a cleft where the fish has taken refuge. He is in fairly deep, and has braced himself with his fins in the usual fashion of groupers. I am trying to reach into the hole when I discover, just in time, the threatening eyes of a moray, obviously also after the wounded grouper. So, counting the sharks, there are seven of us interested in that one grouper.

From a motion behind me I gather that Joerg is back. I hand the line to him, intending to swim up and leave the rest to him, but it is not Joerg, it is the small shark, who does not know what to do with the line. He looks past me, and then dashes off with a sudden flick of the tail. Sure enough, the big shovel-nose shark is coming on again from the other side. Phlegmatically poking his broad, round snout ahead of him, the fourteen-foot brute approaches.

After a brief excursion to the surface, I am back again with lungs refilled. And we have to ascend and descend several times more before we succeed in crowding the slavering moray into one corner of the hole with a harpoon and cutting the grouper loose with a knife. Then we whiz upwards with our booty, leaving sharks and moray bilked behind us.

By the time Alfred has harpooned a second grouper, and it, too, has snarled itself up in the coral, there are already seven sharks circling around us—greedy fellows quite unlike the sharks on the south coast. Some of them come quite close to us, with threatening motions and restless eyes. There is a big blue shark among them too. Camera pressed to my eye, I swim from one to another, and to my delight each one lets himself be photographed without the slightest fuss. I am trembling all over with excitement and tension. This is the moment I have been so eagerly awaiting so long! I mustn't fluff it now. Aperture, shutter speed, range—all properly set? Every nerve tense, with the utmost concentration, gritting my teeth, I swim with my camera from one shark to another. (Illus. 59.)

Half an hour later we are back to the coast. As we are clambering out, a wave snatches Ernst and bangs his head against a rock so that his goggles are smashed. When he stands upright, his left eye socket is a bloody mess in which we discover, only after careful inspection, that the eye itself, as if by a miracle, has remained unharmed. Pepe, who has occupied himself in our absence with as many whiskies as we with sharks, stands beside us, shaking his head.

But Ernst beams in spite of all. "We saw sharks again!" he cries, with the blood streaming down. "At least ten big sharks!"

82

Your last letter took only twenty days (Mother had written before Christmas). *This time it was exactly what I wanted. At least now I know a little more about how you spend your days. But nowhere near enough, even yet! I want to know about the whole day, and an exact description of your friends and acquaintances, and whether you've been invited places, and where, and whether there are any girls, and whether you're having a flirtation, and what she looks like. We all met again yesterday, but I don't entirely agree with the other parents. I say, if you think it's right you should go on and risk the trip home, I'll be glad enough to have you here again. You know how I feel—if a person is destined for it there is no such thing as real danger. But the other parents won't hear of it, and they insist that the boys should stay over there until the end of the war. And who knows how long the war will last? As far as I am concerned you can do what you think best, only talk to some sensible people about it, listen to what they say, and take notice of the risks—I'll rely on your guardian angel, who has always protected you so far, and your common sense.*

Just as our parents had been discussing the problem of our return, we, too, were racking our brains over the future. It was not a simple problem at all. An acquaintance had invited Joerg to Argentina, where he could practise as a doctor, but Alfred and I had no business there, and we did not want to split up on any account. Alfred was once more bombarded with invitations to the United States from some American college girls whom he had once escorted through Austria in the summer. As for myself, I wanted to finish photographing the fish at Curaçao and then go back to Vienna.

We finally agreed that Joerg should try to borrow the fare from his acquaintance in Argentina, while Alfred was to take on the job of having his college girls get us into the United States. There we would earn the money for the rest of our journey by lecturing and selling our under-water pictures.

So we launched various letters, and meanwhile went calmly on with our work. Unfortunately the secret sale of fish and langoustes grew more and more difficult. So we were glad when we chanced upon a new way to make money. We presented Pepe on his birthday with a particularly handsome coral, and he showed it to some American tourists in his shop, whereupon they immediately inquired the price. From that day forward we systematically went hunting with an axe and a big sack for beautifully shaped coral. (Illus. 60.) We would boil them in Pepe's back room, bleach them in the sun on the roof, and dispose of them along with ice cream and whisky-and-sodas in the shop for two or three guilders. Once we even earned ten whole dollars. This, it was true, involved a really very beautiful piece and an elderly American woman with pince-nez, who insisted on having a picture of Alfred in swimming trunks and with a spear. Her wish was granted, but (on Pepe's advice) only in connection with the purchase of the "coral personally dived for by Alfred".

Christmas Eve was distinguished by the fact that for once there was no quarrelling on board. It is really bad when people are penned up close together for months with no change or diversion. But it is particularly bad when they are sailors forced to live aboard ship without moving anywhere, and who, in addition, know that a port is right within reach, but cannot go there because they haven't the money. And on top of that our ship moved over at Christmas to Caracas Bay, where the crew could not go ashore at all any more, because there were oil tanks there, nor swimming, because of the sharks that hung around the ships. We, indeed, were an exception. We went swimming, and could go ashore if Pepe fetched us with his car. As there were also fine coral reefs not far from Caracas Bay, we were once more the only people satisfied with their fate.

Christmas!

We all sat around a little tree with candles, and presents from Germans living in Jamaica were distributed. The alcohol that the gifts included and the Christmas tree had their own magical effect. People forgot the unpleasing present, and warmed to the recollection of better days. A boatswain and a steward who had not spoken for months suddenly shook hands, and the grumpy stoker began telling about voyages to the South Seas. Then the old Christmas carols were heard, and more than one tear was shed. Everyone looked steadily at the little crèche with the Christ child, which for hundreds of years has awakened, ever anew, man's yearning for peace—that beautiful and hopeless yearning.

83

"Where do all the Venezuelan girls at the Hotel X come from?" Alfred asked the barber, who always had the best information on such matters. "New ones keep turning up, don't they?"

The barber smirked. "Between you and me and the gatepost, they're smuggled in on the steamer *Y*. A new shipment every fortnight. Two weeks are enough. Then the girls have earned enough to buy a cheap trousseau here."

"And sell it for big money in Venezuela?"

"Maybe sometimes. No, I think most of them get married."

There were a lot of parties in Willemstad after Christmas. We first accepted some invitations in good society, but that was so tiresome that we soon shifted to less good society. This consisted of the mixture, so characteristic of Curaçao, of Dutch, Portuguese Jews, Venezuelans, mulattos, and descendants of the Indian aborigines. Only real Negroes were not present there, because the half-breeds discriminate even more rigidly against the whites than the whites do against the half-breeds.

This demi-society, incidentally, was thoroughly proper and respectable. There was a lot of dancing (all sorts of rumba-like dances, but fox-trots and waltzes as well), and there were parties that went on without pause for several days. On this occasion Alfred lost his heart to a mulatto girl, who really was unusually beautiful and had bewitching almond eyes. The girl was no less taken with Alfred, and the sole misfortune of the pair lay in the fact that she came from a family whose members tried to make up for Mamma's black face by the particularly spotless reputation of the daughter. The two could only sit or stand side by side, sighing; always and everywhere some member of the family was at hand. This is not to say that Alfred's efforts were unappreciated— quite the contrary! He had constant invitations, and the sighing grew worse and worse. Until one day it all came to an abrupt end.

215

Alfred came home pale with horror.

"Just imagine! She kissed me!" he cried, beside himself.

"Well? What more do you want?"

"But it wasn't her! The mother kissed me! On the forehead, in blessing—like a future son-in-law!"

84

If Curaçao looks as it does today, it is because of the Spaniards and the goats. Before these two were visited upon the island, Curaçao was fertile, and its luxuriant tropical vegetation corresponded to that of the Venezuelan coast. Then the Spaniards cut off the bigger trees to build warships, while the newly introduced goats ran wild, multiplied tremendously, and gnawed off the young tree shoots everywhere. They also destroyed the underbrush and the plant cover that held the soil to the naked rock; the humus was washed away by tropical rainstorms and blown into the sea by the trade winds; and the sparser the vegetation grew, the more the cloudbursts disappeared. Finally the island dried up.

The Spanish conquistadors and their war fleet are long since gone, but the wild goats remain, taking care that no new vegetation shall get a foothold on Curaçao. Unfortunately the police had taken our guns from us the moment we arrived, and then, after the outbreak of war, confiscated them altogether, so that roast goat was never on our bill of fare. Several times we did try to take after the beasts with stones and harpoons, but then, when they would bleat in terror, we would be sorry for them. We continued to feel this way until Heinz Gervais joined us, a nineteen-year-old apprentice mate from Bremen, who became our second diving assistant. Heinz saw the world with soberer eyes than we, and judged goats not by their bleating but by the meat

65. Since it was hard to hold the camera straight and steady, I used a wooden tripod, which I must say showed a regrettable tendency towards higher things

66. Joerg's tarpon pulled him hither and thither through the water

67. Landscapes whose alien magic had never been profaned
by man

on their bones. This became obvious once when we were camping at Plow Plantation, which was illegal because we were always supposed to go back aboard ship in the evening. In the morning a pitiful bleating awakened us, and before we had rubbed the sleep from our eyes Heinz had vanished like a flash into the bushes. Soon afterwards the bleating grew even more pitiful. The wild goat in question had got its horns caught in a wire fence belonging to the neighbouring plantation, and Heinz showed his determination not to waste this opportunity. I do not care to describe in detail how he tried to kill the beast. Suffice it to say that you can turn a goat's head around twice without doing the animal any harm—if you let go, it promptly spins back, and all is as before. Finally we took Heinz a knife, and felt considerably better when the bleating slowly died away. We jointly skinned the goat, and were about to eat the liver for breakfast when a loud rattle announced the approach of a car. With guilty consciences we hastily hid the pieces of goat in a bush, and had barely finished when two policemen got out of the car. Somehow they had caught wind of our forbidden camping, and we were politely and firmly carried off to the immigration service. There we listened to a sermon, which was not nearly so depressing as the thought of the goat liver now decaying in the bush, when its perfume had already been tickling our noses.

Tragic as the death of this unlucky goat was, the subsequent second goat martyrdom was far worse. The only excuse I can offer in either case is that every goat less is a blessing to Curaçao, and that the second goat was even sacrificed upon the altar of a praiseworthy resolution.

I have already mentioned that we hoped to earn money to go on in the United States by selling our under-water pictures. It occurred to us that the Americans would surely be much interested in films showing sharks in action, that is to say while rending other creatures. Heinz maintained that we ought to butcher a goat and sink it off the north coast, which was certainly not a bad idea.

Temporarily this plan bogged down owing to the difficulty of laying hands on a goat. Then when we were hunting on the lonely north-west tip of Curaçao, a lucky chance came to our aid. Heinz's keen ear caught a remote bleating, which he immediately recognized as the cry of a wild goat in distress. Sure enough, we found the creature standing quaking on a little projection in a cliff, unable to move forwards or backwards. We released it, by which it was greatly delighted, but its pleasure was quickly spoiled when Heinz put a rope around its neck and led it forthwith to the seashore.

"I can't swim," bleated the goat piteously as we approached the water, and we had a hard time not weakening in our resolution.

"Believe me," I told the goat, "we're all awfully sorry for you. But it has to be; we have to take these pictures. Besides, you won't need to swim far because you'll be slaughtered out there anyway. And I wish I could spare you the swimming, but if we were to kill you here, you wouldn't be bleeding out there, and your blood is what we want to attract the sharks."

The goat bleated one last time—heaven knows whether accusingly or in forgiveness—and then had to swim whether or no. By the time we got out to deep water, however, the goat was not swimming but floating, for it had suffered heart failure. When Heinz stabbed it nevertheless, not a drop of blood came, but a great air bubble, and the lifeless corpse drifted down to the bottom. There a current caught it and carried it as if on one last gallop across the coral forests.

There was not a sign of a shark far and wide.

85

A fine and difficult sport is under-water hunting of sea turtles. Two varieties are found in the waters around Curaçao: the soup turtles (Illus. 61, 62) from which turtle soup is made, and the hawkbills, from whose shell come jewellery, combs, and brushes.

Hunting sea turtles is difficult because the creatures have unusually keen senses, and in spite of their clumsy shape can swim faster than most fish. Besides, they have to be hit in the thin neck, the one spot where they are vulnerable. The special handicap of turtles is that, being air-breathing reptiles, they have to come up for air every ten minutes. That makes it possible to outwit them. The best way is to follow them cautiously for a while and try to arrange things so that you are above them when they are forced to surface. In this way you can even catch turtles by hand. Joerg, the first of us who achieved this, held the creature by its fin-like hind legs and had himself towed through the water. In order to get away, the turtle swam very hard, and Joerg simply steered it in the direction he wanted to go. Finally he even mounted on its back, held fast with his legs, and rode it. But he would not allow the creature to be killed or sold; after it had grown tired towing him, he let it go in spite of our protests. (Illus. 61, 62.)

86

The longer our stay in Curaçao lasted, the more friends and pupils joined us. One of the most eager was Mr. Capriles, a businessman and passionate photographer, a little man with a small bay window, tremendously capable of enthusiasm and almost constantly excited. One day he invited us on a trip. As he was taking along not only four different cameras with all accessories but three photographer friends with their cameras and accessories, we travelled in two cars, which raced at a breakneck pace through the countryside.

Our first goal was Boca Tabla, one of the few spots on the north coast that we had not yet been to. There was a fairly high surf running that day. As we went into the water, we were snapped and filmed from four directions. Mr. Capriles, with two cameras in front and two behind, constantly switching lenses, clambered from one rock to another, indicating to us with fierce gestures the best way, photographically speaking, for us to hold our harpoons, turn our heads, and flap our fins as we went in. With a constant "Like this, please." "That arm higher, leg lower!" "And now just once more, please!" we went into the water, came back, went in again, out again, and finally, on the third round, dived immediately to dodge all further requests. Out at the pitch in the bottom Joerg harpooned a grouper, which this time we kept from snarling itself up in the coral by a new method. We had fastened the harpoon head to a short line, the other end of which Alfred and I hung on to, and we dived together with Joerg. At the moment when he thrust, we gave a violent yank at the line, so that the grouper was snatched out of the coral region and could not brace himself anywhere.

We swam upwards, and had not yet reached the surface when something rather unusual took place. Three sharks appeared in the distance, and came straight at us, so incredibly fast that we could not see their wildly lashing tails, but could plainly hear them. The sight of these onrushing monsters was so frightening that we were incapable of stirring. One of us gave a piercing yell under water. (Illus. 63.)

The effect of the yell was amazing.

As if repulsed by a magic spell, all three sharks whirled around just as they got to us, and raced off as fast as they had come. One, indeed, a laterally striped fellow easily ten feet long, turned round again, and charged towards us. But this time the three of us yelled in chorus, and this finally put him to flight.

Ernst, who had seen everything from the surface, was pop-eyed when he welcomed us. Hadn't they meant to attack us? he asked naïvely.

Unfortunately in the excitement I had taken only one hasty picture, so when we saw another shark, circling most peaceably around us, I decided to make better use of the

220

opportunity. After a brief conversation Joerg and I swam far apart, and arranged matters so that the shark swam between and below the two of us. Just beforehand we dived simultaneously, and swam at him from both sides. This startled the shark almost as much as the tempestuous onrush of his colleagues had startled us. He promptly took to his fins; by this time, however, I had the desired picture on film. (Illus. 64.)

"That was a well-behaved shark," Joerg observed as we were swimming back. "The others, now, what can they have been thinking of?"

We were received on shore with great to-do, and photographed and filmed again from all directions. With fish, without fish, in twos, in threes, and finally all three together with fish and Mr. Capriles.

I had really intended to stay on the spot and swim out again after a short breather, but Alfred indicated that the photographers would like a swim and a view of things under water themselves, which of course was not possible in the surf along the north coast. We drove on to Knip, a pretty little cove on the west coast, where the sea is almost always perfectly quiet. Fitting goggles to Mr. Capriles and his friends took a fairly long time, so I swam out alone and paid a call upon a squirrelfish couple that lived in a neighbouring coral bush. When I came back the cove was already teeming with under-water hunters. The centre of it all was Mr. Capriles, who lay on an inflated rubber ring, his goggled head under water, and kept taking breath with loud puffs every three or four seconds. Round about him floated his three photographer friends, also clinging to the rubber ring, and likewise peering under water in brief bursts.

"This is the life!" Joerg shouted to me.

Alfred, ten feet below this group, was in the act of putting on a show. With his harpoon he had chased a langouste out of its hole, and now, first glancing upwards to make sure everyone was looking, he impaled it with one mighty thrust. Then he surfaced and held the flapping creature right under Mr. Capriles's nose.

But this was too much of a good thing. Mr. Capriles literally collapsed.

"Please get me ashore!" he gasped. He sank senseless upon the ring, and we towed him ashore, in company with the langouste, amid great outcry.

Here he quickly recovered, and now there was no holding him at all.

"I don't care if a shark is the death of me," were his parting words that day, "I'm going to take pictures under water too!"

None of our observations attracted so much interest and attention when published as the discovery that aggressive sharks could be scared off by yelling under water. And in fact this peculiar weapon proved its usefulness not only in the one case but also afterwards, on several occasions when we were similarly attacked. Each time the sharks fled.

Why were the sharks scared by our yells?

I must begin by pointing out that we were not the first to notice this sensitivity of sharks. A number of South Sea travellers have reported that the natives scare off sharks with noise. Francé, in his *Wonders of Life in the Animal World*, expressly remarks that the pearl divers of Mannar in Ceylon, "who ply their trade amid swarms of sharks", confine themselves to chasing the creatures off by shouts. I also found in the accounts of two professional divers the statement that sharks could be scared off by bubbles, which might best be "fired" at them from the sleeve of the diving suit. This last observation raises the question of whether in our case, too, it was not the yell itself but the bubbles projected into the water that did the scaring.

This question is connected with another problem that likewise concerned us at that time: Why did sharks never come whizzing up except when we had just harpooned a fish? Sometimes we would swim along the north shore for half an hour without seeing a single shark, but the moment we harpooned a fish there would be some on the spot almost instantly. There must be some connection.

One widespread view is that sharks are attracted chiefly

by the smell of blood. In our case this explanation was out of the question, because it could hardly be supposed that the smell of blood would spread so fast and far. The sharks often appeared within a few seconds after we had harpooned the fish, and by their speed we judged that some of them came from considerable distances. In one instance, furthermore, a shark appeared when we had missed a thrust, so that no blood had flowed at all. It seemed more as though the predatory creatures were attracted by the frightened fin beats of the harpooned fish. This conclusion was strengthened by the fact that fish flapping on the line were favourite targets of attack, which is most remarkable, because normally fish scarcely do one another any harm by daylight. In all the months we spent on Curaçao, it was very seldom that we saw one fish devour another. But we often saw small fish swimming around in front of the maw of a shark or barracuda, quite unhurt. Obviously these predatory fish go hunting chiefly at night. By day peace reigns—to be immediately broken, however, if a fish is injured or flapping on the hook; then the robber fish come rushing up at once. William Beebe, who also noticed this, made the following interesting experiment on his Zaca expedition. Having hooked a grouper, he would alternately haul it in and then let it swim freely for a while. At the same time he observed the behaviour of two sharks and a sea perch that happened to be near by. Each time he hauled in the fish and it resisted, flapping, one of the predatory fish would come shooting up; if Beebe slacked off on the line, so that the grouper regained its balance and its normal appearance, the robbers would stop immediately, and watch the fish "like growling dogs that mean to bite, and are waiting only for another movement to snap". Apparently it is the rule of the sea that anything sick, weak, or in any way abnormal positively provokes the healthy creatures to destroy it.

And does not this observation cast new light on the use of live bait? Does the pike really eat the living fish simply because he happens to come by and takes it for an ordinary fish? Or is he not more probably attracted by the desperate flapping of the impaled creature?

This was true of our experience with the sharks, in any case. They were not really attacking us, but the fish we had harpooned. It was the fish's flapping that attracted the sharks. And since we were holding the fish, they simply rushed at us. Nothing but a misunderstanding, really. I then tried to lure sharks by flapping my own fins, but failed. From this we concluded either that our theory was wrong, or else that the shark's sensory organs are so highly developed that even at a great distance he can distinguish our flapping, which means nothing to him, from that of a struggling fish.

What, in fact, are a shark's sensory organs like? I have already remarked that sharks usually go hunting at night. How can they do it in the dark? How does a shark find his prey?

Numerous observations indicate that a shark's eyes are of only minor importance to him, and that he is guided chiefly by other organs, situated on the head and along the sides. These are tiny channels and pits in his skin in which grow highly sensitive hairs. With these he perceives the vibrations of the water, and with their help he feels at long distance, even by night or in muddy water. How these "lateral organs" work is easy enough to visualize. When the shark swims, his motions cause vibrations in the water, which spread in all directions like the light of a lamp. If they encounter a rock, a coral, or a fish, they are flung back to him, just like the lamp's rays when they hit an object. The shark, receiving these returning vibrations with his sensitive organs, can form an image in depth of his surroundings, just as we view the room that we light up with a lamp. Probably, in fact, the shark's radar gives him a much better perspective than we get, because our eyes are close together, whereas his organs are spread the whole length of his body. And because the vibrations, unlike light rays, travel unhindered through the water, he can also "see" much farther with his radar than he could with his eyes, even under the best conditions. To him it does not matter, therefore, whether it is day or night: the more vibrations in the water, the more plainly he "sees". If he rushes at high speed towards his prey, it is, as you might say, in the beam of his own headlights.

What I have said about sharks also applies to other fish,

which likewise have these lateral organs. They, too, can swim around by night and in muddy water without bumping; they, too, can feel at long distances. And since each variety of fish produces different vibrations according to the shape of its fins, presumably they can recognize one another by the nature of their fin strokes. If this is true, then the shark's ability to track down his prey even at night is no longer a mystery. He simply recognizes the fish by the particular "tune" of their fin beats.

Presumably, furthermore, the mood of the fish is expressed in the nature of its motions. For instance, in the love play of fish you see the fins vibrating as they move in a particular way—probably whispering sweet nothings—whereas if the fish are eating, swimming around, frightened, or injured, they move quite differently. This, if true, also explains how predatory fish immediately notice an injured or hooked fish, and why I could not attract sharks by beating my fins.

And if all these conjectures and conclusions are right, we have a plain explanation of why the sharks fled from our yells. In that case it would be neither the sight of the bubbles (sharks have poor eyesight) nor the shrill tone (whether sharks can hear at all is highly questionable) that scared the sharks, but the vibrations in the water produced by blowing out air, which would have a startling effect on the shark's highly sensitive organs.

"Would be" and "probably", remember. For so far, with all its logic, this is merely a theory.

87

One day there was great excitement in Willemstad. A car had fallen off the floating swing bridge that blocks the harbour mouth and gone to the bottom with all hands. We drove over at once, but the car was nearly eleven fathoms down, and several divers were already at work anyway. They forced open the doors, held shut by the water pressure, and hauled out one after another. All hands.

The next day there was a stir aboard our ship. It and another moved from Caracas Bay to St. Michele, a remote, idyllic bay where there were no oil tanks and where the crews could go ashore and swim as much as they pleased—under the guard, that is, of a black soldier.

And a third day we three were fairly excited.

Mr. Jonghoudt, a new disciple who was so eager that his new marriage nearly came to grief, told us about gigantic swordfish that he had caught along the Colombian coast. Quite savage fellows they were, he said, twenty-five or thirty feet long, and if you annoyed them they brandished their swords in the air and sometimes smashed a boat in the process. Mr. Jonghoudt used to fish for these creatures with dynamite that he hid in bait. When the fish had bitten, he would simply press the button in the boat, and then hunt among the fragments for the sword.

Time passed, and the day of our departure approached; it almost found me one-legged.

Native fishermen had told us that the fiercest sharks on the north coast were in Ascension Bay, and a few days later we were on the spot. We swam out into deep water, but for the moment nothing stirred. "Go on and shoot some sort of fish, and get things going," I told Joerg, posing my camera for action. Joerg shot a fish, and got things going with a bang that left nothing to be desired.

The first arrival was a small shark that snapped impudently at the wriggling fish. Joerg yanked this titbit right away from under its nose. The second candidate, a larger shark, came charging in from the other side, closely followed by a third. This many rather flustered Joerg, so he yelled piercingly into the water twice. All three sharks whisked off, and the scene was as deserted as before.

I was just feeling annoyed that Joerg had shouted so loud when a new shark came into view, approaching calmly

226

and steadily across the bottom. It was a thirteen-foot shovel-head, an altogether phlegmatic and tiresome beast. But when I looked more closely, my interest was stirred after all. Close behind this shark's dorsal fin swam a perhaps twenty-pound fish with a hooked nose, a pompano, which kept persistently and spiritedly nudging the giant in the back with its head. It was a complete mystery to me what this might mean—for that matter, I have never found out—but at all events I was determined to get it on film. I snatched the camera to my eye, and swam downwards as fast as I could go.

It was certainly rash of me to dive without looking around (the moment you harpoon a fish on the north coast you have to keep looking around all the time), but at the moment I was thinking only of the picture I meant to get, and my haste nearly cost me dear. At no more than ten feet down I took a violent blow on my left hip, and was hurled aside by an irresistible force. I barely saw two checkered shadows whisking dimly past me and vanishing with dizzy speed in the distance. Then it was over.

Back on the surface I found Joerg and Alfred rather white. Without another word they swam straight to shore. It was not until we had solid ground under our feet that they would tell their tale. Two tiger sharks were going straight at me from behind when Joerg and Alfred first noticed them on my very heels. They both declared that the foremost shark had opened his mouth and rolled sidewise to get a better grip on my upraised leg. A yell from both of their throats had luckily scared the brute at the last moment. The tiger shot past me so close that he knocked me sideways with his tail. The marks were plainly visible on my thigh, which looked as if a great rasp had been drawn over the skin.

"I've had enough for today," said Joerg very decidedly, and Alfred quite agreed. "I simply cannot see," Joerg went on, "why we should risk our good necks these very last weeks, and all for a few damn-fool snapshots."

Whereas I had had no time to be really frightened by the attack, which was all over before I could take it in, Joerg and Alfred had sustained a real shock, and I realized that our future work might suffer badly. Recalling that student pilots who have crashed are sent up again immediately—if living—to master the shock, I suggested swimming out at once. But the two of them flatly refused. So I swam out alone.

I knew perfectly well that not much could happen to me unless I harpooned a fish, but still I did not feel easy. My own nerves showed traces of the attack. Under water I kept looking in all directions, but on the surface I purposely avoided looking shorewards. And sure enough, my expectations were realized. When I went down to deep water, I heard a call from behind. It was Alfred, followed at a short distance by Joerg. They both damned me for a complete lunatic, but their shock was overcome, and the hunt went on.

How fast had the sharks been swimming when they attacked?

We judged their speed at between forty and seventy knots, and later discovered that our guess may well have been correct. Many modern warships move at more than forty knots (46 m.p.h.), and sharks have been seen to overtake them with ease. We also managed to get a few photographs of sharks under full steam, whose blurring allowed us to calculate the approximate speed to the creatures from the known shutter speed of the camera and the length of the shark.

Forty-five to eighty miles an hour! You can scarcely conceive what this means under water. At all events it should be obvious that there is no defending yourself against so tempestuous an onslaught with a knife. Owing to the limited visibility under water you don't even see the shark with the best of luck until it is from one hundred and thirty to one hundred and forty-five feet away, and three seconds later the shark is upon you. Even if you have the presence of mind to snatch the knife from its sheath within this brief span, what can you do against such a monster? Remember, it is roaring in with the speed of an express train; the skin of many sharks is too hard for even a revolver bullet to penetrate; the heart is comparatively small, and bedded in cartilage. Even if you hit it, the vitality of sharks is such that the effect of the blow would not be felt until long after the shark had done its work.

For this reason it is fairly unimportant whether you do or do not carry a knife. The important thing is always to have enough air left in your lungs for a good under-water yell—and to keep away from sharks that happen to be deaf to human shouts.

88

Two hundredth day in Curaçao!

Yes, we have been two hundred days in the West Indies, almost seven months under the fiery sky of the tropics. It was a wonderful time, rich in adventures, and we have learned to love the barren island of Curaçao like a second homeland. We know its dusty highways with the tall, sometimes blossoming wall of cactus on both sides; we know its hot, bare slopes, where iguanas sun themselves; its thickets where parrots screech; and its plantations where luminous yellow mangoes ripen; and we know the colourful turmoil of Willemstad just as well as the dreamy fishing villages along the coast. Everywhere we have found friends, among white, black, and brown people alike. And so far as the under-water realm goes, surely we know the coasts of Curaçao better than any other person. There is scarcely a stretch that we have not carefully investigated, whose inhabitants are not familiar to us, and whose reefs we could not chart perfectly from memory. When we are far away from here we will think back with longing to these days. To hours that will never return, to people we shall probably never see again, and to the wonders of the sea, of which we shall surely never again have such a fresh experience as now, since we have encountered them without forewarning and thus without prejudice.

Today, on our anniversary, we have driven once more to the north coast. It is to be our last hunt in this wild, foaming region. Joerg to the right, Alfred to the left, I in the middle— it is always the same, and yet always different. No matter where we swim, the great unknown is always ahead of us; we never know beforehand what we shall encounter the next moment, nor can we ever say with assurance that we shall get back to shore whole. But it is precisely this undefined peril that has kept driving us into the water for seven whole months. Sometimes for two and three hours without a rest, sometimes eight hours in a single day, sometimes until the best will in the world can no longer master our cold and exhaustion. Where on dry land nowadays could there be such adventures as here in the ocean? Today, in the twentieth century, where are there regions still so virginal and untouched, places whose magic has never been profaned by man, where everything still remains as it was when no man lived on earth? (Illus. 67.)

How well I remember our first expedition to the north coast near Hato! How awkward we were! Now the waves no longer bother us; on the contrary, they help us along. As a ship sails before the wind, so we let the force of the waves push us. If they sweep us forward, we surrender to their power; if they sway back, we make ourselves tiny to offer as little resistance to the water as possible. And so, subconsciously shifting our weight and resistance all the time, we glide of our own accord in the direction we want, and the higher the waves, the faster we go.

On this our farewell day the north coast is perfectly calm for a change, and the visibility under water is gloriously clear. Even close to the cliffs, where the breakers usually befog everything. And everywhere among the cleft rocks and shattered stone fragments the water gleams with fish large and small, some of them shimmering in the colours of the rainbow. Joerg and Alfred have each shot a tarpon, so that I hardly know which one to photograph. A funny situation: each of them is drawn hither and thither through the water by his tarpon (Illus. 66), with each fish in turn leaping into the air like a silver streak. There are sharks, too, including the smallest I have ever seen, a baby eighteen inches long.

Unfortunately my camera is not at its best. It, too, seems weary of long service. I hastily rush ashore, open the box, and give the spring another little poke.

Then I am back in the water, arriving just in time for a spectacle such as we will never see again. In a little cove, below a cliff, rests a medium-sized grouper. Alfred hands me his tarpon, and sneaks up on the creature. All eyes are upon him: our eyes, those of the grouper, still undecided as yet, the eyes of the many bright-coloured fish around—and also one hidden pair of eyes. Quite unexpectedly a massive blue body fades in out of a cleft in the cliff, swoops forward, and the grouper vanishes like greased lightning, and just as Alfred is about to thrust, he has before his harpoon not the grouper but a thirteen-foot blue shark! For a moment Alfred shoots upwards with a sudden motion.

I just have time to hear him say something about "of all the nerve", then I am under water myself, pursuing the big blue shark, who propels his fat body into deep water. I snap twice, then hurry back.

"We're better men than the sharks, all the same!" Joerg grins at me, having meanwhile caught Alfred's grouper.

"Quick, look, look!" Alfred interrupts, waving his arms excitedly.

Close behind us a creature has suddenly appeared that reminds one more of a steam roller than of any fish. It is a hammerhead! And bigger than the one we saw with Meyringh! Its body is almost as thick as we are tall—like the trunk of an ancient oak. And of course the camera balks again. I pound furiously on the case with my fist, and the steam roller slowly swims off.

Here indeed is a situation worthy of an anniversary and a farewell hunt. Round about us the crystal water, ahead and to one side the little cove with the great rock mass and the many bright, shimmering fish. On Joerg's harpoon the medium-sized grouper, on Alfred's face even now the traces of his utter amazement, at my belt the bunch of fish with the big tarpon.

231

And then the tiny, the big blue, and the even bigger steam-roller hammerhead shark. And now this illustrious company is joined by a three-foot hawkbill turtle. Slowly, overgrown with barnacles, it paddles through the water, and Joerg and Alfred are off after it, trying to take it alive.

How happy I am that this expedition came true! How fully every effort has been repaid! Everything we had hoped for has happened.

89

The two hundredth and second day we saw in the papers the awful news that the English had removed all the German passengers from the Japanese steamer *Assama Maru*, and that the Japanese had agreed not to transport any more Germans across the Pacific. How were we to go on from California? In fact, should we be allowed under these circumstances to enter the United States at all?

That same day we were faced with another momentous decision. The two German ships lying at St. Michele were planning to put out secretly in the next few days and run the blockade to Germany. Now, cowards that we were, we must decide whether we would go along or leave the ship at once.

We sat under a manzanilla tree on shore, toying with its poisonous fruits. After some backing and filling we fought our way through a decision, and an hour later we went ashore for good.

The two ships were overtaken by the English soon after their departure, and the crews interned in Jamaica. Ernst, who was along, sent us a post card from a camp there a year later. (By that time we were long since back in Vienna.)

We now slept either on the flat roof at Pepe's beside our

corals that were put out to bleach, or on the front stoop of a German sailor who had a black wife and a small brown boy.

One day, to our great delight, Dr. Diemont arrived unexpectedly with his new ship. It had finally been finished, after all.

"Katchi, the boatbuilder," he told us, "invested all the money in schnapps. Of course they haven't got a cent left now, and are building away at another boat. . . . People in Bonaire are still talking about you. The jewfish is gone and hasn't bitten off any more hooks."

We all went aboard his vessel, and sailed to Plow Bay, where we had a most eventful day. First we discovered an unusually beautiful coral, and Heinz and Mr. Jonghoudt went down and sawed it off the bottom; then Dr. Diemont and I encountered a big shark in quite shallow water. At almost the same time Joerg had an accident. He saw an unfamiliar fish with elongated fins, dived to harpoon it, and, since the fish kept swimming downwards and downwards, Joerg followed to almost sixty feet. When he surfaced, or rather tried to, he had no fish, but he did have a punctured eardrum. It had burst with a terrible bang, water had entered the middle ear, and Joerg, deprived of his sense of balance, swam hither and thither with a strange sort of list. Luckily he could see through his goggles which way was up, and so he got back to the air. Dr. Diemont and Mr. Jonghoudt took him straight to a doctor. It turned out that the puncture was small, and would probably soon grow over. Joerg being the person he is, he tried to go diving again within a week, "just a little", as he said, but it was enough to burst the eardrum again. But three months later, when we were diving on the California coast, the ear was quite all right again, and two years later, in Greece, we even dived to sixty-five feet.

The closer our departure came, the worse grew my conscience. The greater part of our sixteen-millimetre film still lay unexposed in an airtight ice-cooled box. Since Alfred's accident on Bonaire we had hardly taken any films at all. As we could not develop the films ourselves, and I therefore did not know whether the pictures would turn out at all, I had usually

233

preferred to go hunting with the still camera only. But now, no matter whether the material was still good or not, I was determined to grind off those last 3,300 feet. Only a few hundred yards from the last houses of Willemstad I went into the sea, and pointed the camera at everything that stirred on the sea floor. As it was hard to hold the camera still when diving, I used a wooden tripod, which I must say showed a regrettable tendency towards higher things and places. (Illus. 65.) Nevertheless the pictures came out, and in a week I finished an educational film that was afterwards widely shown.

As it was to be feared that the English would take us off the American vessel on the way to New York, we did not want to attract the premature attention of any possible agents in Curaçao, so we concealed the time of our departure to the last day, and also proposed putting off until the last moment the purchase of the tickets.

Everything was prepared, we had all the necessary papers at last, and sufficient money besides; then in the last night agonizing fears began to assail me. We were sleeping on the aforementioned stoop, and I tossed sleeplessly to and fro all night. When we went to the steamer line the next morning, it turned out that still further formalities were necessary. The agency was afraid we would not be let into the United States in spite of our visas, and insisted on a written guarantee from the American consul, who, however, declined to issue one. In our distress we went to Mr. Van de Croef, the head of the immigration service, where we experienced an amusing reversal. He, who had been our worst adversary when we arrived, now turned out to be the most zealous spokesman of our interests. He was obviously overjoyed to get rid of us at last, promptly called up the shipping line, and talked to the people for a good fifteen minutes, during which he said so many nice things about us that we could scarcely contain our mirth. And finally the agent actually did give in. As before in Hamburg, we were now to pay for the round trip, although this shook our budget to its foundations. In addition Mr. Van de Croef gave us a certificate that in case of need we could come back to Curaçao.

234

For this time, they indicated, it was too late, but we could leave by the next vessel in five days.

Heaven knows what got into us—probably my nocturnal fears were the main thing—but in any case we did not quietly accept this either. That day we ran ceaselessly from one office to another, drove the shipping people absolutely frantic, and finally had our way: we were allowed on board at the last moment. Pepe and Mr. Jonghoudt had just time to drink a stirrup cup with us, then the screws began to churn, the gangplank was pulled in, and we were off.

Joerg and Alfred teased me that evening about my alarming premonitions, and yet they, too, were to be confirmed. Some weeks later Mr. Jonghoudt wrote us in New York to ask if we realized what fool's luck we had had. We had got away from Curaçao aboard the last ship! The route had suddenly been changed, and the very next vessel went by Bermuda, where of course all Germans were removed. If we had not got away by the vessel we did, we should not have had any chance to leave Curaçao. Six weeks later the war with Holland broke out; we would then have been interned in a camp on Bonaire with all the other Germans, and instead of a voyage by way of America, Hawaii, Japan, China, and Russia, instead of lectures and books, university study, and further work on the sea floor in Greece and southern Italy, we should have spent five years behind barbed wire.

90

P.S. A squirrel whisked down from a tree, awakening me to the fact that I was not on the sea floor but in the New York Zoo—on my way to William Beebe.

With pounding heart I entered the laboratory, where I was immediately confronted with the great savant. I shook his hand, and was introduced to his assistants, Dr. Tee-Van and Miss Hollister, as well. I showed my pictures, and had the great joy of seeing that they made a good impression. They were the best he had ever seen, said William Beebe; and I believe my work could not have had any finer reward.

THE END